WHITE RELIGION AND BLACK HUMANITY

Harry H. Singleton, III

University Press of America,® Inc.
Lanham · Boulder · New York · Toronto · Plymouth, UK

**Copyright © 2012 by
University Press of America,® Inc.**
4501 Forbes Boulevard
Suite 200
Lanham, Maryland 20706
UPA Acquisitions Department (301) 459-3366

Estover Road
Plymouth PL6 7PY
United Kingdom

Library of Congress Control Number: 2011938195
ISBN: 978-0-7618-5737-2 (paperback : alk. paper)
eISBN: 978-0-7618-5738-9

Cover image © iStockphoto.com/jpa1999

⊖™ The paper used in this publication meets the minimum
requirements of American National Standard for Information
Sciences—Permanence of Paper for Printed Library Materials,
ANSI Z39.48-1992

In memory of

my sister
Leontyne Singleton
(1957-2006)

and

my mother
Annie Oliphant Singleton
(1934-2007)

You're sorely missed and will never be forgotten.

Contents

Preface

This book is my first signature statement on the interrelationship between white Christian values and the dehumanization of black people. My first book, *Black Theology and Ideology: Deideological Dimensions in the Theology of James H. Cone*, (The Liturgical Press, 2002), examined this interrelationship primarily through the lens of James Cone and Latin American liberation theologian Juan Luis Segundo. It was in that work that I established Cone's black liberation perspective as the most viable theological perspective for black freedom in American life. It was also in that work that I established Segundo's deideological hermeneutics or the process of exposing theological perspectives that have given divine sanction to human oppression as the most viable theological method for constructing theological approaches capable of realizing human liberation. But more important, it is Segundo's challenge to liberation theologians throughout the world to apply his methodological principles to their particular contexts that has inspired me first as a doctoral student and today as a theologian.

That particular context for me is the United States of America, its ubiquitous "Christian" presence and its oppressive racial history. One is led to altruistically think that the presence of a Christian morality would preclude the existence of an oppressive racial history (and it should!). Yet my intent with this work is to demonstrate that quite the opposite has been, and is, the case in America. Far from being the moral conscience in American history, Christian faith has been in this context a faith of black oppression and in so being has been a socio-historical farce! It has been used primarily in this context by the white Christian establishment to divinely legitimate a superior-inferior relationship between white and black people and has been from its origins in American history the most vocal opponent of black advancement. It has rooted black debasement not in white will but in divine will seeking an intricate interrelationship between the two. My attempt, with the pages that follow, is to structurally articulate that interrelationship in as clear and as passionate a manner as possible. It is my fondest hope that this work will serve as a catalyst for more candid public discourse on the presentation of Christian faith in America to both black and white Christians with the goal being its permanent disentanglement from oppressive structures in American life and its unashamed affiliation with those who are the victims of those structures.

I would like to acknowledge the following persons of which this work would not have been completed: Dr. Peter Paris of Princeton Theological Seminary who strongly encouraged me to seek the manuscript's publication; Ms. Davida McDonald Manning who helped me bring the manuscript to publication form; all of my colleagues at Benedict College who constantly encouraged me to, "finish what I had started;" my students who were admirably patient with not getting "all of me" for the past year and a half; and my siblings, Vera, Ken, and Terri, who have been my anchor through the loss of our sister and mother in successive years. To you I owe my ability to persevere and my capacity to love.

Harry Singleton
Columbia, South Carolina
March 19, 2011

Introduction

Christian faith in the history of the colonies and America has been both kind and unkind to its black citizens. It has been kind in the sense that it has provided a sense of purposive hope to a community struggling with its identity in a hostile national environment. It has brought from immaturity to maturity black men and women who were previously living unproductive lives who were clearly detrimental to themselves and others. It has provided ultimate hope for eternal bliss through faith in the resurrection of Jesus that transcends the power of white supremacy. It has insisted on the development of a spiritual connectedness to the origin of all existence. It has even, on occasion, prophetically denounced systemic encroachments on black people's humanity as anti-Christian.

Yet, my argument in this work is that Christian faith in the history in the colonies and America has, in the predominance, been unkind to black people. Its practice has lent itself over to the seminal understanding of the superiority of whiteness and the inferiority of blackness and in so doing has given theological validation to the institutions in American life that have affirmed the legitimacy of that understanding. Put another way, when the ideological progenitors of colonial and American life committed themselves to a racist will to power socio-historically, they were also committing Christian faith to a theological will to power as well. As such, the foundation had been laid for an approach to Christian faith that authenticated white racism as synonymous with divinity. This has made Christian faith on American shores anything other than a contemporary reflection of the life of Jesus. Instead, it has been a racist ideology masquerading as Christian faith! Thus, the historical application of Christian faith in the colonies and America, despite its good deeds, has theologically given itself over to the ontological assumption of white racial superiority. In doing so, Christian faith in the colonies and America committed itself unconditionally to establishing an historical link between Christian values and black oppression. This becomes particularly crucial for the structuring of normative thinking insofar as the predominant religious faith in the life of any nation serves for its citizens as its primary guide in determining what is right and wrong thinking in God's eyes. By constructing Christian faith as a condoner of black oppression, it implies that God is a condoner of black oppression as well. This theological implication and subsequent affirmation provided the ultimate validation sought by white racist power brokers (including white Christian leaders!) in establishing black oppression not only as an American norm but a Christian norm as well. This is why I take this work to establish that the practice of Christian faith in the history of the colonies and America has been the single most potent ideological weapon in sanctioning the dehumanization of black people.

In fact, a Christian theology of white supremacy had to affirm the legitimacy of an inferior black humanity as it simultaneously affirmed a superior white humanity. In pragmatic terms, the Christian theology of white supremacy sought incessantly to depict every Christian symbol of positive expression in white form. The whitening of Jesus and the theological implication that God must be white, the angels imaged as white, and the biblical affirmation of purity being symbolized by the color white represent just a few of the symbols that became normative in Christian life in America and made mammoth contributions to the establishment of a Christian theology of white superiority. Communion Sunday in most churches white and black, then and now, provides us with a full display of the matriarchs donning white dresses, shoes, and head wraps, and the men in their white suits and white ties (although occasionally dressed with a black shirt!) and baptismal candidates donning their white sheets with unrequited glee as they are "taken to the waters."

This expression of faith served the dual purpose in establishing that everything associated with the color black had to be deemed unworthy, dirty, impure, and inferior. In fact, the very first Christian theological treatment of the demonic in American history was black skin itself! The problem with such an approach is that, even with its "neutral" historical presentation as the only medium to salvation regardless of one's race, Christian faith came to be indissolubly linked with an America of white privilege and not one of human equality.

Instead, the white gatekeepers of Christian theology in America sought an aggressively intentional approach to faith that wedded black oppression with divine will. Whether it was the contention by influential white clergy and theologians that biblical revelation condoned black oppression through the dividing of humans into races at the Tower of Babel, that the "curse" on Ham for mocking father Noah in his drunkenness was a future prognosticator of God's desire for African enslavement, or that the ordinance of slavery as a divine institution is evident in Jesus not publicly condemning it and in Paul's seeming affirmation of it, Christian faith was making its theological debut in American life as a faith that condoned black enslavement and white racial superiority, and that promised the wrath of God to anyone who dared question its legitimacy.

With white superiority receiving a divine boost from Christian theology, the theories of the white intelligentsia regarding matters of established significance, particularly their theories concerning the origin and worth of black humanity, were established as normative thinking in American life. Indeed, their theories regarding the diminished intellectual endowment of blacks, uncivilized precolonial Africa and her abhorrent cultural expressions, and, more particularly, the dreaded aesthetic appeal of blacks often linking them to apes in both image and mating, became the established understanding of African ontology in American life.

The white church, and thereafter, the black church inherited this theology of black dehumanization. Even though in certain epochs black people used select black churches with pastors that possessed a liberating conscience to plot insurrection and to secure freedom from the slavocracy and, later, civil rights, both black and white churches have inherited and, for the most part, lived out the directives of this theology. That is to say, neither has seen themselves (by careful design!) as mediums for the transformation of racial and gender oppression. In fact, both were created to give sacred legitimacy to racial and gender oppression! The racially separated reality of worship in American churches and the blatantly subordinate pedagogies concerning women, particularly those seeking to enter the ministry, has made the church an institutional participant in human oppression in the name of Jesus. The Christian theology of white supremacy has called on churches more specifically to create a religious language that was comforting, conciliatory and socially detached to impress upon the Christian the issues with which she should be primarily, if not exclusively, concerned. Its historic success has been evident insofar as it has served as a theological tranquilizer to social reform allowing whites to enjoy unprecedented economic prosperity and making blacks "comfortable" with providing that wealth despite the improper compensation they have historically received for their labor. The depiction of Jesus as white and who supposedly demonstrated pious qualities was constructed for the purpose of fashioning this type disposition in the black Christian in particular. Hence, Christian faith in American history has been primarily concerned with establishing an anti-revolutionary, passive disposition in black Christians for the purpose of perpetuating white privilege. Contrariwise, it has not been concerned with the destruction of oppressive behavior on the basis of human distinctions that Jesus' fulfillment of the law was to free us to do. In so doing, Christian faith from its inception in American history has been inauthentic in its application insofar as it has compelled both black and white Christians to internalize an understanding of faith that glorifies racial and gender inequality and, further, that has made the face of poverty its slothful "Negro" citizens!

To be sure, this theology of black dehumanization has been built on three major presuppositions: 1) God alone brings about social transformation only at the eschaton and will reward black people for their "patience" at that time; 2) Christianity is primarily an otherworldly religion and is not principally concerned about human affairs on earth; and 3) Christianity is concerned only with the religious individual and her internal demons, not her collective human suffering. Yet these presuppositions represent not only a distortion of the gospel but an inaccurate presentation of biblical revelation. The Exodus narrative conveys the story of an Israelite people in Egyptian bondage i.e., slavery, in which God commissions Moses to lead the Israelites out of slavery and into a land of freedom that God had promised the Israelites. Moreover, Jesus proclamation of his own ministry as one that seeks to, "set at liberty those who are oppressed," and his encounters with the rulers of first century Palestine regarding the treatment of the poor cannot be dismissed as insignificant dimensions of biblical revelation. Moreover, the significance of divine will to be effectuated, "on earth as it is in heaven," and as exemplified in Jesus' own life concerning his commitment to the human condition on earth are clear indications that human relationships on earth are important to both God and Jesus. Further, the Prophets insistence on God's judgment on nations as well as individuals does create the mandate for nations to be just in their dealings with its citizenry. The church's approval of the abduction of Africans and their deportation to America, their enslavement, their segregation, lynchings and castrations, the mocking of their aesthetic features and *the denial of citizenship* (until the saving grace of the fourteenth amendment!) are an indictment on the practice of Christian faith in America rather than an affirmation.

Morehouse President and author Dr. Robert Michael Franklin is right: there is, indeed, a crisis in the village. But there is a crisis in the community village because there is a crisis in the larger national village. Sitting at the core of this crisis is a Christian community that devalues people of color and women, insists on the primacy of the religious individual, teaches religious superiority through the condemnation of other faiths, and demands otherworldliness as the locus of attention for the true Christian. While America is to be lauded for the human progress it has made, I contend that this progress has come not because of Christian pedagogy but in spite of Christian pedagogy. An approach to Christian faith designed to separate the religious conscious of the believer from socio-political oppression (in both world and church!), is not only theologically suspect but pedagogically irresponsible. It removes social responsibility in the salvation/liberation process and compels the Christian to think that true faith has little to do with human oppression (which, of course, has been the intended goal of white Christian leadership in American history!)

In such a theological and religious milieu, we have witnessed Christian faith become diminished to frequent prayer and worship, tithes paying, socially irrelevant sermons, emotion-driven spirituality, sexual morality and institutional maintenance. We have even built on the presupposition of the primacy of the religious individual, connecting it to individual accomplishment through the pedagogy of "prosperity" ministries. Yet the notion that God and Jesus want us to be prosperous is not novel. What Jesus did show us with his life is that prosperity can only be measured by the overall success of the human family in its striving to live in global community with each other and not in the hoarding up of excessive material wealth in the midst of so much global poverty. Jesus would want us not to naively conclude that this poverty exists simply because the poor lack industry or because they do not pray enough or pay their tithes, but he would want us to more rigorously examine the relationship that exists, nationally and globally, between human oppression and economic structure. Given his concern for the poor, he would want us to struggle heartily with an economic mode of production that creates a few wealthy individuals at the expense of an exponentially burgeoning number of poor people. He would more importantly want us to commit our lives to its eradication. In short, any prosperity that does not take into account the primacy of the destruction of oppressive human relationships is a prosperity that serves the interests of white supremacy more than that of the Christ-event. It vacates the realm of theology and descends into ideology!

What is needed, then, is an ideological separation of the "wheat from the chaff," to expose the ideological elements in Christian faith that have sanctioned black oppression and to arrive at a faith that maintains its liberating fidelity to the gospel.

1

The Question of Black Humanity

> In the adjustment of religion to ethics that was made for the new slavery, under the cotton kingdom, there was in the first place a distinct denial of human brotherhood (personhood). These black men (humans) were not men (humans) in the sense that white men (humans) were men (humans). They were different —different in kind, different in origin; they had different diseases . . . they had different feelings; they were not to be treated the same; they were not looked upon as the same; they were altogether apart and . . . yet so far as this world is concerned, there could be with them neither human or spiritual brotherhood (personhood).
> W. E. B. DuBois, "Religion in the South"

DuBois' statement represents the central area of our investigation. Indeed, not only has the question of black humanity been the most significant anthropological issue for the colonies and America, but because the responses to that question have been intertwined in so much religious language, it has also been the most significant theological issue for the colonies and America. To be sure, the answers to the question of black humanity have departed from the presupposition of the cultural, aesthetic, and intellectual superiority of the white race. Conversely this meant the necessity of "creating" an inferior race of people to ultimately legitimate the supremacy of whiteness. Hence, a well—designed method of black dehumanization was imperative if the notion of white supremacy was to take institutional and societal root.

The choice of people of West African descent as the objects of dehumanization has profound economic and cultural dimensions. Economically, cheap slave labor was needed to build the early infrastructure of the colonies and what would become America. In this regard, an ontological conclusion may be drawn — whites were not as given over to the "fruits" of hard work that would come to characterize the Protestant ethic of human dignity as has been historically asserted. In fact, it marked the origins of the successful white man not as consummate worker but as consummate overseer and with the advent of the slave trade set into motion the racial legitimation of a process of labor relations between white overseer and black laborer that would become the norm for many a generation to come. Moreover, the foundation was being laid for a highly immoral racial relationship between whites and blacks wherein the latter would become little more than a dispensable commodity, an anthropological other worthy of dehumanization as no means was egregious enough to secure the end of incalculable white wealth. As Lester Scherer explains, although the exact value of the free slave labor and the economic prosperity of slave planters can not be ascertained, one thing was for sure: the enormity of white wealth could never have reached its maturity apart from the cheap labor brought by the slave.

> Here as with the slave trade no gross estimate of the value of slave labor can be made from the available data. Clearly, however, every socially and politically prominent figure in the southern colonies rose on the backs of enslaved Africans: Byrd, Laurens, Washington, Jefferson and scores of others. Further, without the staples whose margins of profit depended on cheap labor, the colonies would not have been able to pass beyond the level of subsistence economy, to attract the necessary flow of voluntary migration, or to develop the political institutions essential to the emergence of a new nation. No one interested in a faithful picture of the American past will miss the irony: the institutions of American liberty were built on the toil of those who were never intended to share in them.[1]

Scherer's analysis painfully reminds us of the sinister intentions involved in blacks laboring to build the economic infrastructure of a nation that was never committed to blacks sharing in the fruits of that labor. This chapter takes a look, first, at white supremacy as a virulent social phenomenon and closes with an examination of white religion as its most outspoken proponent.

White Supremacy and Black Humanity

Culturally, the process of black dehumanization was made all the more easier by the inability of white explorers to see any redeeming values in black culture as it was lived in pre-colonial Africa. This owes itself in large part to cultural ignorance stemming from a lack of exposure to a culture radically different from that of European culture. While the English were the biggest player in the slave trade, it was Spanish and Portuguese explorers visiting Africa in the fifteenth century that laid the foundation for characterizing black culture as inferior. To be sure, the valuation of African culture as inferior by Spanish and Portuguese explorers had both ontological and racial components. Ontologically, humans in general tend to brand that which is different from their own customs with a pejorative stigma. Throughout human history, difference has never been truly embraced by humans but rather has been discouraged in favor of a more familiar, and therefore authentic, cultural expression. Hence when Spanish and Portuguese explorers observed Africans in their pre-colonial habitat, African culture's stark difference from European culture was immediately taken note of and the process of black dehumanization was born. Thus the valuation of black humanity as inferior had in part to do with a natural inclination for humans to see difference as an aberration but in large part to do with the creation of an economic infrastructure that would insure white privilege for generations over.

Racially, the cultural assault on the humanity of Africans began, not surprisingly, with the aesthetic differences between that of Africans and its European racial counterpart. Spanish and Portuguese explorers saw the African's dark skin as a freakish anomaly that bred more of a consciousness of paternalism than that of mutual respect. It would not be long thereafter when the terms savage and heathen became synonymous with black humanity. But what the Spanish and Portuguese started, the English finished. Because of its ownership of the colonies and the abduction of West Africans for the slave trade to the colonies, the English proved a worthy surrogate for the Spanish and Portuguese. In fact, the English took the theoretical designations of Africans as savage and heathen and added a pragmatic dimension to the designations that concretized the notion of black inferiority in the life of the colonies and America. As Winthrop Jordan rightly suggests, "A perception of Negro heathenism remained through the eighteenth and into the nineteenth and even the twentieth century, and an awareness, at the very least, of the African's different appearance was present from the beginning."[2] In fact, throughout the period of initial abduction and early colonization, black humanity was existentially dismantled on the basis of its so-called heathenism and black pigmentation would come to characterize the diametric opposite of whiteness — the only true humanity. Yet as has always been the case the debasement of black humanity had to do with more than racial categorization. It had also to do with the inability on the part of whites to take anything about black culture seriously in light of the latter's difference and even distance from white culture. That difference conveniently for whites could only mean the African's descent into savagery without taking into consideration the designation of savagery itself being a necessary by-product of white hegemony. In Africa these qualities had for Englishmen added up to *savagery*, they were major components in that sense of *difference* which provided the mental margin absolutely requisite for placing the European on deck of the slave ship and the African in the hold.[3]

In this regard, we can see a truly ideological progression in the debasement of black humanity. The first stage begun by Spanish and Portuguese explorers was to categorize African culture as *heathen*. In so doing, an oppressive cate-

gory was created that made African culture synonymous with a lack of civilization. This would be crucial. If it could be established that Africans were engaged
in cultural expressions that were uncivilized, it would provide the social justification necessary for destroying African culture for the purpose of indoctrinating
the African to European mores for living. Accomplishing this crucial task would
serve two purposes. First, it would establish the assumed presumption of the
superiority of white culture and second, it would expose heathen Africans to
what a civilized culture really looks like. Hence, a paradox would be created that
would ultimately cost white supremacy its lifeline. If the purpose of exposing
heathen Africans to civilization was to make them more human, then what was
to be made of the process of enslaving Africans to make them more civilized? If
one is given over to the notion that enslavement dehumanizes more than it could
ever humanize, then on what basis is this seeming contradiction overcome?
Spanish and Portuguese explorers, followed by English planters skirted around
this issue by arguing that it was indeed the heathenism of the African that made
her violently skeptical to any exposure to "true" civilization that necessitated her
harsh treatment. Thus, whether it was the violent nature of African abduction or
the violent treatment of the slave once reaching the shores of America, given the
goal of economic prosperity for Europeans, no means was considered out of the
bounds of possibility for such a noble cause. In this regard, it bears mentioning
that the process of black dehumanization has always been couched in extremely
benevolent terms by Europeans and, as we shall see later, Europeans would seek
to establish that process as synonymous with the realization of God's kingdom!
This allowed the European to place the extremely cruel treatment of Africans in
positive terms touting black dehumanization as a necessary initial step to an
overall greater good that both God and Europeans could see but was unable to
be gleaned by the heathen African. Hence, the stench of paternalistic and arro-
gant aggression by whites is purified, and even redeemed, by the greater altruistic effort to expose the African to what being human truly means.

Yet, the true nature of this ideological process of black dehumanization
would continue to reveal itself as time progressed. For what would be a so-
called basis of civilizing the heathen African would come to show itself not as a
process of true benevolence that would eventually acknowledge the equal humanity of blacks but one that would bring to light the true contempt not only for
African culture by whites but for African people themselves. As is well docu-
mented, the historical rationale for the treatment of Africans is to expose them to
civilization and thereby make them truly human. History has shown us that the
primary intent of the slaveholding community was to dupe the African with
clever sophistry about her inferior ontological capacities in the effort to sell African enslavement as an eternal phenomenon. Such skilled sophistry, however,
never found a solid footing in the eyes of many Africans not because they were
heathen and unable to fathom the "greater good" of their treatment but because
of the constant mockery made of African culture by whites and the seeming con-

tempt inherent in white's reflection on African culture. In short, a cursory examination of the ideological process of black dehumanization establishes clearly that the intent was not to humanize Africans but to desecrate African culture. In so doing, it was hoped that such an approach would separate Africans from any historical roots and make them better pawns for eternal servitude to whites in the colonies and America.

Thus, it is in this milieu that the slave trade began — a milieu presented as mutually beneficial to both African and European yet in reality firmly committed to the desecration of African culture. This derogatory view of Africans would be put on full display both theoretically and practically in the history of the colonies and America. Lester Scherer draws a similar conclusion: "It had already been observed that even before colonization, the English had perceived Africans as a different sort of creature, suitable for enslavement. Thereafter, enslavement and racial contempt fed on each other; and it is not surprising to run into many casually disparaging comments by provincial Americans."[4]

Thus, unable to cloak its true intention of economic exploitation, white settlers abandoned the public presentation of "civilizing" the African and began to brand the African a *savage*. This leads us to the second stage of black dehumanization. While heathenism sought to maintain that a group of humans is uncivilized, savagery sought to establish that a group is *incapable* of being civilized. This process would begin in the colonies in the mid to late seventeenth century or shortly into the slavocracy. In this stage, the African was taught that although incapable of civilization on the level of that of whites, her proximity to "superior cultured" whites in a posture of eternal servitude could provide her with some modicum of civilization. This would be the best that the African could hope for given her defective human nature and shorn of any qualities culturally and aesthetically that would make her authentically human. It is on this basis, one of African savagery, that slaveholders would begin to instruct slaves that the slavocracy is the best possible relationship that could exist between the two races. More important, it was hoped that the slave would see the hard work expended by the planters, in both the deportation process and the building of plantations, in order to establish the slavocracy as an extraordinarily benevolent gesture by which the slave should be extremely grateful. In so doing, it furthered reaffirmed the ideological nature of black dehumanization by giving white racism a positive public presentation under a canopy of moral turpitude. It was thus in tandem with the concept of slavery as "a positive good" that the doctrine of permanent black inferiority begin its career as a rationale, first for slavery itself, and later for post-Emancipation forms of racial oppression.[5] Thus what began as a process of government sanctioned black dehumanization reached full maturity by the early nineteenth century. That maturity was made all the more formidable by the numerous literary tracts and oratorical pronouncements by "well-respected" white leaders in every discipline (most notably its religious leaders!) making the case for black people's natural inferiority. In such a fundamentally racist cultural milieu, black inferiority became firmly established as the intellectual norm for white thinking about African people. In so doing, the theretofore generation of black people and their posterity found themselves subject to a citadel of racial prejudice that we have still not yet expunged in American life.

> The attitudes that underlay the belief that the Negro was doomed by nature itself to perpetual slavishness and subordination to the whites were not new, nor was the doctrine itself if considered as popular belief that lacked intellectual respectability; but when asserted dogmatically and with an aura of philosophical authority by leading Southern spokesman and their Northern supporters in the 1830's, it became, for the first time, the basis of a world view, an explicit ideology around which the beneficiaries of white supremacy could organize themselves and their thoughts.[6]

Fredrickson reminds us, not surprisingly, that in order to be effective, the creation of perpetual white privilege through black dehumanization not only required effective planning pragmatically, but in order to be truly effective, it had to be sold intellectually. That is to say, a case had to be made that the harsh treatment of black people was not a process of dehumanization. Rather, it was articulated as a benevolent white response to a people clearly lacking the ontological capabilities to adjust themselves to a natural order that demanded a far superior cultural expression.

To be sure, as stated earlier, the inability of Europeans to see anything of value in African culture had to do with the radically different cultural expressions of Africans. It is in this sense that we are led to, arguably, the most significant dimension of the European-African encounter, and that is the aesthetic dimension. Already perturbed by the difference in the Africans cultural expressions, the most literal visible difference taken note of by European explorers regarding Africans was the latter's much darker skin pigmentation. While Winthrop Jordan and other historians rightly point that although skin hue was not the deciding factor in the selection of Africans for the slave trade, and that the African would be a far more durable worker than the Native American is the most conventional explanation, the dark skin of the African as a natural defect would serve as the cornerstone of white supremacist ideology. This, the African should have found particularly gratifying particularly given the Native American was already on American soil and did not have to be "imported" for the slave trade.

In particular, whites would come to characterize the dark skin of the African as nature's preferred method of informing both Europeans and Africans that it was a manifestation of the demonic. This represents the third stage of the process of black dehumanization. This stage serves as a bridge in the sense that the significance of the designation of the demonic to the African would lay the foundation for a smooth ideological transition for white intellectuals from secular rationales for black dehumanization to theological rationales for black dehumanization. In this regard, what was at stake was not just skin hue of African people but its origins as well. Hence, the branding of the African as demonic was not to be understood as an aesthetic assault on her humanity but rather as a respectable hypothesis regarding the ontological nature of her humanity. In particular, what was at stake here for Europeans eager to "normalize" African enslavement was to treat the demonic in such a way that the African's dark skin was but a visible manifestation of her total inward depravity — an inward depravity that extended beyond the biblical Fall in which all Christians are subject. In fact, it was the dark skin of the African that "demystified" for Europeans why the African was so far afield in her cultural expressions: the radically different skin hue between Europeans and Africans was nature's way of revealing to the former the radically different and, therefore, total depravity of African culture. The difference was as visible and diametric as night and day, wrong and right, demonism and divinity.

> Far from isolating African heathenism as a separate characteristic, English travelers sometimes linked it explicitly with barbarity and blackness. They already had in hand a mediating term among these impinging concepts — the *devil*. As one observer declared, Negroes "in colour so in condition are little other than devils incarnate," and, further, "the Devil . . . has infused prodigious idolatry into their hearts, enough to relish his pallat and aggrandize their tortures when he gets power to fry their souls as the raging Sun has already scorched their cole-black carcasses."[7]

Jordan makes clear that in establishing the demonic as the black outward manifestation of inward depravity, Europeans were well on their way to solidifying the inferiority of black people as a natural "given." In so doing, given the eternal nature of black skin, it became an intellectual formality to conceive of black inferiority as irrevocable and that much easier to sell both blacks and whites on the eternal nature of the slavocracy itself — the ultimate goal of white planters.

More important, by categorizing black skin as an outward manifestation of the African's natural depravity, by inference, it made white skin, the polar opposite of that of Africans, directly associated with divinity. It also by inference made whiteness in all its cultural, intellectual, and aesthetic dimensions naturally superior — the highest breed of humanity on earth! Finally, it also meant that God had created the first, and best, humans as white with all other races of people representing a hierarchical descent and moral degeneration, a falling off if you would, from the purity that whiteness represented. It is in this spirit that white intellectuals in particular considered whiteness to be the color of the original humans — God's first and therefore superior creation. This would become particularly significant in nineteenth century racial anthropology where leading white scholars categorized races in a hierarchical schema on the basis of both the order of creation and, not surprisingly, moral attributes.[8] It was conveniently argued that, of course, whites were the original racial creation of humans by God and in being so imbued whites with superior moral, intellectual and aesthetic qualities. All other races were then possessed of diminished moral and intellectual capacities as it corresponded with their particular rankings. Needless to say, African peoples occupied the lowest rung of that racial hierarchy leading some white anthropologists to conclude that black's aesthetic presentation and intellectual capacities were more on a level of an ape or orangutan than that of humans. Thus, it was through the seminal use of the category of the demonic as black skin that black humanity as polar opposite to whiteness stood very little chance of being considered human aesthetically and/or ontologically. This categorization would be of enormous benefit for the white Christian community in both the colonies and America for the religious sanctioning of the process of black dehumanization. More to the point, it is the categorization of black skin as the demonic that the white Christian community would use as its theological starting point regarding its eternal commitment to black dehumanization.

White Religion and Black Humanity

With a cursory treatment of the origins and development of the notion of white superiority under our belts, we now come to the dimension with which this work is principally concerned. Our purpose is to demonstrate that the white religious establishment has been the most potent ideological source in the legitimation of black dehumanization. The possibility for such an achievement lay in the significance bestowed on religion itself in the shaping of human culture. This has been the case if not throughout human history certainly in the last couple of millenniums.

Religion has universally served two functions in the evolution of human culture. First, religion has served as the cultural expression in both theory and practice that has reaffirmed faith community's affirmation in the metaphysical component of the universe's existence. Put another way, religion confirms the human imagination's contention of the more powerful and wiser "otherness" of existence. Thus, I use imagination here not as the ahistorical, non-experiential musings of the human mind but rather as the source in which we creatively and rationally deduce from our historical experiences and ontological makeup the reality of that "otherness." But more important for our purposes, the human imagination working through specific communities, then, creates religion to provide us with a medium whereby we celebrate and acknowledge our encounter with that "otherness" as the necessary source of our own existence. The second function religion serves is the call to the striving for moral turpitude demanded of us by the source of our existence. In this regard, it can be established that all communities of faith seek to adhere to a moral framework that is understood to be pleasing to the source of our existence. As such, religion has been that phenomenon that we have understood to morally and spiritually connect us to divine reality and hopefully to receiving the ultimate attainment that religion promises its adherents for sincere living. Religion then is the socio-cultural construct that embodies the human imagination's understanding of the distinct but interrelated realities of the human and the divine, the physical and the metaphysical, the earthly and the heavenly, the historical and the eternal. It is the human striving to satisfy the natural inclination to connect with the source that posited that inclination. This is what theologian Karl Rahner had in mind when he referred to the divine-human encounter as the human being in the process of self-transcendence.[9]

Hence, religion serves as the function that facilitates the ongoing process of faith communities between the claims made about objective and ontological reality and the internalization of those claims for the purpose of affirming for those communities their understanding of the divine order of the universe. Thus, religion is that medium by which communities of faith create a world not physically but morally. In this regard, religion serves a profound sociological purpose. Perhaps no one has bore this out more in the past half century than Peter Berger with his classic work, *The Sacred Canopy*. Berger recognizes in this work the inescapability of culture in the shaping of religion and the ontological nature of humanity to desire to create a world for itself. Thus, for Berger, "If one wants to use such a term as designating more than certain biological constants, one can only say that it is the 'nature of man (humanity)' to produce a world."[10] Therefore, human history, for Berger, has been the incessant construction of the institutional and moral world that has provided meaning and purpose for humanity. What appears at any particular historical moment as "human nature" is itself a product of man's (humanity's) world-building activity.[11]

Yet more important for our purpose is Berger's more penetrating analysis of religion's historical use in the maintenance of unjust world orders or what he refers to as *the process of legitimation*. I mean by unjust world orders, a religious community's attempt to socially control or destroy another religious community or other distinct group and to use religious precepts to legitimate that behavior to both groups. While recognizing the theoretically coercive potential for justifying oppressive behavior in other disciplines, Berger rightly concludes that precisely because religion does entail a morality of divine implications, it exerts a significantly higher influence in its ability to convince humans of its legitimacy.

> It will be readily seen that the area of legitimation is far broader than that of religion, as these two terms have been defined here. Yet there exists an important relationship between the two. It can be described simply by saying that religion has been the historically most widespread and effective instrumentality of legitimation. All legitimation maintains socially defined reality. Religion legitimates so effectively because it relates the precarious reality constructions of empirical societies with ultimate reality. The tenuous realities of the social world are grounded in the sacred *realissimum*, which by definition is beyond the contingencies of human meanings and human activity.[12]

Hence, insofar as religion is that phenomenon that grounds the moral and institutional constructions of faith communities, "in the sacred realissimum," it becomes the most effective ideological medium for the legitimation of oppressive institutions. More important, religion (and by inference its hand-maiden theology) becomes the most effective medium for making what influential humans "created" appear as though it is what God has created for all humans. This dimension of the socially constructed nature of religion is crucial. If religious leaders of oppressive communities can so skillfully present the moral precepts of its faith community such that it appears that they are direct spokespersons of the divine, it will so reinforce for the community the divine origins of those precepts that the human dimension (read oppressively coercive dimension) of the process will slowly recede into the background of the religious conscious of the individual while the "divine" dimension comes to the forefront of that religious conscious.

> Let the institutional order be so interpreted as to hide, as much as possible, its *constructed* character. Let that which has been stamped out of the ground *ex nihilo* appear as the manifestation of something that has been existent from the beginning of time, or at least from the beginning of this group. Let the people forget that this order was established by men (humans) and continues to be dependent upon the consent of men (humans). Let them believe that, in acting out the institutional programs that have been imposed upon them, they are but realizing the deepest aspirations of their own being and putting themselves in harmony with the fundamental order of the universe. In sum: Set up religious legitimations.[13]

Thus, Berger aptly demonstrates our contention that religion is the most powerful ideological weapon for justifying oppressive human relationships by virtue of its ubiquitous influence, in general, and its historical use in grounding oppressive pedagogies of divine morality in the sacred in particular.

Berger's analysis has significant implications for our discussion. Having established that black skin is a sign of the demonic, white clergymen and theologians particularly in the early to mid-eighteenth century had come upon a line of reasoning that would satisfy two important conditions for the use of religion as a means of social control of the slaves and giving divine approval to the institution of slavery itself. The first of those two concerns was the obligation many white Christians (both English Protestants and Portuguese Catholics) felt toward the conversion of heathen Africans. The basis of this obligation stemmed from both white Protestant and Catholic contentions that the African had no religion and was therefore lost in a wilderness of spiritual darkness. Enlightenment as they saw it came only through Jesus Christ's message of universal salvation made possible through the grace granted Jesus by God. Even early in the "observation" process of Africans in their native land, whites had already drawn some abhorrent conclusions concerning African culture that fed their Christian consciousness on the one hand and their slave consciousness on the other hand.

Yet the fact of the matter is that Africans were people of profound religious faith in their pre-colonial existence. In West Africa in particular, African people were given over primarily to Islam syncretized with indigenous religions, and Christianity practiced intermittently. But it was not Christianity exclusively, and for English and Portuguese planters that difference was not only glaring but was seen as principally responsible for Africans contentment with "heathenism." More important was the fact that this difference in faith expression confirmed for white explorers not only the heathenism that accompanied the African's spate Christian leanings but also her innate incapacity to build civilization.

> Indeed, the most important aspect of English reaction to Negro heathenism was that Englishmen did not regard it as separable from the Negro's other attributes. Heathenism was treated not so much as a specifically religious defect but as one manifestation of a general refusal to measure up to proper standards, as a failure to be English or even civilized.[14]

Hence, the case was being made by white explorers that Africans were totally depraved and therefore incapable of building and sustaining human civilization. Ultimately, the case was being skillfully made for the reasonability of deporting and enslaving Africans and of black dehumanization in general.

The second concern for white explorers and later white planters was the edifying impact that conversion usually had on a human being. That is to say, to what extent could white planters eternally perpetuate a slavocracy with slaves who would become Christians? To what ends could planters continue to socially control slaves through the institutional pedagogy of the slave's innate inferiority and at the same time expose them to the freedom in Christ that Paul speaks of in New Testament literature? Would it not be reasonable to conclude that even in her innate inferiority the slave would deduce that the freedom of which Paul speaks was meant to be a contemporary revelation that Jesus would want her to be free from the slavocracy? On these queries, a couple of points have significance. The first of those has to do with the African's capacity for civilization and religious instruction. As stated above much of late seventeenth and eighteenth century anthropological literature written by white intellectuals sought to establish that the African had the lowest capacity for sustained intellectual performance. That the African's intellectual capacity was closer to apes and orangutans than humans (read white humans) was a widely held hypothesis by white scholars of the period. Moreover, the fact that many white anthropologists added to this discussion the notion that Africans, in their barbarism, even mated with apes and orangutans fortified all the more that Africans lacked the capacity to live as human beings. While it could be argued that such conclusions concerning the humanity of black people was a sincere attempt on the part of whites to deal with the difference that African culture presented aesthetically and culturally, the fact of the matter is that acute anthropological differences had to be established by whites as a necessary corollary to black dehumanization. Group difference, in other words, is required in order to set oneself apart from the enslaved group and Europeans highlighted the full arsenal of differences between them and Africans to sell the slavocracy to themselves, to Africans, and to the world.

This understanding of the African as irrevocably depraved would also influence major clergymen in the slavocracy. In fact, most clergy owned slaves and were convinced of the "divine nature" of the slavocracy. A leading slave proponent Cotton Mather, in his work, *The Negro Christianized*, observed that, "Indeed their *Stupidity* is a *Discouragement*. It may seem, unto as little purpose, to *Teach*, as to *wash an AEthiopian*."[15] For Mather and other prominent ministers, no matter how steep the challenge was to convert slaves who seemingly had no desire or "capacity" to do so, Christian obligation demanded it in principle and in mission. Yet for many white ministers, what Africans lacked in anthropological capacity to be converted, God would provide to them in spiritual capacity.

> In fact many proponents of conversion were entirely willing to concede that Negroes were ignorant, stupid, unteachable, barbarous, stubborn, and deficient in understanding. More frequently, many advocates of conversion felt called upon to assert with considerable vehemence that Negroes possessed the same capacities as Europeans and lacked only the opportunity of improvement in order to develop them.[16]

Yet it would be the implications of Jordan's quote above that would bring tremendous consternation to most slaveholders and brings us to the second point regarding slave conversion. That implication being that it was becoming increasingly difficult to maintain that Africans needed to be converted and at the same time argue that they were irrevocably barbarous. Regardless of how persuasive the argument that African savagery could be overcome through God's grace, slaveholders were increasingly of the belief that the attempt to convert Africans to Christianity at least implied the "natural" ability to be converted and in so doing implied that the African was capable of civilization on a level at or near the same level as that of whites. If this conclusion regarding black humanity were to become internalize as normative thinking, then it could have signaled the death-knell for slavery given that its legitimacy had been predicated on an eternally depraved African subject. Moreover, slaveholders were particularly cognizant of the ideological inconsistencies that could (and did!) emerge between Christian conversion and the numerous biblical references to freedom. As such, slaveholders were aggressively looking for ways to stem the "freedom" tide implied in Christian conversion. Thoughts of increased rebellions and insurrections by converted slaves who had a divine right to refuse bondage haunted many a slaveholder not only where his immediate economic prosperity was concerned but the economic prosperity of his children as well. This would bring planters into direct conflict with white clergy, theologians, and laypersons in which the clergy would remain firm on the Christian obligation to convert. Thus, the white community was now facing one of its most substantive early challenges.

Yet it is what I refer to as *the sinister unity* of white supremacist ideology that prevented this impasse from destroying the slavocracy. Whatever might be said about the impasse between white planters and clergy, it was clear that they were universally agreed that the slavocracy had to continue but were also universally agreed that the revelation of God in Jesus Christ speaks of freedom for the Christian. What was needed was a treatment of Christian freedom from the leadership of the white mainline denominations that would make the case for the slavocracy's eternal existence and at the same time render *a type* of freedom to the slaves. Put another way, what was needed was a treatment of Christian freedom that denied institutional freedom to the slaves but granted them some form of freedom in Christ. Such a treatment would be constructed in the first quarter of the eighteenth century. In a letter written in 1727 by the Bishop of London, Lord Berkeley and addressed, "to the Masters and Mistresses of Families in the English Plantations Abroad; Exhorting Them to Encourage and Promote the Instruction of Their Negroes in the Christian Faith," Lord Berkeley thought that he had constructed a treatment of Christian freedom that would break the impasse between slaveholders and the white Christian community. More important, he thought that he had found a treatment of freedom that would allay the highest fear of planters — that the conversion of the slave required her immediate manumission. According to Bishop Berkeley:

> Christianity and the embracing of the Gospel does not make the least alteration in civil property; or in any of the duties which belong to civil relations; but in all these respects, *it continues persons just in the same state as it found them.* The freedom which Christianity gives is a freedom from the bondage of sin and Satan; and from the dominion of men's (human's) lusts and passions and inordinate desires; *but as to their outward condition*, whatever that was before, whether bond or free, their being baptized and becoming Christians, makes no manner of change in it.[17] (Italics mine)

To be sure, Berkeley styled this treatment of freedom as the central meaning of Paul's theology. Berkeley saw this as the biblical imperative for Paul in his first letter to the church at Corinth where he admonished the faithful, "Let every man (human) abide in the same calling wherein he (she) *was* called; Let every man (human) wherein he *is* called therein abide with God." (I Corinthians 7:20, 24). Berkeley found in these passages not only what he thought to be a substantive biblical foundation for the eternal maintenance of "divine" institutions but also a substantive theological point of departure for establishing the slavocracy as a contemporary manifestation of such an institution. Insofar as Paul makes a provision for both the past and present by using "was" in v. 20 and "is" in v. 24 he was interpreted by Bishop Berkeley as making the, "calling of humans in their present state," not only God's plan for humanity in biblical history but in all future contexts as well. This meant for Bishop Berkeley that we now had more than a convenient interpretation in not changing "the outward condition" of slaves but a biblical mandate as well.

But more important, Berkeley had constructed a treatment of freedom that not only perpetuated the slavocracy under the canopy of Christendom, but would also establish a theological paradigm that would come to set the tone of Christian theology in the colonies and America. By conceiving of the task of Christian faith as one that calls for transformation of the religious individual in exclusively subjective terms, Berkeley was establishing critical objectives for the cause of white supremacy on a few significant fronts. First, he was, for the most part, able to allay slaveholders' fears of the biblical implications of Christian freedom meaning a change in the "outward condition" of slaves thus preserving unrequited privilege for the white community. Second, he reaffirmed the merits of conversion of the slaves to white Christians and reassured them that this "duty-bound" mission is pleasing to God and that this was the only type of freedom the slaves could experience. The third critical objective accomplished by Bishop Berkeley through this treatment of Christian freedom is that it went a long way in creating in the mind of the slave an existential dilemma between an ontological desire for outward freedom on the one hand but an adherence to the divine mandate of being content with only inward freedom as taught by white clergy on the other hand. More important, Bishop Berkeley's treatment of Christian freedom served as an infusion of new life into the white community and affirmed for many white Christians that because God had given them the divine imperative to convert heathen Africans to Christian faith (and not vice versa), it served as a divine confirmation of the intellectual and spiritual superiority of white humanity.

Pragmatically, this treatment of freedom by Bishop Berkeley would give divine sanction to the slavocracy and subsequently to the establishment of many slave codes that gave slaveholders unbridled power to use whatever means available to keep the slaves on the plantation. It gave planters carte blanche to use any manner of egregious psychological ploys (branding, public whippings, auctions, feet of recaptured slaves severed, removal of tendons from ankles with no anesthesia) to instill in the slaves an acute sense of existential fear in the name of God and country. A fear that would come to be explained as a microcosm of the fear the slave should have for the wrath of God for "violation" of divine will i.e., for leaving the plantation or worst yet trying to topple the slavocracy. That is to say, the fear of God, a recurring biblical theme, would be parlayed by slaveholders as a means of social control and to "eternalize" in the minds of both slaves and slaveholders the divinity of the slavocracy. Put more succinctly, "the inward freedom-fear of God dialectic," was used to continually impress upon the slave that rebellion against the slavocracy was tantamount to rebellion against God's ordinance and that eternal damnation was the nonnegotiable price to pay. Hence the ultimate goal of white clergy was to establish as the theological norm for the slave the violation of a slave law as a violation of divine law.

As this approach to faith became more and more codified in the religious life of the colonies and early America and as an orthodox Christianity began to emerge more distinctly, a "substantive" Christian faith emerged that would have a devastating and lasting affect on the way faith would come to be envisioned in American life. Specifically, Christian faith would come to divinize black dehumanization and white privilege by denying societal freedom to the slaves on theological grounds. But more important, over generations of this understanding of Christian faith and its institutionalization in the life of the early church, an inferior-superior racial relationship would come to be so normal, so common and so proper that its naturalness seemed evident. It is in this regard that Berger's analysis becomes particularly (and painfully!) apparent. By justifying the slavocracy on religious grounds and by making the questioning of the moral and ethical demands for the living of faith a fearful proposition, it led the person of faith to fearfully presume that the theretofore black-white relationship was indeed an extension of the very mind of God and therefore as natural as the revolutions and orbits of the planets themselves! In short, the justification of the slavocracy on religious grounds blurred the distinction between a material world created by God and a socio-historical world created by whites. In doing so, God came to be seen as creator of *both* worlds. Thus, one was led to the conclusion that if the creation of the material world was a wise creation then the creation of a world rooted in white superiority was a wise creation as well.

On the one hand Berger makes clear that we are all in the process as human beings of some type of "world construction." On the other hand, he also makes clear that human history has been witness to groups of humans not being above coercive, controlling, and death-dealing engagement with other humans in the process of world building where even placing the canopy of divine sovereignty over such a world has not been precluded as an option in selling the "citizens" of that world on its appropriateness. One could make a very cogent argument that the black-white relationship in American history is the highest qualified candidate of such a "world construction." Its affect on the social conscience of many a slave is what caused Harriet Tubman to lament toward the end of her life that, "I could have freed many more slaves on the Underground Railroad — problem was that they didn't know they were slaves!"

It is in this regard that Bishop Berkeley's treatment of Christian freedom has profound post-slavery implications. Although history has shown us that Bishop Berkeley's treatment of Christian freedom could only stand the test of immediate time, its theological impact in terms of understanding of faith, I contend, has outlived the slavocracy. In its short-term application, the inward freedom hermeneutic revealed its major weakness insofar as slaveholder's fears that conversion of the slaves did eventually come to mean physical freedom from slavery were realized. It also revealed its weakness in the sense that conversion to Christianity for the slave meant at the least a tacit concession by white Christian missionaries that blacks were now in some way human and therefore difficult to make the case that they remain slaves. The passel of anti-slavery literature in the beginning of the nineteenth century and up to the Civil War revolved principally around these two weaknesses.

Yet American history has also shown us that the process of black dehumanization was far from over. As quiet as the secret is kept, slavery was graciously kind to whites. It allowed whites to procure untold wealth on the backs of free slave labor and to build successful institutions in practically every arena of human existence. But more important, it allowed whites to perpetually bask in the bright rays of their racial superiority through its systematic denial of black entry into those institutions as their equals. Thus, despite the fact that the slavocracy had ended institutionally, whites were not about to abandon a paradigm for "successful" living even if it meant an "ideological tweaking" of slave pedagogy. Whites knew also that its successful paradigm for living had, of necessity, to include a consistent assault on the incapacity of blacks to live as free men and women. Moreover, whites also realized that they certainly could not entertain any notions of black equality in the forwarding of a post-slavery hermeneutic of racial oppression and were willing again to employ its most learned scholars, *including its theologians and clergy*, to legitimate that hermeneutic.

Many white theologians and clergy in the post-slavery context committed themselves to a reworking of Bishop Berkeley's inward freedom hermeneutic. What we would witness is an approach to Christian faith that reaffirmed white superiority and black inferiority through a system of racial separation in all public arenas of American life and the white religious establishment's ordaining of it by God. In particular, this "updated" racist hermeneutic granted black people inward freedom from individual sin but not outward freedom from white control of the dispensation of social, economic and political justice in American life and more important, white control of the aesthetic mediums that would influence both black and white self-images. The legitimation of this post-slavery reality would be most stringently promulgated in theological tracts of white theologians and in sermons of white clergy. Through their tireless efforts, they were able to establish as the norm in Christian life in America an approach to faith that was acutely anti-revolutionary, anti-black, ruggedly individualistic, and, beyond the affirmation of God's favor on white aesthetic, cultural, and intellectual superiority, decidedly other-worldly.

What follows on the pages of this book are the major categories in which I argue that the white religious establishment in America has been white supremacy's most effective advocate.

Notes

1.   Lester B. Scherer, *Slavery and the Churches in Early America: 1619-1819.* Grand Rapids, Michigan: Eerdman's Publishing Company, 1975, 52.

2.   Winthrop Jordan, *The White Man's Burden: The Historical Origins of Racism in the United States.* New York: Oxford University Press, 1974, 53.

3.   Ibid., 54.

4.   Scherer, *Slavery and the Churches in America*, 65.

5.   George M. Fredrickson, *The Black Image in the White Mind: A Debate on Afro-American Character and Destiny: 1817-1914*, New York: Harper & Row Publishers, 1971, 47.

6.   Ibid.

7.   Winthrop Jordan, *White Over Black: American Attitudes Toward the Negro, 1550-1812.* 1968, 24.

8.   One of the leading works of this era was Josiah Nott's *Types of Mankind,* wherein Nott not only argued that blacks were created later than whites but that blacks were actually of a separate origin altogether from whites. Nott also argued that if left to their own devices and void of contact from civilized whites, blacks would remain a barbarous people. See also Claude H. Nolen's, *The Negro's Image in the South: The Anatomy of White Supremacy.* Lexington: University of Kentucky Press, 1968.

9.   See his mammoth work on this subject, *Christian Faith: An Introduction to the Idea of Christianity.* New York: Crossroads Publishing, 1985.

10.   New York: Doubleday and Company, Incorporated, 1967, 7.

11.   Ibid.

12.   Ibid., 32.

13.   Ibid., 33

14.   Jordan, *White Over Black*, 23-24.

15.   Taken from Jordan, *White Man's Burden*, 90.

16.   Ibid.

17.   Taken from James O. Buswell, *Slavery, Segregation, and Scripture.* Grand Rapids: Eerdman's Publishing Company, 1964, 31.

2

The Necessity of a Dehumanized Black Humanity

It was well understood that if by the teaching of history the white man could be furthered assured of his superiority and the Negro could be made to feel that he (she) had always been a failure and that the subjection of his (her) will to some other race is necessary the freedman (free person), then, would still be a slave. . . .When you determine what a man (human) shall think, you do not have to concern yourself with what he (she) will do. If you make a man (woman) feel that he (she) is inferior, you do not have to compel him (her) to accept an inferior status, for he (she) will seek it himself (herself). If you make a man (woman) think he (she) is justly an outcast, you do not have to order him (her) to the back door. He (she) will go without being told; and if there is no back door, his (her) very nature will demand one.
Carter G. Woodson, *The Mis-Education of the Negro*

In close connection to the question of black humanity in existential comparison to white humanity is the necessity of black dehumanization itself. When whites in the colonies committed themselves to the idea of white superiority, it meant that the social, economic, political, and *religious* norm of the colonies had to be given over to the task of establishing the legitimacy of that superiority. This meant not only the "selection" of another race of people with which to compare one's superior humanity but also to the "social construction," of that other race's inferiority. To be sure, such a process entailed the "selection" of West African people and the necessity of their dehumanization in order to confirm their inferiority. A well-crafted systemic method of black inferiority pervaded every significant institution in the colonies and later America.

The social engineering of black inferiority began with the theory of a diminished ontological endowment of black humanity in comparison to that of whites. This, in turned, enhanced the argument by whites that black inferiority was not socially engineered but, by virtue of differing ontological endowments between the races, a divine given. It is in this vain that the religious dimension of white superiority had particularly telling consequences in compelling blacks to think that its dehumanization was not an avaricious and egoistic machination of a racist mind but rather a gratuitous manifestation of divine wisdom. The religious dimension of white superiority has also been successful in creating a religious norm in national life that has either condoned the treatment of black people as necessary for their salvation or has placed national discourse on the moral implications of black dehumanization outside the purview of authentic religious expression. In fact, white racial superiority would become the hinge on which moral discourse turned, and, subsequently, the hinge on which Christian theological discourse turned. The gospel of Jesus Christ, then, became terribly perverted and associated not with the establishment of the kingdom of God as the oneness of humanity but associated rather with the kingdom as the eternalizing of black dehumanization and white superiority in the name of Jesus. As a result, the history of the colonies and America has been witness to a sinister approach to Christian faith that has equated white will to power with the will of God. In so doing, an ideological distortion of Christian faith became the normative expression of that faith.

With this backdrop, we proceed with this chapter examining: 1) the relationship between Christian pedagogy and economic life in Europe; 2) that relationship's co-opting by white clergy and theologians in the colonies and America to justify the dehumanization of Africans; and 3) the deleterious effects generations of working in a slavocracy had on the psyche of African people.

Christian Pedagogy and Economic Life in Europe

Central to an understanding of the relationship between European Christianity and economic life was that the will of God meant, above all, that the golden rule must be extended to human interaction beyond the church and to the living of morally acceptable lives in ones economic dealings. Thus, the dungeons of hell and excommunication in the immediate were often levied on white Christians in Switzerland, France, and England by church leadership for contentment with poverty, on the one hand, and the glorification of excessive wealth and the selling of goods for more than their worth on the other hand. Hence, the golden rule meant from a standpoint of personal wealth an Aristotelian golden mean between poverty and riches and meant from a standpoint of corporate profit, a fair price for goods sold with a heart-filled disposition in selling to the poor. At stake then for the European Christian community was the forwarding of a efficacious

Christian interpretation of humanity through the virtue of work in the context of a stratified society economically where workers, whether tenant or landlord, laborer or manager, servant or master, were to see themselves as part of a process not only bigger than themselves but a process having salvific import as well. That is to say, productive living on earth became a staple part of expression of faith for the European Christian community and subsequently a significant dimension of Christian theology for both Catholic and Protestant alike. Whether it was the link between good works both in occupation and benevolence towards others as a meritorious accumulation of good works as necessary for salvation (Catholicism); whether it was the notion that good works on earth could not merit salvation but God's grace did provide for both a kingdom on earth and a kingdom of heaven (Luther); or whether God's grace manifested itself in the elect in the way it lived its individual lives (Calvin), Christian faith saw its role for the believer expanded beyond the church while not sacrificing the church as the most significant institution on earth.

To be sure, this debate was frequently connected with usury which primarily meant a fair charge of interests for loans. The growing debate on usury reached its pinnacle in the fifteenth century when the Catholic Church was being pushed to be critical of monarchies that many felt were unfairly taxing the poor and charging exorbitant interest rates. This, along with the highly critical practice of indulgences, hindered Catholicism's ability to be a true moral arbiter in such matters and was a crucial issue in both the start of the Reformation tradition and for Catholicism's own counter-reformation. Yet for both the Catholic and Reformed traditions usury, in its seminal meaning, was not considered illegal. But it becomes so, when the lender does not allow the borrower "such a proportion of the gain of his labour, hazard, or property doth require, but…will live at ease upon his labours"; or when, in spite of the borrowers misfortune, he rigorously exacts his pound of flesh; or when interest is demanded for a loan which charity would require to be free.[1] In this regard, the European Christian community was seeking the construction of a religious ethic for the proper conducting of business and fair treatment among each other. This presupposed that: 1) successful living required an intricate knowledge and fair demonstration of economics; and 2) insofar as Europeans were children of God, fair economic dealings were required by divine ordinance. Hence, the Christian…is committed by his faith to the acceptance of certain ethical standards, and these standards are as obligatory in the sphere of economic transactions as in any other province of human activity.[2] Thus, one is able to see that despite theological differences in the manifestations of the particulars of the salvific treatment, there was universal agreement among all quarters of European Christendom that Christian faith must create ethical norms for appropriate socio-economic dealings, and, more significantly, must establish work itself as having an edifying effect on the human subject.

Of particular significance for our thesis is the axiom of proper treatment of other human beings in the process of conducting business transactions. Both Catholicism and the Reformation tradition would be insistent that all business dealings that morally compromised other human beings or that brought about huge profit through the unfair use of other human beings was unlawful. Naturally, therefore he [the Christian] is debarred from making money at the expense of other persons, and certain profitable avenues of commerce are closed to him (her) at the outset for . . . it is not lawful to take up or keep up any oppressing monopoly or trade, which tends to enrich you by the loss of the Commonwealth or of many.[3] Hence, European Christendom's attempt to fashion an ethical criteria for proper living economically, and that fruitful labor is demanded by the Creator as a means for successful living is to be commended for both its content and intent.

But when white Christians in the colonies and America imported this understanding of the religion/economic relationship, they adapted it in such a way that it would come to mean historical and existential disaster for people of African descent. The religion/economic relationship in European Christendom and its ultimate coalescence with capitalism are treated most elaborately in Max Weber's classic, *The Protestant Ethic and the Sprit of Capitalism*. While Weber goes to great pains to point out that it was not Christianity or the Reformation tradition that gave birth to capitalism but that capitalism had already established itself as an accepted form of economic production in the medieval period and before, he does set out to establish that the Reformation tradition would ultimately influence capitalism such that it would go from cherishing the ideas of thrift and humility to the accumulation of material wealth via divine decree. In fact, for Weber, the destructive acquisition of wealth and excessive material consumption has nothing to do with capitalism and is more accurately described in its seminal understanding as more akin to restraining this type of economic end. To be sure, capitalism's intent is to indeed turn a profit in the exchange between raw materials and overhead on the one hand and a fair price of the final product to the buyer on the other hand. Whether it be an individual entrepreneur or a multi-tiered conglomerate, Weber makes clear that the purpose of each entity under capitalism is to profit only what is necessary for all parties involved to live by comfortable but modest means and to not fall prey to the sins of avarice and greed. Yet it is here that the relationship of European Christendom to economic life becomes admittedly complex but clearly contradictory. For it is at the start of the Reformation tradition and Luther's attack on Catholicism's internal handling of its finances and its continuing conflicts with the monarchy over "secular" issues that led him to the conclusion that both society and church were in need of a Christian "ethic" regarding the handling of money and its concomitant affairs. Unfortunately for Luther, this would have to take the formal name of a "Protestant" ethic after his scathing attack on the papacy on the use of indulgences and subsequent excommunication from Catholic fellowship. Weber recognizes in these events that Catholicism although deeply involved in the socio-economic life of fifteenth century Europe, did not possess any well-established doctrine on the church's relationship to the world and certainly did not see a divine imperative to articulate such a relationship. This is to be understood, for Weber, not necessarily as a criticism but rather an observation of Catholicism. However, for Luther, this would become a major criticism of Catholicism in the first couple of decades of the Reformation tradition. If Luther was not wholly swayed by Catholicism's failure to construct an ethical guide to pecuniary responsibility, then his contact with the laity in its daily work activity in the early years of the Reformation decisively convinced him that the church was in need of an "ethic" of socio-economic life.

Luther then makes one of the most significant theological constructions of his theological career when he extends his treatment of the ministerial "calling" to the socio-economic realm. Although the novelty of Luther's conception of the calling was neither the calling itself nor the expanded nature of the calling to the socio-economic realm (Aquinas), the conception was novel in the sense that it carried a superlative moral weight to all other callings in Christendom. Weber explains it this way:

> But at least one thing was unquestionably new: the valuation of the fulfillment of duty in worldly affairs as the highest form which the moral activity of the individual could assume. This it was which inevitably gave every day worldly activity a religious significance, and which first created the conception of the calling in this sense.[4]

To be sure, Luther's conception of the calling represented yet another area of divide between the Reformation tradition and Catholicism but it broke new ground in Christian theological tradition by establishing that God is not only concerned with what we do socio-economically but that it now has incomparably weighted salvific implications for the confessing Christian. The only way of living acceptably to God was not to surpass worldly morality in monastic asceticism, but solely through the fulfillment of the obligations imposed on the individual by his position in the world.[5] Thus Luther's conception of the calling extended the moral compass of God beyond the ascetic life to the socio-political realm giving the latter a moral and ethical significance it did not have with Catholic doctrine. More to the point, it is still at this point in the development of the socio-economic relationship to religion that Luther mandates that modest living and refraining from exploiting others to obtain that living is not only ethically appropriate but had ascended to the lofty level of a manifestation of God's grace. This means conversely, for Luther, that, "the pursuit of material gain beyond personal needs must thus appear as a symptom of a lack of grace, and since it can apparently only be obtained at the expense of others, directly reprehensible.[6]

Yet one key dimension of Luther's conception of the calling for both himself and later for Calvin begins to lay a foundation for the theological justification of human exploitation. Luther's break with monasticism and his "entry" into the world made him particularly cognizant of the socio-economic hierarchy that existed. Yet at the same time, he was also insistent that God's providence over the world must never be compromised. To that end, Luther was at best a lukewarm advocate of upward mobility of the masses. He saw the ascension of peasants to nobility as a questioning of God's providence and never brought a critical bent to the unjust nature of the existing system. He understood the existing order to be God-made and not human-made and in doing so unwittingly perpetuated a socio-economic system that de facto placed value on humanity that corresponded to the class in which one existed. Thus, on the one hand, Luther saw economic exploitation of the peasants by the nobility to be theologically reprehensible but, on the other hand, saw the existence of an economic system that inescapably lent itself to that exploitation as an unquestioned prerogative of divine will. The unfortunate corollary to such a line of reasoning led Luther to see the Peasant's Revolt not as ordained of God but as a "disturbance" of that ordination. This is why, for Weber,

> After the conflict with the Fanatics and the peasant disturbances, the objective historical order of things in which the individual has been placed by God becomes for Luther more and more a direct manifestation of divine will. The stronger and stronger emphasis on the providential element, even in particular events of life, led more and more to a traditionalistic interpretation based on the idea of Providence. The individual should remain once and for all in the station and calling in which God had placed him, and should restrain his worldly activity within the limits imposed by his established station in life.[7]

In this regard, although noble in intent, Luther would create a stratified theological paradigm in Christendom that when placed in providential light, eternally cemented God's favor on a socio-economic system that valued human beings according to their "stations in life" with the nobility, of course, having more human value than the peasants. More important, Luther "righteously" demanded that Christians internalize this stratification as a profound manifestation of God's grace therefore eliminating it as an issue for theological debate. To his credit, Luther did recognize the inherent contradictions in such a treatment of socio-economic human relations. He sought to soften the blow for those on the lower rungs of the socio-economic ladder by maintaining that, regardless of social status, we all go to God after death for judgment as sinners and that we are ultimately justified by faith in God alone and not one's station in life. Yet, the impact of the "stations in life" hermeneutic on subsequent human relationships, precisely because of religion's powerful influence on the shaping of human worldviews, cannot be underestimated.

Whatever Luther's influence did not accomplish in placing God's providence on stratified human relationships, John Calvin's influence would. Calvin would accentuate God's providence to the highest degree arguing for a predestined elect of God prior to the mother's womb, minimizing human works in the salvation process to nonexistence and maintaining that the elect have already been chosen by God for eternal life and are recognizable by the character and integrity with which they carry out those works. In other words, Calvin understood the worldly life to be God manifested in an already heaven-bound elect. In short, Calvin argued that we are chosen by God for salvation not after life but *before* life!

Crucial for our thesis though is that when translated into earthly terms, since the life of the individual was only an ontological manifestation of one already elected by God for salvation, it reaffirmed the insignificance of human works and in so doing placed the dehumanization of African peoples in moral and ethical obscurity. This is because a major Reformation theme would be co-opted and become the kernel of a worldview that justified African dehumanization as a divine ordinance insofar as the inaugurators of the slave trade were a part of the elect and simply demonstrating their elect status! In very similar terms, when Jesus said, "I and my Father (God) are one," (John 10:30) white Christian progenitors of the Reformation tradition in the colonies and America understood themselves to be an earthly crystallization of God not only in deed but in aesthetic presentation as well. Therefore, God was a charter member of the Reformation tradition, had European aesthetic features and inaugurated the "stations in life" hermeneutic. Moreover, God was a proponent of European socioeconomic prosperity and therefore a proponent of the socio-economic prosperity of the colonies and America. This meant theologically that God was not only a proponent of the acquisition of cheap, productive (African) labor but demanded it of the colonists as a display of obedience to God's sovereignty. In short, given God's favor on the elect, the latter wanted to make clear that everything being done by them was a manifestation of the very mind of God as demonstrated in the totality of their behavior. Moreover, given that their works are only a showing of what God would do if God were on earth, any attempt to question or compromise this process would come to be dubbed blasphemous and a direct violation of divine will. This would become extremely significant in the late seventeenth and into the eighteenth centuries when Christian faith would come to be African slavery's most prominent proponent.

More to the point, Calvin's treatment of the socio-economic relationship to religion would follow Luther's retreat from traditional asceticism and come to be termed Protestant asceticism. It would seek, like Luther's treatment, to maintain the divine ordinance of stations in life and to take the discipline and humility of the traditional ascetic life and posit them in the world of everyday human relationships. None moreso than on the salvific value placed on work itself. Of particular significance, Calvin would break with Luther on the absolute denunciation of wealth particularly for the clergy questioning Luther's claim that it hindered the minister's effectiveness but was clear that this wealth attainment shall not be the cause of the clergy or the nobility slipping in to indolent and slothful behavior. The real moral objection is to relaxation in the security of possession, the enjoyment of wealth with the consequences of idleness and the temptations of the flesh, above all of distraction from the pursuit of a righteous life.[8] Hence we see in Calvin's ascetic Protestantism not only a shift from the monastery to the world but also the pursuit of the righteous life that denounces the unwillingness to work as a lack of grace and affirms the pursuit of wealth attainment through cheap labor. We further see with both Luther and Calvin, an insistence on the divine ordinance of work, how it is intimately connected to an earthly expression of God's grace and, more significant, that a stratified society on the basis of wealth and social status was part of God's master plan for human relationships. In so doing, European Christendom was making a huge statement, both implicitly and explicitly, in areas that have come to characterize what in modern times Weber terms, "the spirit of capitalism." We see an easy affinity with wealth attainment for an "elect" particularly for Calvin, in which it chimes symmetrically well with his overall salvific scheme. But more to the point we see with both Luther and Calvin an unyielding allegiance to the providence of the existing order — an order characterized by an unequal distribution of wealth, acute poverty, and human degradation. This owes itself to the reasoning that wherever we find ourselves i.e., our "stations in life," we should humbly accept them in complete obedience as the pinnacle of divine wisdom. Hence, the Reformation tradition, particularly following Calvin, the Puritan movement and the advent of modern Christianity had firmly established the coming earthly kingdom as the uncritical acceptance of a stratified society on the basis of social status and wealth attainment. That these significant theological developments would lay the foundation for modern capitalism in the colonies and America cannot be denied.

> For, in conformity with the Old Testament and in analogy to the ethical valuation of good works, [Protestant] asceticism looked upon the pursuit of wealth as an end in itself as highly reprehensible; but the attainment of it as a fruit of labour in a calling was a sign of God's blessing. And even more important: the religious valuation of restless, continuous, systematic work in a worldly calling, as the highest means to asceticism, and at the same time the surest and most evident proof of rebirth and genuine faith, must have been the most powerful conceivable lever for the expansion of that attitude toward life which we here have called the spirit of capitalism.[9]

Hence, Weber establishes clearly that religion provided the European aristocracy with a theological worldview that placed God's favor on wealth attainment and social stratification. It is also very significant to note that this stratification occurred in a context in which there was very little if any racial heterogeneity. At the same time the anti-African sentiment was rapidly growing in Europe and the colonies. And as commerce and the economic infrastructure of the colonies was taking root, it would begin to flourish with the importation of African slaves thus creating a social context of acute racial heterogeneity. What we would witness, to be sure, is the application of Protestant asceticism structurally but, in enslaving a people who were racially different and culturally despised, an entirely different set of rules emerged for governance in the colonies and America and necessarily so on two fronts. In the first instance, with the drive for wealth attainment given a proverbial green light by Calvin, colonists demonstrated their "elect" status, i.e., the high priority given to work, through the building of a new economic infrastructure that demanded, in the spirit of capitalism, minimal overhead costs. This required the labor of a people that colonists were comfortable enslaving and who were extremely durable. This meant Africans who were comfortable "enslavees" because of the huge anti-African sentiment in European culture and the African's ability to produce high volumes of labor in adverse weather conditions. In the second instance, although Protestant asceticism would serve as the structure for colonists regarding the legitimacy of hierarchical social relationships, colonists had to more directly establish a "stations in life" hermeneutic that entailed a racial as well as a socio-economic hierarchy. This would serve as the most significant factor in building its early economic infrastructure. Thus, the structure of Protestant asceticism and its ultimate development into the spirit of capitalism would make full use of the notion of the divine origin of the existing situation and extolling the virtue of work as a divine calling. As such, the question was never whether the African should be enslaved to bring about wealth attainment for colonists; the only question was how that enslavement would be rationalized as a profound expression of divine providence.

Such a rationalization would begin in the colonies with the slave trade being articulated as serving two noble ends. First, the rise of European expansionism in the colonies was considered God's elect carrying out the divine ordinance of demonstrating that they were indeed the proprietors of God's grace. Buoyed by God's grace and the "new" land obtained through the confiscation of Native American properties, the colonists were well on their way to realizing Manifest Destiny but needed a laboring class to till the lands and bring the crops to harvest. That this process required heavily intensive labor is an understatement. Colonists were also acutely aware that free laborers in Europe were not enough in number to effectively carry out their plans. The logical choice, for many, would have been the Native Americans given the fact that they were already in the colonies and did not have to be "imported." Yet the Indians proved not to be a suitable selection for slavery on several fronts. The Indians rapidly succumbed to the excessive labor demanded of them, the insufficient diet, the white man's diseases, and their inability to adjust themselves to the new way of life.[9] This left, for the colonists, Africans who had already been branded as inferior to Europeans culturally, aesthetically, and intellectually. This leads us to the second noble cause of colony expansion. Not only could the possibility for the development of a successful economic infrastructure be built on the backs of cheap African labor but given the latter's pitiable way of life, African enslavement would also come to be seen by many colonists as a benevolent gesture in exposing Africans to true civilization. Further, on the heels of its unproductive slave experience with Native Americans, the coercion needed to "make" slaves would come to be seen by colonists as the predictable resistance by a group of people content with its inferior existence. Yet the effort to make slaves of Africans in spite of this resistance would be seen as a challenge by God to colonists to expose Africans to the virtues of work as both groups toil through the slavocracy to build a divine kingdom on earth. But more important, in learning from its Native American experience, the repressive, torturous process of making slaves was an anthropological inevitability, even for Africans, given most people's inclination, in their sinfulness, to resist industry in general and slavery in particular. The labor supply of [people of] low social status, docile and cheap, can be maintained in subjection *only by systematic degradation and by deliberate efforts to suppress its intelligence.*[10] (Italics mine) In this regard colonists were relentless in their anti-African sentiments culturally, aesthetically, and intellectually. They were also relentless in the suppression of any expressions that presented African humanity in an intelligent light. Slavery as an institution demanded it and white racial superiority required it.

The Christian Quest for the Contented Slave

Yet because slavery demanded systematic degradation of the enslaved class, colonists found themselves in a slight dilemma. How were they to degrade African culture and the African's capacity for sustained work when the very reason that the African was seen as the best choice for slavery was precisely because of his stamina for sustained work? In fact, colonists would maintain that one African could do the work of four Indians and even more whites and that the Dark Continent was an inexhaustible reservoir of untapped labor. Yet in the final analysis, for the purpose of divine will and the maintaining of "stations in life," the theretofore existing situation had to be strictly maintained. That meant a private concession to the African's industry but not to her culture, aesthetics, and especially intellect. More important, it meant a constant degradation of African culture for the purpose of not allowing the slave to think she could be anything other than a slave. After all, the "stations in life" hermeneutic was understood to be eternal and was the theological matrix, whether explicit or implicit, that guided the colonists thinking regarding the valuation of African people.

In this regard, the maintaining of "stations" required for colonists a public affirmation of their benevolence to expose heathen Africans to civilization while theoretically affirming the lack of capacity of the African for sustained civilized behavior as reflected in her inability to bring any collaborative endeavor to fruition except by constant supervision thus establishing a solid pretext for her enslavement. This would be accomplished by establishing, "the colour as a mark for servitude," paradigm that would come to primarily characterize racist socialization in the early years of the colonies. A paradigm that would be articulated to both the slaves and colonists as the exclusive methodology for prosperity in the south and reaffirm that slavery was the eternal "station" for Africans. South Carolinian William Loughton Smith, an antislavery advocate, while denouncing slavery as an abomination, recognized its deeply rooted entrenchment in southern life and its inescapable degradation of black humanity.

> The truth is that the best informed . . . citizens of the Northern States know that slavery is so ingrafted into the policy of the Southern States, that it cannot be eradicated without tearing up by the roots their happiness, tranquility, and prosperity. It is well known that they are an indolent people, improvident, averse to labor: when emancipated, they will either starve or plunder.[11]

Smith reminds us of the inversely proportional relationship between the affirmation of white superiority and the debasement of black humanity. In particular, the public presentation of the African in non-industrious terms was predictable given that we have already established that enslavement entails systematic debasement and reinforces the eternal stations of human relationships which means for the African, an eternity of enslavement. Quaker John Woolman, a leading critic of slavery maintained that in light of the way slaves are treated and publicly presented by their masters, it left little conclusion for anyone objectively to draw other than the African's natural inferiority. Placing on Men the ignominious Title, SLAVE, dressing them in uncomely Garments, keeping them to servile Labour, in which they are often dirty, tends gradually to fix a Notion in the Mind, that they are a Sort of People below us in Nature.[12] Hence, the intent was to use the pretext of making the African more industrious in carrying out collaborative projects to justify working her in such inhumane conditions when in actuality the reason for her selection for enslavement was precisely because of her capacity for sustained physical labor.

In particular, if the pretext of black enslavement as divine ordinance was to succeed, overseers, in tandem with white clergy, had to demonstrate a certain contentment of the African for her enslaved status. This is why at every opportunity, overseers sought to invoke not only the African's affinity with her enslaved status but also her lack of envy of those in higher providential stations. Properly trained, inoculated with just conceptions of themselves and others, and so protected against the malignancy of modern philanthropy, they were still the best farmhands in the world.[13] Not only did Africans make the best farmhands, but every effort was made to present them as people of pious and docile disposition. This owed itself almost exclusively to the proximity of highly intelligent whites and their indoctrination to the slave that she was involved in a process that was eternal and therefore required an attenuation of any harbored desires to occupy a more material or prestigious position in the social hierarchy.

> Having the kindliest disposition of all workers, the Negro alone among laborers was docile in temper. He did not take offense nor seek revenge; among all the races there was none so loyal. Trained by the high intelligence of the Anglo-Saxon, the southern Negro proved by his fidelity, his incomparable courtesy of

manner, and his accommodating disposition that he occupied his true place in society.[14]

To be sure, this indoctrination was crucial not only for the slave but for the white community as well. Central to an understanding of the ideology of white supremacy was whites convincing themselves of the happiness of Africans in their enslavement. This would become pivotal in the late seventeenth and into the eighteenth century as anti-slavery sentiment grew and sympathetic white Christians grew more and more leery about the easy affinity between Christian pedagogy and African enslavement. Samuel Hopkins, an eighteenth century minister who raised the question as to why whites saw blacks as "fit for nothing but slaves" answered by stating that, "we have been used to look on them in a mean contemptible light; and our education has filled us with strong prejudices against them, and led us to consider them, not as our brethren, or in any degree on a level with us; but as quite another species of animals, made only to serve us and our children; and as happy in bondage, as in any other state"[15] In this regard, Hopkins is to be commended for recognizing the ideology of white racial superiority as a clever subterfuge. In so doing, he is also forwarding the implicit suggestion that oppressive human relationships are not a product of divine providence but rather of distorted socialization. Yet the socialization of white racial superiority became ever so difficult to separate from Christian pedagogy in the colonies and then America. At stake was the legitimacy of a way of life that necessitated the African being content with her enslaved lot. For most white clergy and theologians this was established biblically through the Hamitic curse on African people in the Old Testament and Jesus and Paul's seeming approval of slavery in New Testament history as evidenced in their not publicly condemning slavery. Failure to convincingly establish slave contentedness undermined the credibility of black dehumanization on Christian grounds and lent credence, conversely, to the legitimacy of slave rebellion.

> If in a Christian society a subordinate people were turbulent, dissatisfied, striving for improvement, this would show that is was not their nature to be ruled by another people. Necessarily dependent Negroes, slaves or semislaves, were said to be as lighthearted as children, while the radical political Negro was denounced as a devil incarnate.[16]

Hence we see an integral part of the ideology of white supremacy was not only to use Christian faith to instill in the African an acute sense of docility through the use of piety but also to brand as anti-Christian, even demonic, the militancy exhibited by those blacks who dedicated their lives to dismantling the slavocracy.

Yet, as already stated, the attempt to Christianize slaves to make them more docile brought with it its share of ambiguity. Christian faith had always urged the freedom of humans in Christ and the biblical witness contains more defiant acts in the name of freedom than capitulation to temporal authority. Some white ministers struggled with this ambiguity but for the most part gave in to their racist socialization.

> Sermons addressed to black slaves were invariably freighted with assertions of inherent equality before God and the utter rightness of inequality on earth. When the Reverend Cary Allen urged upon a group of Virginia blacks the central fact that Christ had died for them, as well as for whites, he was no more a "Christian" than the Reverend Jedidiah Morse (who hated slavery) when he cautioned Negroes, "Many eyes are upon you . . .Be contented in the humble station in which providence has placed you."[17]

Most important, this admonition by Morse to the slave to be humbly contented in her station meant not only the acceptance of a debased social status but also the acceptance of the psychical toll such hard labor (and the inability to share in the fruits of that labor!) exacted on the slave's consciousness. This would become particularly significant when examining blacks emerging attitudes toward work itself in the aftermath of the slavocracy.

Contemporary Racial Discourse and the Impact of Slave Labor

The Christianization of the slave brought with it its own set of challenges for black humanity. It was able to convince not a small number of slaves that it was their lot to be slaves and the exposure to European civilization was in fact God's way of edifying their worldly lot. Yet the quest for a Kingdom of God on earth rooted in white racial superiority was met with stiff resistance by the so-called "radical black leader." The slaveholding community was particularly concerned about the emergence of this type of influence in the slave community. At stake was not only the socio-economic prosperity of the white community but the legitimacy of the "stations in life" hermeneutic and God's providence in the creation of the slavocracy. If the radical black leader were successful in leading a revolt that toppled the slavocracy (which eventually happened!) it would not only deal a death blow to white socio-economic prosperity but shed a pejorative light on a white supremacist worldview in its totality. In response, slave laws were enacted to sever the connection between the slave and the "demonic" leader by not allowing the slaves to gather in numbers larger than five on plantations for fear that rebellion was being planned. This understandably created much angst among the slaves who were made to repress their desire to be free for fear of severe consequences but were constantly being called to a freedom-seeking mode by the radical black leader. Should they adhere to a Christian pedagogy of a slave "station" that seemed unnatural and resist all attempts to topple the slavocracy in the name of "righteousness" or should they do the seemingly natural thing and fight for freedom? (The fact that running away from the plantation was a crime and was punishable by death did not do much to diminish that internal struggle!)

Sitting at the core of this struggle in the slave community, and particularly for the black leader, were the psychological effects of slavery on the slave's psyche in general and the developing attitudes toward work itself. Although every attempt was made by the slaveholding community to convince the slaves that they were participating in a process that was divinely ordained, the practical realities of slave life did not mesh with that teaching. Whether it be through intuition or socialization (or both), we see clearly the affects an enslaved status can have on slaves when one is not allowed to share in the fruits of what is harvested. Even if one is sold on a "stations in life" hermeneutic, the slave's status and treatment were clearly meant to impress upon the slave that she was in fact not human in the way whites were. Furthermore, the complete control exacted over the slave's life both socially and legally is suggestive of the slave's unwillingness to participate freely in a process in which work did not edify but dehumanized. As a result of not being a part of the major decision making processes of her work, with no say in the amount of physical labor she exerted, and living in a constant atmosphere of white imposition, the slave, not surprisingly, came to take a negative attitude toward work itself. Hence we come to one of the biggest existential ambiguities in human relations in the past half millennium: how is one to assess the merits of a "station in life" pedagogy bequeath by the Reformation tradition to white Christian colonists and white Christian Americans that placed divine value on the virtue of hard work to affirm one's humanity that had the opposite effect on African slaves?

On the one hand, the easiest way out of this quandary was to argue that the African's uncivilized status and her natural inclination to idleness were so intractable that noble white efforts to use the slavocracy (and God!) to transform her were not effective. In many regards, this affirmed for many white clergy and theologians the polygenesis argument for black ontology or the notion that black people originated from a different source than whites. Yet, on the other hand, the best way to articulate this ambiguity is to argue that the slavocracy itself as a legitimate interpretation of the "stations in life" pedagogy of the Reformation tradition was and still is the problem today in American life. It was one thing to create a peasant class of persons of European descent in a theocratic monarchy and to see them as humans in every way because of their common racial heritage. It was quite another thing to create a slavocracy of African people of diminished human worth and create a society founded on their inferiority and white superiority. While both contexts held to the "stations in life" pedagogy with God demanding contentment of laborers/slaves, they never paralleled each other in labor intensity and deprivation of basic human rights precisely because of the differing valuations of the humanity of white peasants on the one hand and African slaves on the other hand. In the first instance, the humanity of the peasant class was never questioned insofar as their common European origin and similar aesthetic presentation compelled those of the ruling class to see humanity in the peasant class for to not recognize true humanity in them was to not recognize true humanity in itself. But in the second instance, the differing culture, geographic location and aesthetic presentation of Africans represented the diametric opposite of European culture. Thus, not only was the humanity of blackness questioned but was the target of a full-scale assault on the basis of those differences. This served to solidify in the minds of both slaves and slave-holders, the ontological impossibility of black humanity. In short, the making of a slave required the suppression of anything positive and valued about black humanity.

Yet the Peasant's Revolt itself should serve as a clear indication that even within the context of an European "stations in life" pedagogy, a few sharing in the wealth created by the cheap labor of the masses, even of the same race, intui-tively disclosed itself to the peasants as an unethical approach to human rela-tions. This disclosure occurred despite the fact that Christian theologians and clergy went out of their way to admonish the faithful that failure to live the duty of one's station without envy will surely result in excommunication from God's grace. This disclosure occurred also despite the fact that the peasant class found itself unquestionably in the household of human affirmation as a result of its white skin. It would stand to reason then that incessantly rebellious behavior would occur with enslaved Africans who fell clearly outside the household of human affirmation as a result of its black skin.

Meantime, while the slavocracy was rolling to its eternal destiny, no stock was being taken on the psychical toll it was exacting on the slave. But in retro-spect, why should there have been. Given that the slave trade was intended to be an eternal institution, there was no need to make the slave's exclusion from the prosperity of the slavocracy a significant issue of public discourse. Yet in the aftermath of the slavocracy we are of necessity having to deal with not only the African American's capacity to work but her will to work. It has become an is-sue of intense public discourse in the days of so-called big government and handouts to lazy Americans. It is also interesting to note that African Americans are the only race in America in which contemporary public discourse occurs regarding its lack of industriousness. African Americans are also the only race in America chided for a lack of integrity brought to the workplace
(for those who do work!) and for draining the government of its precious re-sources. (for those who don't work!)

Yet a keen perspective on this issue requires that we briefly examine the history of Africans in America and the "work" imposed on us by the slavocracy. Failure to do so will not only render more ahistorical and therefore ill-informed contemporary discourse but will not do justice to the historical connectedness between the hostility towards African Americans by whites in the slavocracy and how that same hostility conveniently makes itself into contemporary public discourse in America. In both contexts, I contend a pejorative view of African Americans is the ultimate goal. A concise but substantive treatment of this issue is found in Na'im Akbar's work, *Chains and Images of Psychological Slavery*. Akbar rightfully begins his treatment with the societal understanding that work is meant to be an edifying endeavor. It is the medium in just about all civilizations wherein humans construct meaning and purpose in life. But more important, Akbar maintains that that meaning and purpose are inextricably bound with the individuals having a choice in their line of work, and a fair share of the profits for all parties involved. It is in this context that work becomes edifying and meaningful for all humans. However, for Akbar, when persons are placed in a context in which work is forced upon those individuals and they have no input into how long their work day is, what type of work is done and no sharing in the profits of their labor, then work becomes a demeaning rather than an edifying phenomenon. This explains, for Akbar, the work history of African Americans.

> Work in a natural society is looked upon with pride, both because it permits a man (humans) to express himself (themselves) with pride and because it supplies his (their) survival needs. As a natural form of expression, work is not too distinguishable from play. During slavery, work was used as a punishment. The need for workers was the most identifiable cause of the African American's enslavement. Work came to be despised as any punishment is despised. Work became hated as does any activity which accomplishes no reward for the doer. Work became identified with slavery. Even today, the African American slang expression which refers to a job as a "slave" communicates this painful connection.[18]

Further, watching white slave masters engage in what could be considered acute leisure in the process of making African slaves work relentlessly and then completely securing the profits of their labor reoriented a natural human desire to work. Thus began the surreptitious and cunning acts by slaves to avoid work by feigning sickness or injury or by seeking escape from the slavocracy. In short, work came to be seen by the slave as a process of dehumanization rather than humanization.

> Consequently, slaves equated work with enslavement, and freedom with the avoidance of work. Work was identified as the activity of the underdog and was difficult to be viewed with pride. Work is something approached unwillingly and out of necessity only. It is also a badge of disparagement.[19]

Because of this legacy and many other battles fought racially by African Americans in the aftermath of slavery, particularly indentured servanthood, many African Americans continue to see work as a dehumanizing endeavor and is done out of necessity only. This owes itself in large part to being excluded from educational and training programs that would enable African Americans to pursue lines of work that would be considered humanizing. But having lived so many generations as slaves and enduring white backlash at every epoch in American history, we are also dealing with a matter of realistically concluding what African Americans could aspire to be and trying to construct meaning and purpose within the parameters imposed by whites for "acceptable" black aspirations.

Further, we must also take stock of the fact that after Emancipation, many African Americans took the attitude that their foreparents who had worked from cradle to grave as slaves would want their now free children to do as little as possible in the way of work. This also had a huge impact on attitudes toward work for many African Americans. In light of this, some African Americans sought to live as leisure-oriented as possible. Hence the legacy of slavery toward work for African Americans becomes apparent. The slavocracy exacted such a psychical toll on African Americans that it created a hostile attitude of the African American toward work. But more important, it created a rebellious disposition toward a system of white privilege that exploited African American humanity at every turn. As such, it caused the African American to take not only a negative attitude toward work but a negative attitude toward Americanism itself socially and legally. Given that its enslavement and segregation were made legal, it also caused African Americans to become criminals not in the committing of random deviant acts that sought to destroy American life but as morally conscious communal acts designed to affirm black humanity in the wake of an unjust system of governance.

Hence, as public discourse continues on the future of race in America we must as African Americans continue to be vigilant in response to the criticism that we are less industrious and/or given over more to idleness and lack of productivity than those of other races and must continue to remind America and the world that the economic infrastructure of America was built on the productivity of African slaves. In fact, we must continue to hammer home the reality that in American history there has been no people more industrious than African Americans, and no people who have had more jobs than African Americans. And for that indispensable contribution to American prosperity in the most adverse conditions we have only a modicum of the wealth we should have in light of the aggregate benefit of our work in American history.

Notes

1. R. H. Tawney, *Religion and the Rise of Capitalism.* New York: The New American Library, 1954, 185.

2. Ibid., 184.

3. Ibid.

4. Max Weber, *The Protestant Ethic and the Spirit of Capitalism.* New York: Charles Scribner's Sons, 1958, 80.

5. Ibid.

6. Ibid., 84.

7. Ibid., 85.

8. Ibid., 172.

9. Ibid.

10. Eric Williams, *Capitalism and Slavery.* Chapel Hill: University of North Carolina Press, 1994 (Originally published in 1944), 7-8.

11. Ibid., 7.

12. Winthrop Jordan, *The White Man's Burden: Historical Origins of Racism in the United States.* New York: Oxford University Press, 1974, 129.

13. Ibid., 115.

14. Claude H. Nolen, *The Negro's Image in the South: The Anatomy of White Supremacy.* Lexington, Kentucky: University of Kentucky Press, 1968, 11.

15. Ibid., 12.

16. Taken from Jordan, *White Man's Burden*, 115.

17. Nolen, *The Negro's Image in the South*, 13.

18. Na'im Akbar, *Chains and Images of Psychological* Slavery. Jersey City, New Jersey: New Mind Productions, 1984, 9-10.

19. Ibid., 10.

3

White Religion, Racial Morality, and Black Dehumanization

The characteristic feature of the Negroes is that their consciousness has not yet reached an awareness of any substantial objectivity – for example, *of God or the law* – in which the will of man (humanity) could participate and in which he (she) could become aware of his (her) own being. . . . Thus man (humanity), as we find him (it) in Africa has not progressed beyond his (her) immediate existence. As soon as man (woman) emerges as a human being, he (she) stands in opposition to nature, and it is this alone which makes him (her) a human being. But if he (she) has merely made a distinction between himself (herself) and nature, he (she) is still at the first stage of development: he (she) is dominated by passion, and is nothing more than a savage.

Georg Wilhelm Friedrich Hegel, *Lectures on the Philosophy of World History*

We now turn our attention to what can be considered the most significant aspect of our argument. The construction of moral frameworks is the single most important factor in the shaping of our worldviews as human beings. Hegel, in his quote above, clearly demonstrates how a white racist moral framework influences one's anthropological and theological conclusions about other races of people. In fact, Hegel's European ancestral inheritance socialized him into a moral understanding of human worth based on racial categorization with European morality and culture occupying the top rung of a racial hierarchy. His contention that Africans possessed no substantive knowledge of either God or of law was/is a widespread and long-standing conclusion of Europeans and served as a bedrock pretext for both the physical brutality and the Christianizing of slaves. The physical brutality was seen as an inescapable dimension of bringing Africans into slavery given that their so-called savage nature would compel them to resist all attempts at civilization. The Christianizing of slaves was seen as a benevolent duty carried out by whites in service to God. White clergy and theologians were convinced that there was something salvific for both them and Africans in bringing the latter out of savagery and into a consciousness of God and law. It is on these two themes that the morality of black dehumanization in American life was constructed.

In this regard, Christian theology in American history has played a crucial role in sanctioning a morality of black dehumanization. For not only are moral pedagogies constructed by religious communities, but in light of the sacred designation attached to religious instruction, these moral pedagogies have served, in many white religious communities, as the most significant dimension in shaping a racist worldview. Insofar as Christian leadership understands itself to be imparting a moral pedagogy to its adherents that is rooted in divine knowledge it is also imparting a moral pedagogy it understands to be sacred and therefore pleasing to God. Thus, we find ourselves dealing with two areas of supreme significance regarding moral discourse in America. First, in equating moral pedagogies with divine reality, we are equating them with God's eternity and thereby implicitly suggesting that those pedagogies existed at the foundation of the universe itself. Second, in maintaining that a moral pedagogy emanated from the very mind of the Master Moralist, we are taught not to question its content for in doing so we make a mockery of faith. While both these factors are not actually foundations of a moral pedagogy but aspects of a moral pedagogy, they are presented as the former in most ecclesiastical structures in American life. I shall deal with that point later in this work. For now, it suffices for me to treat racial morality here in broader strokes.

When we add to the two factors above the widely accepted theological axiom that we are bound by universal sin, the complexity of moral frameworks becomes apparent. That complexity emerges not only in our inability to ultimately live up to the precepts of those frameworks in both their individual and collective dimensions but also our apparent sinfulness in their creation as it relates to human oppression and the propensity of those who benefit economically from that oppression to morally affirm it as a divine precept. In this regard, I speak directly to the collective dimension of human existence in the colonies and America as it relates to a racially superior moral framework that has either condoned the dehumanization of black people or that has affirmed only individualistic transgressions (namely sexual transgressions) as morally inappropriate. The intent of structuring a racially superior morality in this way is to conveniently render collective moral discourse and the dehumanization of black people in particular a nonexistent aspect of American public life. This chapter explores what I consider to be the fundamental axioms of a morality of black dehumanization.

Christian Theology and American Morality

Two white American theologians, ironically, provide us with a suitable foundation for our treatment. We find in Reinhold Niebuhr's 1932 classic, *Moral Man and Immoral Society*, a timeless treatment of both humanity's moral strivings and moral failings. In particular, Niebuhr takes this work to skillfully argue that the crux of humanity's moral failings has primarily to do with its inability to exhibit moral turpitude in its collective dealings particularly those in positions of power governmentally and ecclesiastically. Sitting at the core of these moral failings, for Niebuhr, is the propensity for those in power to engage in "collective egoism" and "the power of self-interest" in the carrying out of their duties. He insists that the ubiquitous presence of the propensity to collective egoism is a part of the sinful reality of humans and, as a result, not able to be transcended. As such, Niebuhr saw all collective relationships as more political than moral, i.e., as the quest to either obtain or wrest away power.

At issue for Niebuhr is the seeming overwhelming propensity for power elites to engage in ongoing struggles between those perceived equals who challenge their power on the one hand and a paternalistic attitude toward those who are perceived as having less power on the other hand. Yet it is precisely this paternalistic attitude, for Niebuhr, which affirms that power elite's status as a legitimate power and a constant reminder to those with less power of the consequences of challenging the legitimacy of that power.

> With only rare exceptions, his highest moral attitude toward members of other groups is one of warlike sportsmanship toward those who equal his power and challenge it, and one of philanthropic generosity toward those who possess less power and privilege. His philanthropy is a perfect illustration of the curious compound of the brutal and the moral which we find in all human behavior; for his generosity is at once a display of his power and an expression of his pity. His generous impulses freeze within him if his power is challenged or his generosities are accepted without grateful humility.[1]

Niebuhr's analysis is penetrating in its ability to extract the kernel of oppressive human relationships and the seminal factors contributing to the moral conscience of power elites. Most significant for our purpose, Niebuhr's analysis brings moral clarity to the acutely paternalistic attitudes of white power elites in their treatment of black people in the history of the colonies and America. The abduction, deportation, and enslavement of Africans to the new America have been interpreted in the predominance by whites as an extremely benevolent gesture to bring heathen slaves out of "dark" Africa and into American civilization.

Moreover, Niebuhr finds as the common trademark of all contexts of slavery in human history a unique will to power in the sense that it entails of necessity the coercion of the enslaved class to submit to its enslavement and subsequently to its deprivation of basic human rights in the process.

> The history of slavery in all ancient civilizations offers an interesting illustration of the development of social injustice with the growing size and complexity of the social unit. In primitive tribal organization rights are essentially equal within the group, and no rights, or only very minimum rights are recognized outside of the group.[2]

In this regard, Niebuhr is laying claim to the universality of oppressive moral frameworks that legitimate slavery first to the enslaving group and then to the enslaved group. An in group-out group morality is established that first legitimates the moral appropriateness of human oppression which in turn provides the structure to create an oppressive world and to maintain that world through what Berger refers to as "world historical maintenance." Yet the legitimacy of that moral framework for Niebuhr quickly reveals its shortcomings insofar as it necessarily means the construction of two moral frameworks instead of one — a framework for the group in power and a framework for the enslaved group. This is why, for Niebuhr, power elites are guilty of sinful human relationships from the outset of the process of enslavement. It constitutes an excessive will to power that snowballs downhill to a deeper entrenchment in that oppressive world. A process Niebuhr argues is inescapable for a sinful humanity.

> Thus the more humane attitudes that men (humans) practice within their social groups gains a slight victory over the more brutal attitudes towards individuals in other groups. But the victory is insignificant in comparison with the previous introduction of the morals of intergroup relations into the intimate life of the group by the very establishment of slavery.[3]

In this regard, Niebuhr is affirming the inescapability of the construction of moral frameworks but is also making a sobering assessment of the application of moral frameworks in the evolving of human history. That assessment being that the construction of moral frameworks that affirm the legitimacy of human oppression is a necessary corollary to the initial immoral decision to create that oppressive relationship.

In fact, the vicissitudes of human history convince Niebuhr that the human family is not capable of transcending its immoral behavior in its collective relationships and is therefore incapable of realizing the kingdom on earth. Niebuhr is insistent that the grace of a loving and just God is humanity's only solution. Niebuhr's conclusion is closely akin to both Reformation and Neo-orthodox conclusions regarding the ability (or lack thereof) of humans to realize the kingdom.

While I am impressed with Niebuhr's analysis of the moral situation and his mammoth contribution to moral discourse in twentieth century America, I am concerned with the quietistic implications of his conclusion. While Niebuhr's divinely engineered solution is termed Christian realism, such an approach to the divine-human relationship ultimately glorifies a panacea-God religious conscience. Moreover, because it concedes the persistence of oppressive human relationships until the eschaton, it tends to be more nihilistic than realistic. The realism that Niebuhr seeks to establish robs oppressed communities of the hope that lies in the struggle to ameliorate its plight and, in doing so, affirms the moral appropriateness of an escapist religious conscience. Finally, Niebuhr's treatment does not put into full scale systematic terms an approach to theology that places the divine-human encounter squarely in the socio-political dimension of human existence — the dimension in which collective/oppressive human relations occurs.

We do find such a treatment, however, in the works of Walter Rauschenbusch in general and his *Theology for the Social Gospel* in particular. Rauschenbusch's treatment of Christian morality departs from his contention that not only are we as humans capable of realizing the kingdom but it is an essential demand given us by God. It is precisely the social dimension of human existence, for Rauschenbusch, in which we are called to decisively transform not only for our personal salvation but for the salvation of the human family as well. Rauschenbusch is intentional in his emphasis on a gospel that is social insofar as he finds problematic Christian tradition's treatment of faith divorced from social-political human advancement. Hence, Rauschenbusch sees this unapologetic emphasis on the social aspect of the gospel as a necessary corrective to a historical Christianity that has reflected the interests of power elites and served for the most part as the theological hand-maiden of moral frameworks that legitimate oppressive human relationships. This has manifested itself primarily for Rauschenbusch, in a Christian theological method that places ultimate emphasis on God's acceptance of the elect for eternal life rather than socio-ethical duty in working to realize the kingdom:

> It [the Social Gospel] ties up religion not only with duty, but with big duty that stirs the soul with religious feeling and throws it back on God for help. The non-ethical practices and beliefs in historical Christianity nearly all centre on the winning of heaven and immortality. On the other hand, the Kingdom of God can be established by nothing except righteous life and action.[4]

Thus, in contrast to Niebuhr, Rauschenbusch's treatment of faith centers the kingdom on earth to be established by humans working collaboratively with God to eradicate social injustice. In this regard, Rauschenbusch is at the very least implying that we are capable of transcending our universally sinful natures to establish the kingdom and that, although these untoward social relationships emerge from our universal inheritance from Adam, we should see the evolving of human history as a steady incline from universal sin to universal righteousness. Rauschenbusch maintains that the overwhelming propensity of the will to power of power elites that Niebuhr claims is inescapable is not only a crass alignment with the forces of oppression but undermines the power of God working through humans to transform those relationships. It is the task of Christian theology, for Rauschenbusch, to expose oppressive relationships not just for the purpose of better social relations but to bring power elites face to face with its conscience regarding their historical interactions with oppressed groups. This is crucial, for Rauschenbusch, in transforming oppressive relationships and helping power elites to better understand God's will for humanity.

> An unawakened person does not inquire on whose life juices his big dividends are fattening. Upper-class minds have been able to live parasitic lives without any fellow-feeling for the peasants or tenants whom they are draining to pay for their leisure. Modern democracy brings these lower fellow-men up to our field of vision. Then if a man has any religious feeling from Christ, his participation in the systematized oppression of civilization will, at least at times, seem an intolerable burden and guilt. Is this morbid? Or is it morbid to live on without such a realization? Those who to-day are still without a consciousness of collective wrong must be classified as men (humans) of darkened mind.[5]

While Rauschenbusch recognizes the deeply entrenched nature of socially oppressive relationships that favor a few at the expense of the poor, he also recognizes the power of God to change that relationship with the help of socially conscious humans. This, for Rauschenbusch, is consistent with the work of the Old Testament prophets and their condemnation of socially oppressive relationships as God brings down judgment not only on individuals but on unjust nations as well. Thus, Rauschenbusch pushes past Niebuhr to the conclusion that the social concerns of the prophets is affirmation that oppressive historical relationships can change and that the change need not wait until the eschaton. But more important, for Rauschenbusch, the eradication of historically oppressive relationships is bound up with our individual salvation as well. That is to say, for Rauschenbusch, as we grow in contributions to the improvement of the social order it brings about a social salvation that at the same time brings about growth in individual salvation as well and with far less angst associated with traditional understandings in Christian theology regarding one's ultimate destiny.

> In the Old Testament, we have a number of accounts describing how men (humans) of the highest type of God-consciousness made their fundamental experience of God and received their prophetic mission. In none of these cases did the prophet struggle for his personal salvation as later Christian saints have done. His woe did not come through fear of personal damnation, but through his sense of solidarity with the people and through social feeling; his hope and comfort was not for himself alone but for his nation. This form of religious experience is more distinctively Christian than any form which is caused by fear and which thinks only of itself.[6]

Hence Rauschenbusch's task is clear: he seeks a reinterpretation of Christian faith that does not slavishly tie us to an individualistic sin/redemption dialectic characteristic of Christian tradition but rather frees us to socially transform the world with the assurance that our participation in bringing about the coming kingdom is also our participation in bringing about our individual salvation. Put another way, our individual destinies are inextricably bound with our collective destiny insofar as we improve our lot in the former dimension as we engage in our God-given duty to improve the latter dimension.

Rauschenbusch is challenging two long-standing interpretations of Christian theology: 1) the highly individualistic pedagogy of Christian thought; and 2) God's grace as a panacea for human problems. Not surprisingly, Rauschenbusch's social gospel was not greeted well by the white religious establishment in early twentieth century America. Its inclination to the condemnation of unjust social orders and its branding of human inequality as sinful would predictably not be regarded as authentic Christian theology in a nation that refused to recognize the sinful activity inherent in its treatment of black people. In fact, the history of Christian theology and ethics in America had long before the arrival of Niebuhr and Rauschenbusch committed itself to a sinister theology of black dehumanization founded on the moral appropriateness of white superiority. The white religious establishment for two centuries prior had been creating a pseudo-theological avant-garde that was ready to affirm the moral appropriateness of white racism and to destroy the legitimacy of any moral discourse that lent credence to racial and gender equality.

In Niebuhr's case, Christian realism's transformation of human oppression only at the eschaton provided those committed to white supremacy an ideological "out" in the perpetuation of racial and gender hegemony. In Rauschenbusch's case, the treatment of sin as a collective evil was co-opted by a racially superior morality that resulted in a paternalistic benevolence by whites towards blacks but not a change in the latter's social status.

Yet what else could be expected of a nation that had prepared schools and erected churches on a theology that sanctioned unparalleled white privilege through the oppression of people of African descent. As Niebuhr rightly pointed out, any oppressive context needs a moral framework that legitimates its existence. The history of the colonies and America is built on a morality of white racial superiority that has garnered our attention.

White Morality as Racist Sacralization

The history of the colonies and America has always been accompanied by an "underside." African slaves would become the prime targets of this undercurrent insofar as they would come to be the objects of a moral framework that legitimated their dehumanization. At the core of a white supremacist morality is the reduction of African humanity to chattel i.e., more closely akin to lower animals. In short, a morality was built on the ethical acceptance of conquering black people and presenting them to the world as savages. Hence, a racially superior morality in the colonies and America became predicated on the conquering of African humanity as a means of affirming that superiority. Thus, white humanity in its seminal commitment to racial superiority needed a different race of people to not only build its economic infrastructure but to reduce them to subhuman status in order to solidify the claim of its own superiority. But more important, when white racial superiority became an accepted way of being in the world morally, white racist ideology became the paragon of aesthetic, cultural, and intellectual normativity and necessarily relegated the humanity of people of color to the periphery of social existence. Thus, while Descartes was busy constructing his cogito in order to establish thinking as the trademark of being human, it had already been preceded by the morally superior cogito of conquering as the trademark of being human for the European mind. Hence, what Descartes thought to be an original construction of what makes one fundamentally human, turned out to be only a restatement of a larger theme of a European culture that had committed itself to the legitimacy of a superior conscience. Hence, Descartes "thinking" took place within the larger cultural reality of "conquering" that has come to define much of European thinking in its relationships to people of color globally. Enrique Dussel sums up this ontology of white racial superiority.

> That ontology did not come from nowhere. It arose from a previous experience of domination over other persons, of cultural oppression over other worlds. Before the *ego cogito* there is an *ego conquiro*; "I conquer" is the practical foundation of "I think." The center has imposed itself on the periphery for more than five centuries.[7]

In short, Dussel was establishing that the worldview of white racist morality that had come to dominate the global scene for over half a millennium can be best characterized as a dichotomous morality — one for those in the center and another for those on the periphery.

George Kelsey, in his mid-twentieth century classic, *Racism and the Christian Understanding of Man*, makes the case for what he refers to as idolatrous faith regarding the interrelationship between Christian faith and black dehumanization. He refers to the center-periphery relationship between whites and blacks as the in-group, out-group dynamic wherein the actual dehumanizing acts may manifest themselves in the institutions of that society, but are only manifestations of the depravity of humans. For Kelsey, the inability of whites to recognize the common humanity in people of color coupled with the proclivity to perpetuate a system of white privilege in the name of God reflects a larger failure of the human spirit itself. Kelsey refers to this as "the faith character of racism."

> It is this faith character of racism which makes it the final and complete form of human alienation. Racism is human alienation purely and simply; it is the prototype of all human alienation. It is the one form of human conflict that divides human beings as human beings. That which the racist glorifies in himself (herself) is his (her) being. And that which he (she) scorns and rejects in members of out-races is precisely their human being. Although the racist line of demarcation and hostility inevitably finds expression through the institutions of soci-

ety, it is not primarily a cultural, political, or economic boundary. Rather, it is a boundary of estrangement in the order of human being as such.[8]

Hence the faith character of racism brings to full legitimation the justification of black dehumanization as the highest moral virtue insofar as it is touted as a natural phenomenon and not as a socio-cultural construct of white racists. Since the white people possessed a superior economic and military technology and were therefore able to conquer and enslave the people of color, it was a simple matter to explain the superiority of the cultural apparatus in terms of a superior human endowment.[9] In short, Kelsey is articulating the process by which white privilege is affirmed as a divine given and not as a socio-cultural construct. It is what I have termed *racist sacralization* or the process in which white racial bigotry is divinized as the will of God. In such a context, black dehumanization becomes the apparent creation of God's infinite wisdom and therefore the ultimate pretext for coercing black people into a quietistic faith. The tragedy of this outcome is that racism had now in the words of Kelsey developed a "faith character" and in so doing had/has developed an unquestioned status in regard to proper living. Hence, the moral imperative of black dehumanization became not a question of the moral depravity of the slavocracy itself but an affirmation of the righteousness of slaveholders in maintaining the slavocracy. In short, white supremacy had now been given the lofty status of divine decree and the faith character of racism meant that white racial power politics had now been given a righteousness that even slaveholders themselves were bound to uphold morally and ethically. To this end, white racial superiority had been given a moral significance that was synonymous with the kingdom itself and therefore considered ungodly to work for its demise.

White Morality and Social Control

One of the first moral issues for slaveholders was the regulation of slave behavior. To be sure, slaveholders were not surprised by the presence of white antislavery advocates but considered them penultimate threats to the slavocracy at best. By far, the perceived biggest threat to the slavocracy (and subsequently to the kingdom) was the emergent black leader who would constantly seek to instill in the slave a rebellious spirit. Slaveholders, along with many white clergy, had worked extremely hard to instill in the slave a morality of acquiescence and capitulation to her situation. Slaveholders and white clergy were relentless in their teaching that the slavocracy was a divinely engineered plan for exposing the slaves to civilization and that given their acutely depraved status, their enslavement was the best possible reality for which they could hope. The black leader in turn always took an uncompromising approach to the morality of racial stratification and urged slaves at all costs to fight for its demise. With this opposition to a racially divine morality, every effort was made legally and morally to reaffirm the legitimacy of the slavocracy. More important, since the slavocracy was considered a divine institution, every effort was made to depict the black leader as an enemy of God. Legally, slave laws were passed in many states in the south disallowing the gathering of slaves in large numbers (in some instances as little as five people!) for fear that an insurrection was being planned. Laws were also passed to establish total control over the slave's life. This was considered necessary to both build the economic infrastructure of the slavocracy and to continue working toward the kingdom.

> Each slave state had a code which was designed to keep slaves ignorant and in awe of white power. Slaves were forbidden to assemble in groups of more than five or seven away from their home plantation. They were forbidden to leave plantations without passes and they could not blow horns, beat drums or read books. Slave preachers were proscribed and hemmed in by restrictions; and slaves were forbidden to hold religious meetings without white witnesses.[10]

Since the slave was understood to be acutely depraved, she would predictably not see her slave status as beneficial and therefore not fully acquiesce to these restrictions. In fact, the brutally violent treatment of the slaves was a morally accepted norm in slaveholding circles precisely because of the assertion that non-acquiescence to the slavocracy was touted as the manifestation of the slave's woefully depraved ontology. Hence, the means of the violence and brutality inflicted on the slave, particularly when she attempted to escape, justified the end of maintaining slavery in its divine ordinance. This is why the attenuation of the black leader's effectiveness was seen as particularly crucial to the life of the slavocracy.

Every effort was made by the masters and clergy to sully the image of the black leader in the eyes of the slave as an immoral and therefore ungodly person. Moreover, every attempt was made to convince the slaves that their only moral voice should be God, represented by white clergy, or to convince the slaves that they should follow an "establishment" black leader who would promote the agenda of the slavocracy. In most instances the latter alternative was pursued. In short, the morality of white supremacy styled the black leader as unnatural insofar as her behavior was in direct opposition to divine will and styled the "hand-picked" black leader as the one who was most deserving of the slave's loyalties.

> Any slave who began to emerge as a natural head, that is, one oriented toward survival of the whole body, was identified early and was either gotten rid of, isolated, killed, or ridiculed. In his (her) place was put a leader who had been carefully picked, trained, and tested to stand only for master's welfare. In other words, unnatural heads were attached to the slave communities. They furthered the cause of the master and frustrated the cause of the slave.[11]

This racially stratified moral framework required not only a categorization of white and black but also a categorization of slave worth as well. In the attempt to control slave rebellion, every effort was made to positively showcase to the slave the hand-picked black leader and to negatively showcase the natural black leader. Behavioral labels would become the norm of slaveholders and white clergy in the valuation of black morality. Moreover, to make sure that their point concerning the authentic black leader was received properly, it was not uncommon for slaveholders to punish the entire slave community for its support of the black leader.

> The slaves were taught to view with suspicion natural heads which emerged from among themselves. Such heads were identified as "uppity" or "arrogant" and were branded as the kind of trouble-makers who were destined to bring trouble to the entire slave community. This idea was reinforced by the public punishment of such indigenous leadership and any of his/her associates or sympathizers. The entire slave community was often required to carry an extra burden, or deprived of some small privilege, because of such "uppity slaves."[12]

On the opposite end of the valuation of slave morality was the public commendation of the slave who acquiesced to her enslavement, carried herself with passive resignation about her fate or adopted a Christian piety that affirmed the providence of the slavocracy. Thus, arguably the biggest devaluation of black humanity in the colonies and America was not the physical labor but the denial of the opportunity of the slave to develop a legitimate moral framework in lieu of the slavocracy and living a daily existence wherein one's "humanity" is affirmed only when acquiescing to one's own enslavement and not the development of one's character and integrity as such.

> When the Negro himself is spoken of as "good" the term refers exclusively to conduct; it does not refer to the depths of the inner life. The good Negro is "ole black Joe." He is the Negro who maintains "the proper attitude toward white people, and knows his place."[13]

But more important, the "goodness" of the slave would come to be measured by Christian moral means as God-affirming behavior. In structuring the moral pedagogy in this way, slaveholders and white clergy were theologically establishing that the slave's salvific destiny was inextricably linked with her pious disposition in regard to plantation life. Kelsey, though, is extremely impatient with this type of pseudo-Christian morality particularly given white America's designation of the slave's inferior status as irrevocable.

> The good Negro is often referred to as "humble," a term which has profound spiritual significance in the context of Christian faith. But when the racist consciousness applies it to the Negro, the term means manifesting a humblelike or deferential manner toward white people. Moral and spiritual terms applied to the Negro mean "manners" not "morals." The racist consciousness has no notion of morality in the life of the Negro in the fullest meaning of the word. The Negro is believed to be stationed somewhere between the beast and man (hu-

man) in the order of being and, therefore, to be devoid of a genuinely human inner life. Accordingly, he (she) does not and cannot interiorize moral norms and values.[14]

Hence, the morality of Christian faith has been co-opted in American history to justify black dehumanization in general and the destruction of authentic black leadership in particular as a means of black social control. As such, the realization of the kingdom through the eternal designation of the slavocracy made black social control a salvific duty for slaveholders and not just an existential desire.

The Wages of Sin Is Life?

Any moral framework informed by a Christian perspective must at some point deal with the implications of that framework in the shaping of a theological treatment of sin. While the mostly popular definition of sin as a transgression against the laws of God will suffice for our treatment here, it's unpacking in the history of the colonies and America as primarily the attempt to topple the slavocracy or to challenge the notion of white racial superiority has far greater significance for us here. That is to say, racial superiority itself was/is not the sin but the attempt to compromise the onward march to a kingdom rooted in white superiority was/is. In this regard, the treatment of sin for white clergy and theologians begins with the presupposition that the slavocracy was a divine institution and that the enslavement of Africans is a consequence of their sinfulness prior to abduction. Here we have again a restatement in theological terms of the sacralization of a racist way of life wherein Africans are the unfortunate beneficiaries of white oppression. But, to be sure, it was not styled that way to the slaves.

In fact, the pedagogy of sin to the slaveholding community was that God made them the representatives of the creation of the kingdom and that if they were real Christians they were bound by righteousness to perpetuate the slavocracy through eternity. Hence sin for the slaveholding community was the refusal to use the socio-historical power that God had given them to defeat all enemies of the slavocracy for it was in this institution that God would manifest Godself to the world. This meant the protection of the slavocracy against white sympathizers and the slaves themselves. In the case of the former, this meant the development of a pro-slavery intelligentsia that would soundly challenge the arguments of white sympathizers and would make the claim for the legitimacy of slavery as a divine institution. In the case of the latter, every avenue of social control was pursued to maintain slaves physically and psychically. Thus, no amount of violence and deprivation of basic human rights to cement in the consciousness of the slave the eternity of her condition were considered out of the norm in the fulfillment of the God-given duty of the white community to protect the slavocracy. Not surprisingly then, the pedagogy of sin to the slaves was that this was God's way of providing them with an opportunity for redemption. In this regard, sin then became for the slave any attempt to compromise the integrity and existence of the slavocracy.

One of the first formal attempts to "Christianize" the slave comes in an instructional book by well-known southern clergyman, Cotton Mather. In his, *The Negro Christianized*, Mather insisted that all whites were capable of teaching the slaves in the proper rudiments of Christian righteousness through the two catechisms provided in his work. After making sure that he conveyed the significance of providing, "Agreeable Recompences, and Priviledges" for slaves who received this instruction with heightened enthusiasm, Mather left no room for misunderstanding his appropriation of sin for the slave. The short manual [catechism] required the instructor to tell the pupil, "That by their sin against God, they are fallen into a dreadful condition," but if they serve God "patiently and cheerfully in the Condition which he (God) orders for them, their condition will very quickly be infinitely mended, in Eternal Happiness."[15] While Mather conveniently does not go into detail about what that pre-slavery sin was and why Africans were chosen for this gruesome journey, he does clearly establish that their reward lies in eternity and not in human history. Thus, in close connection with the sin/redemption interrelationship for the slave is her eschatological or ultimate destiny. That the reward must transcend history is of great consequence for the slave but of little surprise. It seeks to convince the slave that God wants her enslavement and her posterity's enslavement throughout human history and that any activity to derail that process in inherently sinful. Thus, the slave's favor with God rested on the rather spurious ethic of *edifying docility* in the wake of the brutality and oppression of the slavocracy.

The second catechism dealt mainly with the nature of the Christian life. It consisted of a question-answer segment in which slaves were duty-bound to participate. It sought to make the slave fully conversant with Christian duty that was "pleasing" to God. And since this was a call and response process, slaveholders could continue to deprive the slave of the ability to read. It read:

> If you serve Jesus Christ, what must you do?
> I must love God, and Pray to Him, and Keep the Lords-Day.
> I must Love all Men, and never Quarrel, nor be Drunk, nor be Unchast, nor Steal, nor tell a Ly, nor be Discontent with my Condition.[16]

The catechism goes on to similar question-answer discourses on the Ten Commandments and the New Testament exhortations to obedient living with all responses given over to the merits of slave docility as an inescapable disposition for serving Jesus Christ. Mather's catechism represented just one of a plethora of slave catechisms that began to emerge in the early to mid eighteenth century. This would lay the foundation of what Christian theology in the colonies and later America would come to represent: righteousness in the support of an eternal institution of white privilege and black dehumanization and sin in the way of any attempts to topple that institution.

This approach to the sin/redemption interrelationship had become so embedded in the life of the slavocracy that many slaveholders came to see it as paramount for establishing the kingdom on earth. This became the theological rallying cry of the Confederate States of America. Holding true to this treatment of the sin/redemption interrelationship would assure a victory against the "enemies of God," and preserve the confederacy in the contemporary Armageddon. The confederate worldview was clear in its understanding that all races were serving in positions of divine decree necessary for God's reign on earth and that they were agents of God fighting against the Union to preserve the kingdom as represented by the confederacy. Hence, sinfulness did not lie in the confederacy's attempts to perpetuate an institution of black dehumanization but in the Union's attempt to topple the slavocracy (despite Lincoln's rather derogatory views of black humanity!). The confederacy clearly understood itself to be fighting for a righteous cause and understood their defeat to be not a victory for human freedom but of God punishing them for sinful behavior in not fighting hard enough to preserve the slavocracy. Thus, the post-war confederates were still not convinced of the sinfulness of slavery itself. In October, 1865, the Baptist *Religious Herald* of Richmond, Virginia, defiantly asked, "whether any combination of capital and labor ever produced greater freedom from want and suffering, and a higher degree of contentment and cheerfulness among the laboring classes, than did Southern slavery."[17] While The South Carolina Conference of the Methodist Episcopal Church conceded that the defeat was a clear sign of God's providence to make the confederacy a part of the United States, it was by no means a sign that white southerners had been unrighteous in either its creation or attempts to preserve its way of life. More particularly, "It had affirmed that the War had settled the question of 'the powers that be,' whom Southerners were [now] commanded to obey as they rendered unto Caesar the things that are Caesar's. But the conference insisted that the demise of slavery did not invalidate the certainty that God had ordained it in a previous time and place."[18] Nevertheless, the pain of the defeat of its way of life did not deter confederate leadership from recommitting itself to the principles of the confederate way of life particularly as it related to black dehumanization. Even seminary professors weighed in on the legitimacy of racial stratification in post-slavery America. Presbyterian ordained minister and professor at Union Theological Seminary in Richmond, Virginia, Reverend T. E. Peck contended that:

> Religiously and morally, slavery was by no means a settled issue. The intransigence of the divines may be more readily understood if for "slavery" we substitute "some form of personal servitude" and recall the long efforts to bring their preferred social system up to biblical standards.[19]

Hence, Peck expressed the sentiment of a southern white mindset that saw an inextricable link between the confederate and biblical worldviews. More significant, Peck voiced the sentiment of many other white southerners where black dehumanization was concerned despite the confederacy's defeat in the "American Armageddon." That sentiment would become reality with the emergence of Jim Crow segregation that served as more than adequate substitute for the slavery of which Peck spoke.

To be sure, whatever that substitute was, it had to insist on preventing the realization of the biggest fear whites had in the assumed closer contact with black people in the post-war period — racial miscegenation. So significant would this be for whites that racial miscegenation's incorporation into the theology of white supremacy was quick and predictable. The logic was that every sin could be atoned for and could be made right except miscegenation. Allowing miscegenation to occur in large numbers, it was reasoned, would destroy both races and produce a population of mixed race offspring referred to as mongrels. This process was to be regarded as the beginning of the end of human existence for with the white race in particular destroyed, God would no longer have the chosen racial representative on earth to advance human civilization. Thus, the largest sin one could commit was the attempt to dilute the purity of the white race insofar as they held the key to human salvation for themselves and for blacks. The mixing of the "blood" of a superior race with that of an inferior race is a loss of such proportions that nothing can compensate for it and no new thrust of life can spring from the wreckage.[20]

With this line of reasoning, black people were to understand that its indentured servitude, separate but unequal public accommodations and living conditions, separate communities in American cities, racial epithets from the Citizens Council and racial violence from the Ku Klux Klan, poll taxes and literacy tests at voting precincts, racist legal systems and stiff resistance to the civil rights and black power movements was all in the name of preventing miscegenation and subsequently the destruction of human civilization as we know it.

Further, in what I consider a bit of paranoia, miscegenation was perceived by quite a large number of whites as a ploy by Moscow, Russia to infiltrate the American way of life and destroy it sexually. Staunch segregationist John W. Hamilton affirms that concern and its ultimate connection to the divine.

> Remember, mixing white children with Negroes is a form of insanity. It takes the form of religion, democracy, brotherhood, etc. It is a pollution complex directed from Moscow. Remember, discrimination is not a sin. It is a sign of Mind or God working through man (humanity) to protect what is good.[21]

One is to give close attention to Hamilton's easy connection between the categorization of miscegenation as sin and God's inscrutable will in making racial discrimination a moral virtue that protects white purity. As such, white supremacy is presented to the nation as a disclosure of the mind of God with white racists acting only as the Christian servants that execute that disclosure.

Yet such a theological co-opting of divine providence begs the question as to how a superior race could genetically become the victims of mongrelization? That is to say, should not the superior nature of whiteness itself be sufficient to prevent its dilution amid the sexual savagery of black people and therefore avert the catastrophe of an end to civilization as we know it? The most popular response by white clergy and theologians is that the Fall of humanity made whites, although superior still to all other races, vulnerable to genetic annihilation from peoples of color. In other words, although the white race was created with the resources to prevent genetic annihilation, it was impacted by the Fall such that those resources were compromised thus allowing for its complete eradication.

> No environmental or historical factors in themselves can ever affect the virtue
> of superior men (humans). But this one thing superior races lack: they lack the
> endowment of wisdom and virtue equal to the choices necessary for remaining
> superior.[22]

Thus the moral framework of white supremacy takes into account the fallen nature of all humans but sees white racial stratification as the necessary condition by which salvation becomes possible for all humans. Thus, sin was not considered the perpetuation of a society rooted in white prosperity at the expense of people of color. Sin was instead treated as any attempt to create a more egalitarian society.

Hence, if one is given over to the notion that racial stratification is necessary for the creation and perpetuation of human civilization then moral frameworks that aid in the continuance of that notion are considered a profound expression of moral turpitude. But if one is given over to the inherent equal worth of all human beings, then the perpetuation of moral frameworks that enlist God as the czar of black dehumanization will undoubtedly be seen as exclusively benefiting those who are able to impose its will to power. Thus, the wage of sin for the colonists and white Americans has not been death but life. The sin of the dehumanization of black people in the name of God was the basis in which the European man established his dominance over the world's people of color and brought about unparalleled social, economic, and political advancement for himself and his posterity under the guise of righteousness and civility.

Notes

1. Reinhold Niebuhr, *Moral Man and Immoral Society*. New York: Charles Scribner's Sons, 1932, 13-14.

2. Ibid., 12.

3. Ibid., 12-13.

4. Walter Rauschenbusch, *A Theology for the Social Gospel*. Nashville: Abingdon Press, 1990, 15. Originally published by The Macmillan Company, 1917.

5. Ibid., 19.

6. Ibid., 20.

7. Enrique Dussel, *Philosophy of Liberation*. New York: Orbis Books, 1985, 3.

8. George Kelsey, *Racism and the Christian Understanding of Man*. New York: Charles Scribner's Sons, 1965, 23.

9. Ibid., 22-23.

10. Lerone Bennett, *Before the Mayflower*. Chicago: Johnson Publishing Company, 1964, 93.

11. Na'im Akbar, *Chains and Images of Psychological Slavery*. Jersey City, New Jersey: New Mind Publishing, 1984, 15.

12. Ibid., 12.

13. Kelsey, *Racism and the Christian Understanding of Man*, 118.

14. Ibid., 118-19.

15. Lester B. Scherer, *Slavery and the Churches in Early America: 1619-1819*. Grand Rapids, Michigan: Eerdman's Publishing Company, 1975, 97.

16. Ibid.

17. Eugene D. Genovese, *A Consuming Fire: The Fall of the Confederacy in the Mind of the White Christian South*. Athens: University of Georgia Press, 1998, 101.

18. Ibid.

19. Ibid.

20. Kelsey, *Racism and the Christian Understanding of Man*, 127.

21. John W. Hamilton, "The Kiss of Death," taken from Ibid., 128.

22. Ibid., 129.

4

White Religion and Black WOhuMANity

The sexualization of racism in the United States is a unique phenomenon in the history of mankind; it is an anomaly of the first order. In fact, there is a sexual involvement, at once real and vicarious, connecting white and black people in America that spans the history of this country from the era of slavery to the present, an involvement so immaculate and yet so perverse, so ethereal and yet so concrete, that all race relations tend to be, however subtle, *sex* relations.
Calvin Hernton, *Sex and Racism in America*

Thus far, we have examined the impact of the most cherished Christian ideals in the history of the colonies and America and the acute interrelationship between those ideals and the dehumanization of black people in strictly racial terms. The purpose of this chapter is to examine the impact of those Christian ideals on the dehumanization of black women as a unique form of black oppression in American history. Such an examination becomes imperative given the literary history of black oppression and the propensity of both black and white male writers to frame their discussions in exclusively racial terms. This has been the case on both benign and intentional fronts. From a more benign standpoint, the uncritical internalization of patriarchal values on the part of both black and white males led to genuine treatments of black oppression that envisaged black liberation as one that included both black men *and* black women. Hence, the use of exclusive language such as man, mankind, and pronoun references to God in masculine gender were seen by men of this disposition not as part of a larger sexist super-structure that cemented their patriarchal authority but more of an innocuous way of speaking of both men and women on the one hand and God on the other.

Thus, along this line of reasoning, one is to understand man as meaning both men and women, mankind as meaning all humans, including women, and more important, God as "He" simply because God cannot be both a man and a woman.

From a more intentional and inhumane standpoint, patriarchal values are understood by men of this disposition to be normative by divine behest and therefore a Christian duty for them to maintain women in a subordinate status. Hence, the right of women to human equality with these men is to be seen as an aberration at best and sinful at worse. From this view, the struggle for black liberation was seen by most black men as the abolition of the slave trade. After that occurred however, most black men sought to maintain the same hierarchical relationship with black women as white men had already established with white women. In this regard, the use of exclusive language meant exactly what it implied – social, economic, and political exclusion for women! That is, man, mankind, and references to God in masculine indication of person existed to firmly establish in the minds of both men and women the ontological superiority of men. As such, women were not to understand the animalistic aggression of powerful men to exert inordinate control over them as patriarchal privilege but as an historic unfolding of the mind of God.

Inheriting this subordinate relationship from both biblical and contemporary history, black women found themselves in a most horrific situation. While they found a measure of collaborative sympathy from their own black man on racial grounds and white women on sexist grounds, they could not ultimately find genuine collaboration with either. Although black men could coalesce with black women around the racial struggle from freedom and white women could coalesce with black women on sexist grounds, because neither of them historically encountered both racism *and* sexism as black women did/do, their understandings of human oppression were/are shortsighted. Further, when the contemporary analysis of poverty is added to the analytical mix, black women were and are the victims of what Theresa Hoover refers to as triple jeopardy — victims of racism, sexism, and classism.[1] In so doing, Hoover has compelled us to raise our analytical bar wherein any substantive treatment of black oppression must entail far more than black male freedom from white racism. Those treatments rather must encompass a tripartite analysis that frees black people from white racism and neo-capitalist elites who see the creation of poverty as an inescapable residual in their own wealth attainment. But more important, those treatments must also free black women from both white and black men — i.e., it must free black women from racist sexism! Treatments that must, especially for the purposes of this work, expose Christian pedagogies in the history of the colonies and America that have divinely affirmed the patriarchal dispositions of most men and equated sexist behavior with righteous behavior.

The Origin and Development of Racist Sexism

The first obstacle to a true assessment of black women's experience of oppression is the lack of significance accorded women's suffering terminologically. Writing out of a highly patriarchal disposition, most male historians have tended to see black women's oppression as a subsidiary and, therefore, less virulent manifestation of racism. For instance, Calvin Hernton, in his insightful work, *Sex and Racism in America*, sought to articulate black women's oppression as, "the sexualization of racism." In so doing, Hernton was unwittingly assigning the sexism black women have experienced as merely a manifestation of the archetypal evil of racism. Yet this approach to black women's oppression devalues black women in the sense that it never treats sexism as an evil that needs to be eradicated along with racism. It perpetuates the historical notion on the part of most black men that black women's experience of oppression is fundamentally similar to theirs. This necessarily diminishes the depth of most black men's analysis regarding the totality of black oppression and black women's oppression in particular. In short, such a view of black oppression leads black men to the erroneous conclusion that the elimination of white racism frees both black men and black women. Such treatments of black liberation also fail to challenge black men to seriously struggle with the extent to which they have internalized patriarchal values and align themselves with white males in the oppression of its own women. As such, any substantive treatment of women's oppression in general and black women's oppression in particular, must depart from the equally archetypal evil of sexism. This becomes particularly appropriate when examining black women's oppression in the colonies and America and the particularly degrading experience at the hands of white men. Far more appropriate, then, is arguing that the dehumanizing experience of black women would be best treated as *racist sexism* given that most of these experiences occurred and could only occur precisely because of their female status. Acts that black men could only imagine.

> In a retrospective examination of the black female slave experience, sexism looms as large as racism as an oppressive force in the lives of black women. Institutionalized sexism — that is, patriarchy — formed the base of American social structure along with racial imperialism. Sexism was an integral part of the social and political order white colonizers brought with them from their European homelands, and it was to have a grave impact on the fate of enslaved black women.[2]

A cursory treatment of the history of black women in the colonies and America that led to that grave impact is in order.

In particular, black women were called on to do what is typically called "double-duty" in plantation life. Not only was she expected to do work in both the field and the big house, she was routinely called upon to act as a surrogate nanny for white infants as well as her own children given her, "tremendous suckling attributes." In fact, one could go as far as to refer to this as double-double duty. As a recent mother herself, she often had to take her newborn to the field with her and lay it down in a landing a short distance from where she was working. Despite nursing a newborn, she was responsible for normal productivity to prevent a fit of rage from the master that could lead to a severe whipping. In fact, such whippings by the master were conducted in the presence of young field hands to socialize them early in life to the repercussions of slothful slave activity. Moreover, using black women who had just given birth as an example was intentional insofar as a whipping not spared a black woman who had just given birth could be even more brutal for others slaves. Black women, then, were expected to produce just as much as male slaves in the field and take care of "womanly duties" when those needs arose as well.

> But women suffered in different ways as well, for they were victims of sexual abuse and other barbarous mistreatment that could only be inflicted on women. Expediency governed the slaveholders' posture toward female slaves: when it was profitable to exploit them as if they were men, they were regarded, in effect, as genderless, but when they could be exploited, punished and repressed in ways suited only for women, they were locked into their exclusively female roles.[3]

To this end, black women had the unenviable task of assuming the "super-woman" role. She had the task of being equally productive as men in the field and serving as nurturing mother and maid for her children and those of the masters.

A prevailing misconception about plantation life was that black women had a much easier time working in the big house rather than the fields. This, however, was not the case. She could be and was watched with even greater scrutiny in the big house than in the fields by both the master and his wife and, if considered attractive, she would usually be targeted for harsh treatment by the master's wife for fear that a sexual relationship had developed. More particularly, she would be severely punished for the most benign of mistakes. Ex-slave Solomon Bradley reveals this gruesome punishment of a black woman by her master emblematic of the time.

> Yes sir, the most shocking thing that I have seen was on the plantation of Mr. Farrarby, on the line of the railroad. I went up to his house one morning from my work for drinking water, and heard a woman screaming awfully. On going up to the fence and looking over I saw a woman stretched out, face downwards, on the ground her hands and feet being fastened to stakes. Mr. Farrarby was standing over her and striking her with a leather trace belonging to his carriage harness. As he struck her the flesh of her back and legs were raised with welts and ridges by the force of blows. Sometimes when the poor thing cried too loud from the pain Mr. Farrarby would kick her in the mouth. After he exhausted

himself in whipping her he sent to his house for sealing wax and a lighted can-
dle and, melting the wax, dropped it upon the woman's lacerated back. He then
got a riding whip and, standing over the woman, picked off the hardened wax
by switching at it.

   Mr. Farrarby's grown daughters were looking at this from a window of the
house through the blinds. The punishment was so terrible that I was induced to
ask what offence the woman had committed and was told by her fellow servants that her only crime was in burning the edges of the waffles that she had
cooked for breakfast.[4]

While it is to be noted that from a sexism standpoint white women observing
this harsh treatment of black women in close proximity saw this as a possibility
for themselves at the hand of their husbands, that concern was tempered by a
sense of relief that if their husbands whipped a black woman this severely it
meant that the chances of a sexual relationship with that woman were remote.
This is why many black women were leery of offers of assistance from white
women given this sexual dynamic. One, therefore, is able to discern the multi-
dimensional dilemma that racist sexism presented for black women: how to sur-
vive the social and ideological onslaught of anti-black woman treatment at the
hands of white and black men, and white women.

   Socially, black women had to sustain the dehumanization of sexual attacks
by white and black men who had internalized patriarchal values and saw her
mainly as an object of sexual pleasure and therefore not a "good woman." In
fact, because slaveholders owned slaves by law just as one would own a piece of
property, the slaves were considered the property of the master. Thus, it was not
considered illegal for a slaveholder to "coerce" a black woman into sex given
that it was not possible for him to rape a black woman. This represented a huge
part of the racist sexism of the time.

> Mass sexual exploitation of enslaved black women was a direct consequence of
> the anti-woman sexual politics of colonial patriarchal America. Since the black
> woman was not protected either by law or public opinion, she was an easy tar-
> get. While racism was clearly the evil that had decreed black people would be
> enslaved, it was sexism that determined that the lot of the black female slave
> would be harsher, more brutal than that of the black male slave.[5]

Naturally, this created tremendous angst among white women given their husbands "attraction" to black women. On the one hand, one could look at this development as the animalistic aggression that contributes to the sexual connection
we have toward each other as men and women and fulfills our fantasies. Yet,
given that this dynamic is not taking place in a racial and gender-neutral environment but rather in an environment teeming with racial and gender impositions of black debasement, sex became on the plantation and in many instances
today a power relationship. This becomes a particularly difficult process for
black women who, because, of racist sexism are debased because of both race

and gender. In practical terms, this meant for black women becoming the targets of sexual dehumanization by white men and the targets of social scorn from white women who knew that certain black women on the plantation had captured the sexual imagination of their husbands. For these black women, a proverbial rock and a hard place became their constant locus. They were involuntary thrown into an intense power struggle between the slaveholder and his wife. If they did not acquiesce to the slaveholders demand for sex, they would satisfy the slaveholders' wives and themselves but would be subject to a brutal flogging by the slaveholder. If they acquiesced to sex with slaveholders, a possibly more intense flogging would be their fate as ordered by the slaveholders' wife. With this limited choice, it was almost impossible for a black woman to avoid a whipping.

While a few masters treated the black women as his equal and fathered many children by them that were manumitted upon birth, the majority of black women were caught in this losing proposition of sexual power politics. Mary Frances Berry and John W. Blassingame affirm that, "Most slave women were caught on the horns of a dilemma. If they rejected the advances of the planter, they would be flogged until they submitted. If they submitted and the planter's wife discovered the relationship, the mistress would flog or sometimes try to kill them or their mulatto children."[6] One is able to clearly understand the social dilemma faced by black women and the significance of her "sexual output" not in determining her edification but her dehumanization. In short, it represented a form of dehumanization experienced not only because of her slave status and her blackness but the blackness of her womanhood as well i.e., because of race *and* gender. Coerced sex became and was meant to become, an ever-present reminder for black women of their powerlessness. With each act of "coerced" sex black women were being reminded that this was society's way of conveying to them their diminished worth insofar as they had only limited opportunities to determine with whom and when they had sexual intercourse. Hence, the very act that brings new life into the world, meant to be pleasurable as a gift from God, became for black women an arduous and dehumanizing chore.

From an ideological standpoint, racist sexism has had particularly damaging effects on both black women's self-image and their perception from white and black men, and white women. White men used their socio-political power to make sure that clearly different images existed between black women and white women. A huge benefit of patriarchal privilege is being able to envisage an image of womanhood and use one's power to socially construct reality in such a way that it appears to be a natural ordering of human relationships. White men, in their patriarchal mindset, "pedestalized" white women while assigning to black women the opposite image. They gave their women a lofty if not puritanical status that placed her close to the angels in her public presentation and moral conduct. To be sure, such a conception of white women owes itself in large part to the advent of the Victorian era of feminine royalty that emerged in Europe in the sixteenth century and adopted by white male colonists. It laid a foundation that perpetuates itself up to today that equates authentic womanhood with white womanhood. That is, true womanhood was imaged as dainty, petite, reserved, clean, soft-spoken, above physical labor, conservatively dressed, and more important, sexually chaste. White women were reared in contexts that lent itself to the development of these virtues in perpetuity, the inherent sexism notwithstanding. Yet even if there were some white women that did not develop these virtues, particularly in regard to her sexual chastity, to white men's satisfaction, the ultimate purpose was achieved: to ideologically establish white womanhood as the standard for womanhood socially and aesthetically.

Since most slave black women, however, worked in the fields and lived in the substandard houses of the plantation they were conveniently put in a social context in which they would never be able to meet the Victorian standards of womanhood. The obvious end of such a scenario was/is to establish that black women were not the women white women were by nature not social location. In this sense, every effort was made by slaveholders to establish diametrically opposite images for black women and white women that would confirm only white womanhood as authentic womanhood. As such, racist sexism meant that black women were struggling against an inferior status not only racially but, literally, sexually as well.

> The Victorian "extended" family also put the "moral" categories of women into sharp relief. The White wife was hoisted on a pedestal so high that she was beyond the sensual reach of her own husband. Black women were consigned to the other end of the scale, as mistresses, whores, and breeders.[7]

More particularly, black women became the victims of what I term the *comparative moral designation* wherein white women were given a stellar, if not pure, moral status and black women, as the opposite of white women in both skin hue and social location, were designated a degraded moral status. These designations were constantly reinforced in plantation life. For instance, black women would often be given clothing, particularly during the spring and summer months that would show lots of flesh while white women were, for the most part, totally covered which indicated the latter's angelical purity. The intent of course was to reinforce the notion that because of her "revealing" attire, black women were loose sexually and therefore not worthy of moral commendation and not capable of moral turpitude. This reinforcement was not lost on white clergy who incorporated this understanding of womanhood into their religious teaching "sacralizing" it as the wisdom of the creator. Thus many white clergy affirmed the puritanical elevation of white women on the one hand and the inherent whorishness of black women on the other hand. It had become a staple part of the teachings of most major Christian denominations that black women were the embodiment of evil seducers of white men. In the end it proved to be a clever explanation for slaveholders. Their inability to "resist" sexually aggressive black women decreased their culpability and increased white women's mistrust of black women.

> Most white women regarded black women who were the objects of their husbands' sexual assaults with hostility and rage. Having been taught *by religious teachings* that women were inherently sexual temptresses, mistresses often believed that the enslaved black woman was the culprit and their husbands the innocent victims.[8]

Over time we see the religious pedagogy of most Christian churches enlisting the will of God in legitimating the racial and gender stratification of black and white Americans and the acutely dehumanizing treatment of black women.

The comparative moral designation regarding the dress of white and black women as a visible sign of their disparate moral states was often reinforced by rapes of black women that became articulated as black women being evil temptresses. Further, it became customary for slaveholders to publicly present black women with no clothing at all. This was meant to portray black women as morally corrupt by publicly presenting her in the diametrically opposite way of the clean, sexually chaste, and fully clothed Victorian paragon of authentic womanhood. In fact, the raping black women served two purposes for slaveholders. First, beyond the obvious sexual pleasure derived from such trysts, raping black women also diminished their sexual chastity with each act of sex, lending credence to the prevailing notion that black women were whorish. Second, as a result of having more sex, black women were made to be naked more frequently thereby violating the Victorian standard of being fully clothe. This only served to cement black women's presentation as sexually promiscuous creatures that were overpowering in their seduction of white men and to reaffirm Christian teaching that black women were by nature evil and had to be "tamed" by masters. It also served an important function for masters in the sense that they were duty bound as Christian men to "deal" with black women on a more frequent basis in order to "tame" them. But more significantly, the "taming" of black women provided masters a psychosexual reason to engage in violence/sex relationships with black women that satisfied their masochistic inclinations representing yet another unique dimension of black women's oppression.

> As females, slave women were inherently vulnerable to all forms of sexual coercion. If the most violent punishments of men consisted in floggings and mutilations, women were flogged and mutilated, as well as raped. Rape, in fact, was an uncamouflaged expression of the slaveholder's economic mastery and the overseer's control over Black women as workers.[9]

This solidified the intricate relationship between sex, dehumanization, and economic prosperity in plantation life and the indispensable role black women played as infamous leading lady.

More particularly, it was customary for most slaveholders to conduct public floggings of black women in their nakedness. The publicly stated reason for this was so that the black woman's back could receive the full brunt of the master's lashes. But in addition, the ideological reason was to publicly humiliate black women in their nakedness given that plantation life had given itself over to a Victorian view of womanhood.

> Rape was not the only method used to terrorize and de-humanize black women. Sadistic floggings of naked black women were another method employed to strip the female slave of dignity. In the Victorian world, where white women were religiously covering every body part, black women were daily stripped of their clothing and publicly whipped. Slaveowners were well aware that it added to the degradation and humiliation of female slaves for them to be forced to appear naked before male whippers and onlookers.[10]

In addition to rapes and naked public floggings, more often than not, female slaves were auctioned naked. This would usually occur with even more white male onlookers than floggings and rightfully so. The floggings brought slaveholders and slaves together primarily to reaffirm the rigid code of laws and the repercussions inherent in disobeying those laws. Thus, the floggings were meant to be primarily demoralizing. The auctions, however, meant that slaveholders had more of a vested interest since he could be taking a particular black woman/women back to his plantation after purchase. Thus, while serving a demoralizing status secondarily, the nakedness of the female slave at auction gave potential slaveholders an opportunity to, "see exactly what he was getting." This became especially significant when slave importations ended and the black woman's womb became the most crucial dimension of the slave trade. Not surprisingly, a young very attractive black woman with no reproductive problems was given prime consideration and usually sold at the highest value. Yet the demand for such black women became so acute that slaveholders refused to sell them in large numbers opting to keep them in order to grow his plantation. This certainly characterized the last fifty years of the slavocracy.

> When the abolition of the international slave trade began to threaten the expansion of the young cotton-growing industry, the slaveholding class was forced to rely on natural production as the surest method of replenishing and increasing the domestic slave population. Thus a premium was placed on the slave woman's reproductive capacity. During the decades preceding the Civil War, Black women came to be increasingly appraised for their fertility (or for the lack of it): she who was potentially the mother of ten, twelve, fourteen or more became a coveted treasure indeed.[11]

Although a coveted treasure if she produced a lot of children, black female slaves were still not looked upon as respected women in the sense white women were. In fact, the ideological underpinnings of racist sexism were driven to the end of a debased and demoralized black woman. Even though she might have been coveted for her baby-making ability, it was for the increase of the slave population only and brought about no change in her slave status.

> This did not mean, however, that as mothers, Black women enjoyed a more re-spected status than they enjoyed as workers. Ideological exaltation of mother-hood — as popular as it was during the nineteenth century — did not extend to slaves. In fact, in the eyes of the slaveholders, slave women were not mothers at all; they were simply instruments guaranteeing the growth of the slave labor force. They were "breeders" — animals, whose monetary value could be pre-cisely calculated in terms of their ability to multiply their numbers.[12]

Hence black women had to endure throughout the colonies and America an un-relenting assault on their sexual intentions and sexual image, while having their worth measured by their ability to produce large numbers of children for the perpetuation of the slavocracy. In so doing, it began what bell hooks' refers to as a "sexual politics of rape" that continued to devalue black womanhood through segregation up to today.[13]

White Christianity and Black Women's Experience of Oppression

While the Victorian image of the white woman reinforced the notion that white women were just below the angels in terms of their worth, a countervailing im-age of black women had firmly affixed itself in the nineteenth century as well. While white women were expected to display their womanhood primarily through the external virtues of being clean, soft-spoken, petite, conservatively dressed, and sexually disinterested, black women were being socialized into a plantation life and beyond that required adherence to so-called "positive virtues" that would certainly benefit slaveholders more than black women. In particular, "The images of black women that are seen as *positive* are usually those that de-pict the black woman as a longsuffering, *religious*, maternal figure, whose most endearing characteristic is her self-sacrificing self-denial for those she loves."[14] (Italics mine.) The implications for the creation of this type image of woman-hood are not hard to find. In creating an image of black womanhood that is long-suffering and sacrificial, the intent is to impress upon black women that their socially appointed role is to sacrifice their immediate happiness for the sake of others. The intent is also, more important, to impress upon black women that they should be content with not being the progenitors of their image of woman-hood. Otherwise, the fear was that if left to the machinations of their own minds, black women could possibly create an image of themselves that places them on the same level as that of white women — an ontological impossibility! As such, black women were not to interpret this process as oppressive but rather should see it as a positive social arrangement that works most effective with them in a subordinate role. That is to say, black women should not have seen the floggings, coerced sex, and naked presentations publicly as demoralizing and/or dehumanizing but rather should have seen the slavocracy as the only vehicle to an improved black womanhood.

But most significant, hooks points out that one of the criteria in the making of the image of black womanhood was for her to be religious. To most persons of faith, this is surely to be looked upon as the black woman's saving grace — both figuratively and theologically. Yet, as we have already established Christian faith in the colonies and America had been co-opted by the forces of white supremacy masquerading as a virtuous pedagogy. If it is true to say that a white supremacist understanding of Christian faith was unduly harsh on black people in general, it is even truer to say that it was doubly harsh on women because of racial and gender dehumanization. Further, black women were not helped by the general debasement of women in the history of the church and white male clergy's so-called biblical mandate to subordinate women in both the church and society. The stated reason for this was so that slaveholders would not incur God's wrath for disobedience. But the actual reason was to create a kingdom on earth rooted in white male racial privilege in the name of God. Also necessary for masters and white clergy was how to affirm the debasement of women in general as a biblical mandate for salvation while at the same time affirming that white women, by virtue of their whiteness, were not the evil temptresses that black women naturally inherited from the biblical Eve. Hence, we have arrived at a theological complexity that cannot be deciphered separately but must be treated within the interconnectedness of Christian history, in general, and Christian history in American life in particular.

More to the point, because great lengths were taken to create conversely different images of white womanhood and black womanhood sociologically, slaveholders and white clergy sought to create a theological hand-maiden to the sociological images that gave divine legitimacy to the dehumanization of black womanhood. Of utmost priority was making sure that black women be presented with an image of womanhood that advocated passivity in the face of oppression. To this end, the most popular image of black womanhood was that of the nanny or what would come to be known as the Mammy or Aunt Jemima image. Slaveholders saw an opportunity to both mythologize black womanhood as unappealing and unintelligent and at the same time allay fears by slaveholders' wives of a possible sexual relationship between her husband and the black female house servant. This became increasingly imperative for slaveholders given that the prevalent notion already in circulation on the plantation and taught in the church, that the black woman was an evil temptress who was seducing slaveholders into sex for future favors, was losing its influence on the thinking of slaveholders' wives. Rather, slaveholders' wives began to reason that the sexual liaisons between their husbands and black female slaves were, if not reciprocal, certainly initiated in many instances by their husbands. This called for the creation of an image of black womanhood that made white women feel more secure and to convince black women that patience and longsuffering were qualities necessary for salvation.

> Considering white male lust for the bodies of black females, it is likely that white women were not pleased with young black women working in their homes for fear liaisons between them an their husbands might be formed, so they conjured up an image of the ideal black nanny. She was first and foremost asexual and consequently she had to be fat (preferably obese); she also had to give the impression of not being clean so she was the wearer of a greasy, dirty headrag; her too tight shoes from which emerged her large feet were further confirmation of her bestial cow-like quality. Her greatest virtue was of course her love for white folk whom she willingly and passively served. The mammy image was portrayed with affection by whites because it epitomized the ultimate racist-sexist vision of ideal black womanhood — complete submission to the will of whites.[15]

This analysis gives us the best chance to fully understand the sinister politics of black dehumanization as a form of social control. The intent on the part of slaveholders and white clergy was to fashion a mindset in both black and white women that reinforced patriarchal/Christian values that made white women content with their Victorian status over and against the greasy, dirty black woman and black women content with their ultimately inferior status in relationship to white men, white women and black men.

> In a sense, whites created in the mammy figure a black woman who embodied solely those characteristics they as colonizers wished to exploit. The saw her as the embodiment of woman as passive nurturer, a mother figure who gave all without expectation of return, who not only acknowledged her inferiority to whites but who loved them. The mammy as portrayed by whites poses no threat to the existing white patriarchal social order for she totally submits to the white racist regime.[16]

It is interesting to note that this image of black women not only seemed to be least threatening to a white system of racial privilege during slavery but, in many regards, this image of black women is operative even today particularly as it relates to the attributes of longsuffering and submission to male domination.

In addition to the Mammy image, two other presentations of black womanhood in American history are worthy of our discussion – The Sapphire and The Jezebel. The Sapphire and Jezebel images not only show their importance in plantation life but also reveal the duplicitous activity of white clergy in the Christianization of these images in American history. The difference between the Mammy image and those of the Sapphire and the Jezebel lies primarily in sexual appetite and aesthetic presentation. Whereas the Mammy was imaged as an asexual, unattractive, unintelligent and consistently pleasant, the Sapphire and the Jezebel were imaged as combative, argumentative, animalistic in sexual aggression, extremely appealing sexually, and who made demonic use of high intelligence to seduce white men for personal advancement and to take the latter off the path of Christian righteousness. As such, this type of black woman was regarded as extremely dangerous to the plantation and to the salvation of white men. In addressing the connection between the Sapphire image and white Christianity, hooks writes:

> The counterpart to the Aunt Jemima images are the Sapphire images. As sapphires, black women are depicted as evil, treacherous, bitchy, stubborn and hateful; in short all that the mammy figure was not. The Sapphire image had as its base one of the oldest negative stereotypes of woman — the image of the female as inherently evil. Christian mythology depicted woman as the source of sin and evil; racist-sexist mythology simply designated black women the epitome of female evil and sinfulness.[17]

Here we see clearly the convenient collaboration between plantation and Christian leaders in the debasement of black womanhood. By connecting negative images of black womanhood to biblical revelation, the case was being made that black women were not only more inclined to treachery than white women but also that their status was not a socio-historical construction on the part of white men but an ontological construction on the part of God. As such, it absolved white men of any wrongdoing in "creating" these images of black women and provided white men, white women and even black men the theological foundation to conveniently conclude that although we are all casualties of the Fall, black women have evidently either fallen more than the rest of humanity or that they were actually created by God with a depraved nature. In so doing, it served as an effective Christian theological pretext for satisfying the oppressive dispositions of white men, white women, and black men.

> White men could justify their dehumanization and sexual exploitation of black women by arguing that they possessed inherent evil demonic qualities. Black men could claim that they could not get along with black women because they were so evil. White women could use the image of the evil sinful black woman to emphasize their own innocence and purity. Like the biblical figure Eve, black women became the scapegoats for misogynist men and racist women who needed to see some group of women as the embodiment of female evil.[18]

In short, the co-opting of the biblical image of Eve as an evil temptress sentenced black women to the dungeon of human worth on both historical and theological grounds.

In close connection to the Sapphire image was the co-opting of the biblical image of the Jezebel for black women as well. In many ways similar to the Sapphire in attributes, the Jezebel image and designation did not have to be created for slaveholders and white clergy. It rather only had to be established as a com-

parative designation on black women relative to the biblical character herself as
portrayed in Christian history. That portrayal places Jezebel, the wife of King
Ahab, as the most treacherous and cunning woman in biblical history. She is
often depicted in contemporary history as having no regard for sexual chastity or
moral turpitude if they can accomplish hedonistic or male destructive ends. She
is depicted foremost as an enemy of men who intentionally seeks their downfall
through relentless sexual overtures and irresistible charm. (Jezebel is still considered today by many women to be the most derogatory epitaph that can be
directed to them!)

The intent of slaveholders and white clergy in seeking an inextricable link
between this biblical vixen and black women becomes obvious. By contrasting
the Jezebel image with the Victorian demand for virtuous womanhood as a staple component of Christian theological discourse, it not only laid the foundation
for the legitimacy of distancing black womanhood from white womanhood but it
also created the atmosphere for the brutal treatment of black women as a necessary, or dare I say, a salvific duty for slaveholders' given black women's depraved status.

To be sure, this image of black women began in Africa as European traders
saw less dressed black women in a warm African climate and erroneously concluded that black women were less virtuous than the more conservatively
dressed white woman who lived in a cooler European climate. Hence, by not
conforming to the Victorian image of womanhood in regard to dress, black
women were unwittingly participating in the destruction of their womanhood.
Kelly Brown Douglass explains:

> Though the Jezebel image in relation to Black women would come to fruition
> during slavery, like White cultural stereotypes and images of Black people in
> general, it is rooted in European travels to Africa. Travelers often interpreted
> African women's sparse dress — dress appropriate to the climate of Africa —
> as a sign of their lewdness and lack of chastity.[19]

This would come to play a major role in the Christian theological participation
in the dehumanization of black women. By employing the Jezebel image from a
biblical standpoint and using the Victorian criterion of proper attire for determining a woman's moral state, a "world" was being sociologically constructed
to solidify in the minds of black women a Jezebel kinship that was being touted
as their natural lot by white clergy.

> If the habits, way of life and living conditions of the African woman gave birth
> to the notion that Black women were Jezebels, then the conditions and exigen-
> cies of slavery brought it to maturity. The life situation of the enslaved woman
> encouraged the idea that she was a Jezebel, even as the Jezebel image served to
> justify the life situation she was forced to endure. Essentially, the very institu-
> tion that the Jezebel image served to guard gave credence to the idea that Black
> women were in fact Jezebels.[20]

Douglas is in essence reminding us of the powerful affects of social control. Though highly complex, the process entails the placing of a group of people in a context in which you govern their behavior through imposed customs and laws that over time become what you are seeking to fashion with that group initially. This is followed by the use of sacred symbols to maintain that what was fashioned in that group of people is irrevocably natural. In this regard, the intent was to impose negative images on black women that forced them to live a daily existence that confirmed those images. This was accomplished most effectively through the differing attire of white and black women.

> Clothing signified one's moral status as well as class. A "respectable" White woman thus "adorned" in layers of clothing. By contrast, the enslaved female was often given barely enough clothing to cover her body. In addition, the enslaved woman's work in the fields often required her to raise her dress above her knees. Even house servants often had to pull their skirts up to polish and wash floors. Their sparse covering coupled with working in a manner that required that they were even more exposed all fed the sentiment that the Black female was a wanton, loose creature.[21]

This would lay a foundation for an imaging of womanhood in contemporary America in which we are still socialized to determine a woman's worth by her sexual chastity and draw conclusions about her morality based on her choice of clothing. Outfits that show a lot of flesh cause both men and women to conclude that the women who wear them are loose sexually and that if very little flesh is showing then she is considered a virtuous woman. And when given divine sanction by many of our religious institutions that this understanding of female morality emanates from the mind of God, it carries ultimate weight for people of faith in how both men and women image womanhood.

That leaves a final category of theological reflection in regard to the unique oppression of black women and that is the appropriation of the Virgin Mary. Given that Eve was established as the biblical norm for viewing black women, it stood to reason that white clergy would select a biblical character for imaging white women as well. Not surprisingly, this biblical character would have to embody the very virtues white males were seeking to establish regarding white women – pure, above moral reproach, and imaged as white! What better selection than a woman who was a virgin. Just as black women were mythologized into Eve i.e., evil temptresses, white women were mythologized into the Virgin Mary i.e., pure. At the same time, it reinforced the theological contention on the part of white clergy that white women transcended the curse of Eve and were not the evil temptresses black women were.

> The new image of white womanhood was diametrically opposed to the old image. She was depicted as goddess rather than sinner; she was virtuous, pure, innocent, not sexual and worldly. By raising the white female to a goddess-like

status, white men effectively removed the stigma Christianity had placed on them.[22]

In fact, the overall intent was to establish that the highly contrasting skin pigmentation of black women and white women served as a visible manifestation of their differing moralities. Thus, slaveholders and white clergy were fully cognizant that with each positive virtue assigned to white women, a corresponding negative virtue was being assigned to black women. Hence, one could wage a cogent argument that white women were actually used as a tool of oppression by slaveholders and white clergy in theologically establishing white womanhood as ideal (Virgin Mary) while positing black womanhood as its racial counterpart (Eve).

> The message of the idealization was this: as long as white women possessed sexual feeling they would be seen as degraded immoral creatures (as black women were depicted); remove those sexual feelings and they become beings worthy of love, consideration, and respect. Once the white female was mythologized as pure and virtuous, a symbolic Virgin Mary, white men could see her as exempt from negative sexist stereotypes of the female (as black women were depicted).[23] Parenthetical expressions mine.

In this scenario, an unfortunate one for black women, slaveholders and white clergy understood themselves to be liberating white women while at the same time oppressing black women. Theologically, it was understood that a subordinate relationship existed between men and women with God assigning men the higher status in that relationship. So even within the context of promoting white women as paragons of morality in contradistinction to black women, white women themselves were socially helpless in their placement in an ideological scheme that at one and the same time made her a goddess and a tool of exploitation.

The more damaging result of this Christian mythology of the white superwoman was that it lent credence to white clergy and theologians' contention that Jesus was white and male. It is the image of the white male Jesus that has given white males the religious motivation to exploit people of color and women in the name of God and to create a society predicated on the "logic" of white male superiority given that Jesus himself was a white male. That is, given the presupposition of Jesus' whiteness, one should also be given over to the conclusion that Jesus' parents were white — God and Mary. In establishing Mary's whiteness, white women, by racial and gender similarity, became the inheritors of Mary's purity and chastity. This placed black women at the opposite end of a racial and gender spectrum that made them dirty, sexually promiscuous and evil.

So codified has this God-Jesus-Mary construction become in the history of the church in the colonies and now America, many black female scholars of religion really wonder whether the image of Jesus as white and male can be re-

demptive for black women. Womanist theologian Jacquelyn Grant, in her classic, *White Women's Christ, Black Women's Jesus: Feminist Christology and
Womanist Response*, rightly identifies the most challenging obstacle for the realization of a fully human black womanhood as Jesus' whiteness and maleness.
Given that black women are black and female, Grant wonders whether a traditional Christian theological paradigm that seeks to present white male superiority as normative can save black women on either racial or gender grounds. In
seeking a reimaging of Jesus' universal value for all Christians, Grant does not
abandon the God-Jesus-Mary paradigm but does maintain that in order for the
saving grace that God gives all Christians through Jesus to be received, Jesus
must be imaged as human rather than as white and male. That is, given that Jesus has been imaged as white and male throughout most of Christian history to
legitimate white male superiority, imaging Jesus as human brings a far more
inclusive understanding of the incarnation and does not keep us mired in the
racial-gender exclusivism that has characterized much of Christian history in the
colonies and America. In this regard, for Grant, two questions, not surprisingly,
become the point of departure for Womanist Christology: Can women redeem
Jesus? And can Jesus redeem women.[24] That is, in order for Jesus to be able to
redeem women, for Grant, he must first be liberated from the centuries of oppressive treatments of the incarnation by white theologians that sanction white
male superiority and that lead black women to conclude that they fall out of the
purview of Jesus' salvific scope. Thus, Jesus can only redeem women, for Grant,
when he is imaged as a savior of women as well as men. It then becomes essential to reimage Jesus by departing not from Jesus' ontology but to whom Jesus'
came to save — both men and women. More particularly, Grant makes clear
that, "If Jesus Christ were a Savior of men then it is true the maleness of Christ
would be paramount. But if Christ is a Savior of all, then it is the humanity —
the wholeness — of Christ which is significant.[25] Hence, by locating the efficacy
of the incarnation in the life of Jesus and the responsibility of future Christians
to carry out the salvific function of witnessing to the encounter that has the
power to redeem us, Grant reconfigures the Christ-event out of Jesus' maleness
and whiteness and into the universal category that connects us all — his humanity.

> I would argue . . . that the significance of Christ is not his maleness but his hu-
> manity. The most significant events of Jesus Christ were the life and ministry,
> the crucifixion, and the resurrection. The significance of these events, in one
> sense, is that in them the absolute becomes concrete. God becomes concrete not
> only in the man Jesus, for he was crucified, but in the lives of those who will
> accept the challenges of the risen Savior the Christ.[26]

Grant's vision is similar to Hoover's in the sense that they both call for the total
emancipation of humanity as an intricate part of God's reign. Grant's treatment
is primarily concerned with the Kingdom of God and the demands placed on

Christians by the Christ-event to be totally inclusive in its understanding of just what constitutes being human. Hoover's vision entails the tripartite all-inclusive struggle of race, gender, and class as equally significant dimensions of the struggle for human liberation. That is to say, Hoover maintains that all three, although interrelated, are distinct in their manifestations and should be approached as such and not as race trumping both gender and class. Hence, for black male theologians and black men in general, both Hoover and Grant make clear that they are unconditionally supportive of our racial struggle as black men but also make clear that the racial politics of black liberation must extend beyond a struggle of racial inclusion into the fullness of American life for black men only. Rather, both compel us to see racism, sexism, and poverty as equally virulent. A feat that, in my judgment, cannot be accomplished until black men genuinely take into account the unique experiences of black women's oppression and the role white American Christianity has played in its perpetuation.

Notes

1.   See, "Black Women and the Churches: Triple Jeopardy," in Gayraud S. Wilmore, and James H. Cone, eds., *Black Theology: A Documentary History, Volume 1, 1966-1979*, 377-88.

2.   bell hooks, *Ain't I A Woman: Black Women and Feminism.* Boston: South End Press, 1981, 15.

3.   Angela Davis, *Women, Race, and Class.* New York: Vintage Books, 1981, 6.

4.   Taken from hooks, *Ain't I A Woman*, 38.

5.   Ibid., 42-43. This is not to suggest, however, that black men were not victims of sexual politics as well. It is only to suggest that this was a far more ubiquitous reality for black women and contributes to the primary demonstration of black women's unique experience of oppression.

6.   *Long Memory: The Black Experience in America.* New York: Oxford Press, 1982, 118.

7.   Paula Giddings, *When And Where I Enter: The Impact of Black Women on Race and Sex in America.* New York: Bantam Books, 1984, 43.

8.   hooks, *Ain't I A Woman*, 36.

9.   Davis, *Women, Race, and Class*, 7.

10. hooks, *Ain't I A Woman*, 37.

11. Davis, *Women, Race, and Class*, 6-7.

12. Ibid., 7.

13. This sexual politics of exploitation perpetuates itself up to the present day. During segregation, the catchword was miscegenation and the harrowing thought among many whites that too many interracial couples would produce mulatto kids and destroy both races. The larger concern, however, was that black people would begin to develop a better self-image and not be content with a nation of white male privilege. Further, the growing sexual unions between black women and white men did create an extremely distrustful relationship between black women and white women, but the two were able to form substantive coalitions regarding the women's liberation movement in the nineteenth century. For a more detailed treatment of these developments see Davis, hooks, and Giddings works cited above in particular. My intent at this point is only to show the origins of black women's oppression in the slavocracy as a foundation for understanding the social complexities of interracial relationships and sex throughout American history.

14. hooks, *Ain't I A Woman*, 66.

15. Ibid., 84.

16. Ibid., 84-85.

17. Ibid., 85.

18. Ibid.

19. Kelly Brown Douglas, *Sexuality and the Black Church: A Womanist Perspective.* New York: Orbis Books, 1999, 36.

20. Ibid., 37.

21. Ibid.

22. hooks, *Ain't I A Woman*, 31.

23. Ibid.

24. Jacquelyn Grant, *White Women's Christ and Black Women's Jesus: Feminist Christology and Womanist Response.* Atlanta: Scholar's Press, 1989, 180.

25. Ibid., 219.

26. Ibid., 220.

5

The Racialization of God and Black Dehumanization

The Christian must conduct his business [life] with a high seriousness, as in itself a kind of religion. Such teaching, whatever its theological merits or defects, was admirably designed to liberate economic energies, and to weld into a disciplined social force the rising *bourgeoisie*, conscious of the contrast between its own standards and those of a laxer world, proud of its vocation as the standard-bearer of the economic virtues, and determined to vindicate an open road for its own way of life by the use of every weapon, including political revolution and war, because the issue which was at stake was not merely convenience or self-interest, *but the will of God*.
R. H. Tawney, *Religion and the Rise of Capitalism*

In examining the interrelationship between economic prosperity and racial morality, the Reformed tradition, in particular, had already committed itself to a "stations in life" interpretation of human relationships. As noted earlier, the Reformed tradition had given itself over to a stratified understanding of human existence according to a divinely ordered proportionality of the dissemination of gifts. Whether it was, in fact, a divine creation was questioned by many at the outset of the Reformed tradition. But with Calvin's "next logically conclusive" interpretation of Luther's treatment of the righteousness of God, nothing happens in the universe without divine intentionality. For Calvin, God's providence is completely deterministic in regard to human destiny (double predestination). It then followed for Calvin that God is completely deterministic in regard to the events of human history as well.

This would become the structure by which most European Christians imaged human relationships, particularly in the economic realm. Yet there are two "addendums" that would emerge from this worldview that leads us into this chapter. First, it was understood by European Christians that the "stations in life" worldview was not their creation but the creation of God. That is to say, the "stations in life" worldview was never understood and taught as a theological construction of the church's leadership. Rather, it was taught to European Christians as God's plan for humanity mediated to the leadership of the church through divine revelation. In that regard, the Reformed leadership did not, in this case, mind being compared to the papacy relative to divine epistemology! Thus, a society that formed itself on individual and class stratification was not to be questioned but only to be realized through the principled work of devout Christians. In so doing, those Christians would be showing the world, also as stated earlier, that they have been predestined by God for eternal bliss. Second, the "stations in life" worldview would come to take on a more insidious form racially when European Christians came into contact with Africans. The "stations in life" worldview would be theologically co-opted in the colonies and America to theologically justify the dehumanization of people of West African descent. As we would come to learn, although the structure of the "stations in life" hermeneutic was the same in the slavocracy as that of fourteenth century Europe, the treatment of black slaves would be infinitely worse than the treatment of lower class whites in Europe. Moreover, just as in the European context, wherein one's lot in life was not to be questioned but lived according to that station, white Christians in the colonies and America worked to establish a white racial bourgeoisie that placed black slaves in an eternal lot of human oppression. In contrast to the European context in which lower class whites were respected as full human beings, blacks were made slaves in the most crude and dehumanizing sense. Their aesthetic, cultural, and intellectual dispositions were mocked and they were not allowed to share in the profits engendered by their work. They were made to understand, as in the strictly European context, that this relationship was to be understood as eternal and not to be questioned. The reason: God had ordained these relationships exactly in the manner in which they existed for the realization of God's ultimate purpose for humanity. Thus, white Christian leadership in the colonies and America had successfully established a theological paradigm not only for furthering its economic interests off the backs of free slave labor but, more important, a salvific pretext for whatever treatment it accorded blacks to maintain that paradigm. In Christian theological terms, blacks were made to see the unmerited suffering it would be experiencing as God's plan for fashioning a kingdom on earth and eternal bliss for them only after death.

Historically speaking, God, then, was presented to slaves as an avowed white supremacist that sanctioned black oppression as divine will for the black-white encounter. Yet as we moved through the slavocracy and this approach to

Christian faith was criticized by northern whites who saw blacks as inferior but thought that the slavocracy was too harsh, God was then styled by southern white clergy as a broad thinking Sovereign Lord unconcerned about the particulars of human relationships but working all of humanity to God's desired end. It is an examination of each of these conceptions of God that we now turn.

God as Avowed White Supremacist

When it was determined by white clergy and theologians that it would be beneficial to Christianize slaves, an immediate effort was made to establish that God had ordained the institution of slavery and righteousness could only be affirmed by doing what masters had ordered. In this regard, white clergy and theologians sought to make a racial correlation between the minds of white racists and the mind of God. Put in simpler terms, every effort was made to establish that God was the author of white supremacy and that blacks were duty bound to humbly serve those in whose image God existed — slaveholders. Thus, God was an avowed white supremacist because God was white, ontologically, and, in being, so had willfully ordered a master-slave relationship between whites and blacks historically. As for slaves, their bondage was a manifestation of God's benevolence in that despite assigning the superior position to white people in human history, God made salvation possible for slaves through nonresistant duty to whites in the slavocracy. This context was to be seen as preferable to slaves over and against an African context of heathenism and savagery.

> Their duty to God was to look upon him (God) as their "great and chief master," who constantly watched them and searched out all their secrets. This God they must love with all their hearts, not least because he (God) brought them out of a land of darkness and ignorance to a country where they might learn "a sure way to heaven." Out of this love should proceed fear of displeasing him (God) and dread of his (God's) terrible judgments. They owed this God worship, reverence (rather than cursing and swearing), and truth (rather than lying).[1]

Hence we see the makings of a theological paradigm that equated the love of God with a distorted fear of divine retribution for not serving whites well in the slavocracy. This would have a huge impact on the religious conscious of the slave and lead to much of the quietism and passivity that ensued with black internalization of white Christian pedagogy. Worship and reverence were two key components in the acceptance of the God of white supremacy insofar as slaves were subtly made to internalize white values which were decidedly anti-black. It was an unapologetic attempt to sacralize the slavocracy as a product of the mind of God and establish an intricate connection between white supremacy and divine will.

Their duty toward their masters and mistresses was summed up in "one general rule that you ought always to carry in your minds; — and that is, — *to do all service for them, as if you did it for God himself (Godself),*" for they were God's overseers. Good slaves therefore served their owners with cheerfulness, reverence, and humility and without surliness and backtalk. . . . And besides masters had ways of forcing labor, and God would punish slaves in the next world for grumbling and murmuring.[2]

Two issues immediately suggest themselves relative to this theological approach. First, one is to delineate a dogged insistence on slave behavior being servile and passive. This type disposition is not lost on the contemporary scene in the sense that "good" Christian behavior has become associated with meekness, monotone voices, and a panacea-like reverence for God in working human history to God's desired end. To be sure, this began as a pretext for black oppression during the slavocracy but has tremendous implications for today's Christian in identifying these attributes as prototypically Christian. It became codified as the ideal social disposition and became the foundation of the notion of being a pious Christian. Hence Christian piety became the canopy that divinely hovered over every slave decision morally and ethically. Second, although piety was a staple part of Christian pedagogy during the slavocracy to white Christians as well, that piety extended to whites in their interactions with each other and not with the slaves. Whites were anything but pious with black people. In the carrying out of their divine duty to perpetuate the slavocracy in the name of God, whites conveniently understood themselves to have assumed whatever negative disposition short term in order to be positively judged by God in eternity. In short, this theological paradigm divinely freed slaveholders to do whatever they deemed necessary, both physically and mentally to slaves, to prevent the slavocracy from ending.

These things, combined with the insults, the loss of cultural traditions, rituals, family life, religions, and even names, served to cement the loss of self-respect. As the slave master exalted himself and enforced respect of himself, he was increasingly viewed as superior to the slaves. The superiority was based on the utter dehumanization of the Africans. The slave was forced to bow and bend to the slave-owner and treat him as a god. With the image of a Caucasian man as God, and with all kinds of images of Africans as dirty and only half human, it was inevitable that a sense of inferiority would grow into the African-American personality.[3]

Akbar is incisive concerning the imaging of God as a white male and its implication that by virtue of similar race and gender, white males were assigned the highest ontological status among humans and therefore the highest social status. But more important, Akbar's analysis lifts up the inversely proportional relationship between the edification of whiteness through superior racial categorization, its connection to the whiteness of God, and the inevitable devaluing of blackness as a racial category both ontologically and historically.

Everything associated with blackness culturally aesthetically, and intellectually was looked upon as wanting simply because it was not white. What should have been looked upon simply as cultural differences in the human race resulted in racial inferiority if those cultural expressions did not align themselves with white values and culture. I have established in both Chapters One and Two the inability for us as humans to embrace difference and see it as neutral and/or positive. In this context, that inability to accept difference in skin hue was brought to full expression when European traders "discovered" Africa. This inaugurated the process by white clergy and theologians to divinize white values and culture to the degradation of African culture. But more important, Christian theology in America treated God as the creator not only of the world cosmologically but ontologically as well. That is, for many white clergy and theologians the differences between cultural expressions existed not because of diversity in contexts, but so that one would be able to distinguish all other inferior cultures from white culture. In this regard, God imaged as white and male became the empirical confirmation of the superiority of whiteness in all its cultural expressions. The symbols [religion, and law and order] have a particular meaning for blacks, implanted historically, but it is hardly the meaning our leaders would like them to have: for the God is a Caucasian, supervising the purification of white consciences at the expense of their blackness; while law and order are the conditions of white productivity and black degradation.[4]

As we move into the nineteenth century and a passel of anti-slavery literature began to emerge, many white clergy and theologians continued to produce a similar number of tracts promulgating the slavocracy as the manifestation of divine design thereby reaffirming its "benefits" to the slaves. The authors of these works sought to justify its [slavery's] continuance from various sources, but chief among them were (a) the benefits the Negro received from slavery, and (b) the destination of the Negro by God, and by nature to a condition of servility.[5] To be sure, the Negro's destination was established not to be of the behest of whites but of God. This served two purposes. First, black servility would seem more authentic if God ordained it; and second, black servility cast God in a white supremacist light that, even in God's racist will, was benevolent enough to inferior Africans to expose them to superior white culture. In this regard, Africans were to look upon their enslavement by whites as God's way of making salvation possible for them and that they should be especially grateful. But more important, the slave was to understand that everyone's racial standing, because it was the idea of God, was etched in eternal history and "not to be tinkered with through disruptive behavior." Thus, slaves were not to look upon their masters as inimical but as the vicegerents of God's ultimate plan for humanity. Nineteenth century pro-slavery activist George Sawyer explains:

This all goes to show that the Negro race, by universal consent of the civilized world, are considered separate and distinct race of beings, suited only to their own peculiar state and condition. Their freedom is but a name, an unmeaning sound; they are by nature totally incapacitated to enjoy the rights and privileges of freemen, except in secluded communities of their own kindred blood, which ever have been, and ever will be, sooner or later, when left to themselves, in a state of barbarism. Their condition among the whites is necessarily that of pupilage and dependence.[6]

Sawyer's intent is clearly to establish the virtue of the docile, productive slave by equating the slave's eternal bondage with the will of God. But more important, the logic also is to present God to the slave as white, omnipotent, and benevolent. In so doing, it serves as the prototypical "sacred canopy" in affirming these attributes: whiteness as a symbol of racial superiority that confirms the attribute of God's whiteness; the creation of a world of complete white privilege that confirms the attribute of God's omnipotence; and bringing heathen Africans into civilization through slavery that confirms the attribute of God's benevolence.

Yet as Sawyer also brings out, the treatment of God in white terms was seen as the proverbial "star on the Christmas tree" to sell the slaves on the logic of white people being given the superior position in God's ultimate plan for humanity. After all, it would look highly illogical for God to be white and to give black people the superior status in the racial hierarchy. It seems most plausible for the Master Moralist to assign that position to the very race of people in whose image God shares. In short, the God is styled in early Christian theology in America as a white supremacist because logically that is all God can be. Once the presupposition of God's whiteness (and maleness) and omnipotence is established by white clergy and theologians it of necessity makes God a white supremacist. Thus by ontological designation, God's being is that of a white supremacist and therefore the inaugurator of a white supremacist way of life. The significance of this treatment is that it underscores the fact that God has not and has never done theology. Humans do theology with God as its principle subject. As such, humans who are able to wield tremendous influence can go a long way in structuring theological worldviews and subsequently approaches to human relationships both individually and collectively. White clergy and theologians wielded ultimate power for they were seen as the true messengers of divine revelation. With God styled as a white supremacist, it logically followed then that God would elevate the white race to a superior status, make black people inferior to whites, and "reveal" to white clergy that this relationship was eternal. Thus, when presented with this paradigm, slaves were to thank God for creating them for eternal service to whites, be happy about God including them in God's salvific scheme and accept their inferiority with no envy for white culture or people. This would be the most crucial cog in the wheel of the white supremacist argument. If they could establish that God had ordained African enslavement, then it would go a long way in inculcating in blacks an anti-revolutionary conscience with the hope of attenuating the slaves struggle for freedom. That is to say, if whites could get slaves to accept their inferiority from an ontological standpoint, it could convince slaves that their freedom would never be realized because they were incapable of conducting themselves as free men and women. But more important, it would put them on God's "retributive hit list" for attempting to subvert God's intention for all humans. Thus, behind all the presentations of benefits and happy, carefree existence of slaves, there lurks the argument basic and conclusive for all contemporaneous defenders of slavery . . . that the Negro belongs to a race which is separate and distinct from the white race, that he is by nature inferior to the white man and thereby incapable of any social, economic, or political equality.[7] Thus, what I term a racist theocracy was being presented to lay Christians both black and white as the true content of divine revelation. God as white supremacist, then, was a creation of a white racist theological imagination designed to make blacks content with an enslaved status by creating a dilemma in the slave's theological conscience between a natural inclination to freedom on the one hand, but a fear of divine retribution on the other hand. Thus while slave were being made to struggle with this moral dilemma, slaveholders were clearly galvanized by the feeling of what being superior to another race of people produced. It was a haughty and "highly responsible" feeling "knowing" that they looked and thought like God and that God had therefore entrusted them with maintaining God's earthly kingdom. In short, for white supremacists, lucrative economic profit was the sociological rationale for the slave trade while the surreal feeling that comes with "knowing" that you are the Imago Dei racially was the theological rationale for the slave trade. Thus, African enslavement gave whites in general and white Christians in particular an incomparable sense of racial pride that no feudal system or stratified economic system gave them in Europe.

> Not only does Negro slavery elevate the character of the master, and where the master is free, render his devotion to liberty a high and holy feeling, but where, as in our own country, the slave is of a different and inferior race, marked and set apart by his (her) color, physical and mental characteristics, it elevates the character, not only of the master, the actual owner of the slaves, but of all the individuals of his (her) own race who were the color of distinguishing characteristics of freemen (free people). With us color, not money, marks the class: black is the badge of slavery, white the color of freemen (free people); and the white man (race), however poor, whatever be his occupation, is inspired with the just pride of a freeman (free person), a sovereign.[8]

Sawyer thus affirms the "high and holy feeling" whites enjoyed through its systematic domination of people of African descent and in so doing establishes a clearly intended racial stratification as the backdrop into which the economic dimension of the slave trade emerged.

Black indeed was the badge of slavery and has become associated with inferior human characteristics even in contemporary times. This, no doubt, owes its existence to not only the excruciating physical labor imposed on the slave but also the highly demoralizing treatment of the slave psychically and legally. The white American intelligentsia was in large part developed to bring an intellectual respectability to all forms of black dehumanization. But white clergy and theologians were committed to using the gospel to convince slaves of their eternal lot regarding service to whites. As Christian theology had given itself over to the Pauline dualism that humans were possessed of both body and soul, the issue of concern is what was to be made of each given the slave's already inferior status. The treatment of the black body had been already determined when most white clergy deemed the black skin of the slave the most telling sign of the demonic. Not surprisingly, given that purity and godliness had been measured by white skin, it bolstered the original presupposition of the whiteness of God's being. It also continued to lay a foundation for Christian theologizing in terms of white privilege.

The crucial question then became for white clergy and theologians, what are we to make of the soul of the slave? There were generally two responses that unfortunately served no useful purpose for slaves. The first response is that the slave had no soul. White clergy reasoned that the demonic nature of the slave as exemplified by the blackness of her skin was at the same time proof that she possessed no soul. As such, salvation was not an achievable goal for the slave. Yet that approach revealed a major contradiction in white Christian pedagogy. What gave the slave hope in the slavocracy was that good service to her earthly master would bring salvation in the world to come. (It still remains one of the main reasons even today why so much emphasis in black Christian faith is placed on the life to come.) Yet, the slave was also taught that the existence of a soul was necessary for salvation. Thus this treatment of the slave's soul had to be "tweaked" immediately. The response: the slave does possess a soul but not a soul like whites. She possessed a soul that took additional power and energy by God to eternalize even if she were a "good" slave. Thus the slave was corrupted not only physically but spiritually as well. It is what ethicist Riggins Earl refers to as "the white man's hermeneutical circle of double theological self-denigration."[9] In treating the ontology of the slave in this way two fundamental dimensions of white supremacist Christian theology were reaffirmed. First, it reaffirmed the necessity of treating the slave in a relentlessly denigrating way for the purpose of destroying any positive self-image and creating in her a distorted love for white culture and values. The goal, of course, was making the slave completely dependent on slaveholders for the necessities of life psychically as well as physically. The job of the white minister-missionary was to convince the slave to think of self totally in a self-denigrating way . . . the servant must say, "Me think no good, nor do good."[10] Second, it reaffirmed the benevolence and power of God by making salvation for slaves possible, and having the power to save blacks who possessed a far more corrupt soul than whites. In short, slaves should be thankful to a white supremacist God for choosing to redeem them despite the fact that: 1) God did not have to do it; and 2) in doing it God has to exert infinitely more power to redeem slaves in their doubly corrupt state than needed to redeem whites. Thus, slaves were doubly self-denigrated. Not only were they shorn of a healthy self-image because of their blackness, but they could only be saved by a God who was an avowed white supremacist and, therefore, the source of that unhealthy self-image.

> Primarily, this became an act of double self-denigration because it demanded that slaves see themselves interiorly and exteriorly in a worthless light before God and master. This meant that they were solely at the mercy of white people and their God. It was the blood of the white man's Jesus that could whiten the black soul. This severity of the African servant's interior and exterior condition would require God's extra salvation power to save her or his soul.[11]

In making a white supremacist God the only entity capable of bringing about the doubly corrupt slave's eternal bliss, it authenticated even moreso the legitimacy of a racist, yet benevolent God in the mind of the slave. The servant is made to say: "Me believe that Jesus Christ came into the world to save sinners; and though me chief of sinners, though me be only poor black negro."[12] In this regard, the inversely proportional relationship between the doubly corrupt black human and the benevolent, omnipotent white God became a major theological fixture in slaveholding theology.

Given the ontological and spiritual distance between black humans and a white God, obedience to temporal law, not surprisingly, was deemed crucial for the slaves to obtain salvation. This meant for the slave, high worker productivity and a humble spirit. A white supremacist theological paradigm was created to bring about optimum economic gain for the slaveholding community via a theologically manipulated slave community. While the image of a white Christ served as the linchpin that brought the doubly corrupt slave into spiritual union with the God of white supremacy, it was by far the usage of Pauline literature that brought the slave into historical union with the God of white supremacy. Because of the Reformation tradition the primacy of the Bible was paramount in guiding the Christian community's understanding of faith. This meant that biblical "proof" of black servility was indispensable in the forwarding of a white supremacist Christian theology. Not only did white clergy and theologians see in most of Paul's letters God's condoning of slavery, they also saw an acute emphasis on slave obedience in general, and the consequences of unruly behavior by slaves, in particular. The message was consistent and undeniable: servants were to obey their masters in all things; defiance toward civil authority was also defiance toward spiritual authority; the road to salvation was disciplined and orderly; and freedom in the next life did not require freedom from this one.[13] Slaveholders and white clergy saw in this biblical dictum from God through

Paul a more than adequate biblical pretext for its construction of the God of white supremacy. They saw not only the biblical affirmation of a God that condoned slavery but a God that would severely punish slaves for insurrectionist activities. Such a strong biblical precedence would serve as the cornerstone of white Christian pedagogy to slaves. The catechisms of the early church dealt more with the theme of slave obedience than any other dimension of faith. This call-and-response teaching to slaves was emblematic of the Christian pedagogy of the time:

> *Who gave you a master and a mistress?*
> God gave them to me.
> *Who says that you must obey them?*
> God says that I must.
> *What book tells you these things?*
> The Bible.[14]

In sum, the intent of the theological construction of a white supremacist God was to inculcate into the slave the non-negotiable demand of obedience to both earthly master and heavenly master. What better way to achieve that end than by ransoming the slave's salvation to a white supremacist God who, in turn, demands earthly obedience to those in whose image God is for the realization of that salvation. Thus, the doubly corrupt body and soul of the slave demanded simultaneous obedience to both earthly master and heavenly master as the only means of purifying that body and soul. Hence, earthly master and heavenly master were distinct but interrelated around the ontology of white superiority.

Yet another conception of God, one of eschatological reign rather than ontological superiority, would emerge in the nineteenth century and up to the present day that would be a far more covert but no less virulent conception of God. It is to this "colorless" God that we now turn.

God as Sovereign Lord

In the first typology of God, divinity was wed with the goals, aims, and ends of white supremacy. God was the author of white privilege insofar as God created the white race for the purpose of a supreme earthly life and a supreme heavenly life. The reason: God is white and purposely designates whites as the rulers of earthly life and even promises them a special place in the life to come. Conversely, blacks were specifically created by God for a life of toil and enslavement to whites. In this sense, God creates human relationships out of a cosmological intentionality for white privilege and black dehumanization. This means that although this God is equally interested in this world as well as the one to come, racial equality is not a goal of this God in either human history or beyond. In short, this God is a white racist.

However, the second typology of God in slaveholding theology in America is what I have termed the Sovereign Lord typology. This typology, which is our concern for the remainder of this chapter, holds that God is not significantly interested in earthly life. God, rather, is interested only in the world to come and welcomes all humans worthy of salvation regardless of race into the coming kingdom as equals. In this regard, God is a God of ultimate equality and, at least in heaven, "is no respecter of persons." This God is not a God of unapologetic white privilege. This God, rather, has created a racially stratified society of different occupations, classes, and gifts and has assigned those differing occupations based on God's racial dissemination of those gifts. This God by virtue of their "gifts" mandated that the most prestigious positions, those requiring a high-level of responsibility, those that offered the highest salaries and those that afforded the best opportunity to be lauded historically for their accomplishments, be held exclusively by whites. Blacks, the poor, and women were to happily accept their less fulfilling lots in life.

Yet the difference with this approach to the divine is that although God creates a racially stratified society of white privilege, God's racism is not to be measured as appointing whites as the superior designee of responsibility and wealth. Rather, since human history's significance is only for the purpose of serving as the proving ground for God's judgment on one's life in the particular lot given by God, one's specific "station" should not be given serious weight. One should only be concerned with the effectiveness in which one labors in one's assigned lot for only that will be the criterion in which God will determine one's salvific destiny. Thus, with this typology of the divine, the "stations in life" hermeneutic remains intact but God is not a racist that willfully creates a historical reality of white supremacy but a loving and providential God who offers the gift of salvation to all humans whatever their lot in life. In short, with this typology, God is interested in human history only as it relates to individual performance in one's divinely appointed station and not specifically in black suffering.

In a real sense, this typology is a classic adaptation of the Lutheran doctrine of salvation wherein no distinction is made on the particular occupation of the individual but only the effectiveness with which one performs in that occupation. Regardless of the difference in salary, and/or prestige of occupation between individuals, both stand as equals before God in judgment. Yet, in the final analysis, this becomes another and, in my judgment, a more clever pretext for black suffering. It essentially portrays God as the Great Equalizer of humanity but that equality is possible only in eternity. Thus, whether God is conceived as White Supremacist or Sovereign Lord, a white supremacist end is still served — God is still the creator of black enslavement in human history.

To be sure, this seemed to be an inevitable theological development in the evolving of Christian history in America as we move into the nineteenth century on two fronts. First, after witnessing more than two centuries of plantation life, many northern whites and a few sympathetic southern whites were beginning to question the brutal treatment of slaves. While most generally accepted the inferiority of black people as an ontological given, they also began to consciously struggle with the severity in which blacks were dehumanized. Ironically, this struggle began not more than a generation into the era of the Christianization of the slaves in the late seventeenth century and continued into the nineteenth century and into the post-Emancipation era. Laden between economic privilege and black dehumanization was the notion that some Aristotelian golden mean could be reached between the two that allotted for a more humane treatment of the slave, (even advocating the end of plantation life in some instances!) while maintaining economic and political power. This was seen as an appropriate and long overdue response from some in the white Christian community who were beginning to feel the moral weight of trying to "live" Jesus and black dehumanization simultaneously. Second, slaveholding theology had its intended impact on some slaves, i.e., to instill a docile and quietistic disposition about their oppression. But it had the opposite effect on other slaves. The nineteenth century would bear witness to most of the slave insurrections in the history of the slavocracy with some being extremely violent. The fact of the matter is that slaves were tired of being slaves and intuited that God did not intend their bondage. For most whites, this was seen as particularly hazardous to the slavocracy but was also a premonition that some semblance of godliness was manifesting itself in slaves insofar as a good number refused to accept their bondage as a criterion of faith. It is into this historical backdrop that the God of White Supremacy became theologically suspect.

But not white supremacy itself!

The times called for a God that was at once given over to white privilege but who was "concerned" about all humans. A God that saw the equal nature in all humans but who also adhered to a stratified structure of human relationships in history. A God whose providence and wisdom affirmed the equality of all humans in eternity but white racial stratification in history. In short, the times called for a God whose sovereignty affirmed a secondary interest in human history but a primary interest in eternity. It was the duty of the white Christian leaders, then, to impress this newfound understanding of God on both the slaves and other whites. Of course, there were many whites who saw this "softening" on the question of the humanity of the slave as motivation for the latter to increase its incendiary practices. But for white clergy and theologians still committed to the creation of a more humane slavocracy, (however more humane a slavocracy could be!) their response was clear. The rebuttal was simply that Providence had appointed some to be masters and some servants and that, "Christianity does not blend or destroy these distinctions but establishes and regulates them, and enjoins every man (human) to conduct himself (herself) according to them."[15] Thus, the late eighteenth, early nineteenth century ushered into reality an "innovated" approach to the question of black humanity but was by no means one in which the humanity of black and white people were to be understood as equal in human history. This implied that the signs of "true Christianity" — modesty, meekness, humility, and faithfulness — meant something different for black people than for white.[16]

Yet for all its "innovation" this new conception of the divine never abandoned two crucial characteristics — it affirmed white privilege and black dehumanization as unalterable dimensions of Christian tradition:

> Essential to the defense of the system is the claim that it was not instituted by modern-day members of society, but rather came to them as a sacred and ancient tradition from their forefathers; an inherited way of life. Hence what is done is *de facto* right. In the grip of such a tradition, which received tangible form in personal relations, individuals or groups proclaim their impotence to alter the situation or to defy the tradition.[17]

Leonard crystallizes the old intent of the new God for white clergy and theologians. Even though God had moved from White Supremacist to Sovereign Lord, the tradition of white privilege via black dehumanization remained the key goal of racial relationships in American life. While the rationale became more sophisticated, the intent remained the same. If imaging God as more of a color-blind humanitarian created in the slave a greater comfortability with her enslavement and helped slaveholders to present the slavocracy as a more humane institution, then no level of skilled sophistry was considered out of the white theologian's domain. Yet, as black theologian James Cone points out, this color-blind God is just as virulent as the white supremacist God insofar as it images God as neutral in matters of racial hegemony and in so doing makes a caricature out of the God of the biblical witness.

> The blackness of God, and everything implied by it in a racist society, is at the heart of the black theology doctrine of God. There is no place in black theology for a colorless God in a society where human beings suffer precisely because of their color. The black theologian must reject any conception of God which stifles black self-determination by picturing God as a God of all peoples. Either God is identified with the oppressed to the point that their experience becomes God's experience, or God is a God of racism.[18]

To be sure, Cone's treatment of God in black liberation terms highlights the varied way in which God has been envisioned by whites and many blacks in American history. In so doing, he also accentuates the crucial relationship theologically between divine revelation and socio-historical experience. That is to say, Cone makes clear that what we say about our encounter with divine reality has much to do with what we have historically experienced. Given black people's encounter with the divine out of an experience of acute oppression, it would stand to reason that our encounter with the divine is one that implores us to eradicate that oppression. Given white people's history of racial domination and the economic strength acquired from that domination, it would stand to reason that God would be envisioned as one who upholds the idea of white superiority. Thus, in essence one could argue that the racial struggle in American history has been just as much about the struggle between a black God and a white God as it has been about black and white humans. Yet, even with the construction of a God that condones human domination, some white clergy and theologians recognized that an encounter with the God of white supremacy is theologically incongruent with the aggregate presentation of God in biblical history. Yet even as some in the white Christian community were given over to imaging blacks in a more humane way, they were also not about to relinquish the economic and cultural benefits that a racially hegemonic America had produced. Though God may have evolved from White Supremacist to Sovereign Lord the assault on black humanity did not relent. In short, human equality meant something decidedly different for whites than blacks and, more important, meant something decidedly different in history than in eternity.

> The notion that all human beings were equal in some fundamental sense had long been a standard belief of Western Europeans. But before the eighteenth century, universalistic affirmations of equality existed only in forms that had no clear application to the organization of human society. Equality in the eyes of God — an essential Christian belief — was usually seen as no impediment to a hierarchical order in human affairs. It was in fact, *the will of God* and a consequence of original sin that some should rule and others be ruled.[19] (Italics mine)

Fredrickson brings out two points of acute significance. First, he demonstrates that the equality of humans in the eyes of God as an essential Christian belief is not a new theological concept in Western European history. We established this earlier but also went on to show how European ideas about God and human equality changed when explorers came across "dark" Africans and their "heathen" ways. Second, even given over to a concept of an egalitarian God in European history, the notion of European dominance as a manifestation of original sin was also at the same time a manifestation of divine will. Economic gain won out over moral turpitude, and racial stratification won out over human equality in history. The words of John Winthrop bespeak the majority sentiment of white clergy and theologians regarding God as sovereign Lord: "God Almightie in his (God's) most holy and wise providence hath so disposed of the Condicion of mankind, as in all times some must be rich and eminent in power and dignitie, and others mean and in subieccon."[20] In racially stratified terms, this means that we serve a God that sees the equal worth of all humans but that has also ordained white people occupy the top rung of the racial stratification ladder in human history. In light of that, they are the possessors of power and dignity and conversely blacks are the inheritors of poverty and submission.

    In conceiving of God as a condoner of white privilege we must never lose sight of the fact that the real locus of theological and religious attention is not heaven but earth. We must also not lose sight of the fact that the intent of conceiving of God as a condoner of white privilege in either typology serves conversely as a negative valuation of blackness. Hence, God may have been styled in this typology as a God of all peoples but was still the divine confirmation of white values. God, in either typology, is to be seen as the author of white privilege which in turn leads to the creation of an inferior black humanity.

> They [white churches] tell the receivers of their messages that [in essence] all that is significant in this world and the world to come is White. It would appear to church members that God lives in the suburbs, has an occasional Black member or friend, fights crabgrass, has middle-class values and is White. These attitudes, impressions and values when transferred to the larger society lead individuals to believe that God is not concerned with the everyday oppression of Blacks and that the ghettos are the products of Black ignorance, laziness, and immorality.[21]

This understanding of God was intended to convey to blacks that the extent to which God is concerned about their freedom is the extent to which God has placed them in the care of whites. Thus, every effort was made to convey to blacks that any attempts to "disrupt" the stations in life in which God has placed them is the height of sinful activity and the greatest of human folly. As a corollary, blacks were assured of freedom in the hereafter only if they submitted to whites in all endeavors of human existence. They were to see this as their opportunity to be brought into the household of God. It was only through this crucible that they could share in the divine fellowship that God has provided for them. [Just as] the husband's superiority was self-evident, they [white clergy] concluded that Christ had not advocated equality but that each man (person) — master and slave — had certain duties to perform in accordance with the political and social position that God had placed him (her) in and in the relationships with others that this position called for.[22]

Yet despite this seemingly imperturbable biblical evidence of slavery's virtues, it was gradually being criticized by black and white abolitionists as an unjust institution. The brutal physical treatment of the slave and the breaking up of families represented the height of humanity's inhumanity to humanity. In fact, much of the antislavery literature refuted the claim that rebelling against slavery was sinful arguing instead that slavery itself was the sin. In response, proslavery advocates argued that while one could ostensibly argue that slavery was an evil institution, it was not sinful particularly given its many manifestations in human history, including biblical history. When coupled with the understanding that any God ordained institution could not be sinful, the fact that slavery existed meant that God was working human relationships to an ultimate end. But in a slight concession that slavery might be an evil institution, white clergy and theologians insisted that its existence is still divinely ordained insofar as God ultimate purpose for bringing humanity to a higher destiny could not be achieved unless evil first existed. This served as a most formidable argument given that it justified slavery's existence as an evil that could only be overcome by God's power at the end of human history. White clergy and theologians morally questioned slavery's existence but sought its perpetuation until the end of human history. As such, even as conceived in evil terms (and precisely because it is conceived of in evil terms!), slavery's existence was still justified as an eternal institution.

> The idea that slavery could be evil but not sinful was an essential feature of the conservative Christian's theology because, in answering the charge that an all-powerful, all-good God would never permit evil, suffering and injustice to exist, it enabled him (her) to fit wrongdoing into God's greater plan of the ultimate good. That is, in order to root out evil, it must first be there . . . which meant that slavery was one of those evils that should be left alone. It was the ultimate rationalization.[23]

White clergy and theologians committed to slavery's perpetuation were able to take one of the most formidable anti-slavery arguments and successfully stave off slavery's demise with an equally formidable counter-argument.

In sum, white clergy and theologians were convinced that slavery or some form of black servitude was the best possible relationship that existed between the two races and were also convinced that God, as White Supremacist or as Sovereign Lord, mandated that whites carry out their Christian stewardship by maintaining this superior-subordinate relationship no matter the intensity of the criticism received from anti-slavery "enemies of God." Thus, for many white clergy and theologians, the increase in anti-slavery literature was not seen as a call to conscience but simply as a test of faith. As the Civil War approached and the demise of slavery stood as a concrete possibility, white clergy and theologians steadfastly clung to the test of faith hermeneutic. Alabama Baptist minister Reverend Isaac Taylor Tichenor proclaimed to the Alabama General Assembly in 1863 that God would vindicate the Confederacy and blamed the war's existence and the South's losing of the war as a punishment from God for slaveholders not properly teaching slaves the proper rudiments of slave life and their connection to salvation. Tichenor, however, was convinced that this "losing" was only temporary and that God would fully restore the fortunes of the Confederacy once it made the slavocracy more humane. Tichenor was not conceding that the slavocracy was a sinful institution. Quite the contrary, he was making the case that the slavocracy, if more humane, would result in a Confederate victory and vindicate slavery as a superior institution created by a superior God. Tichenor expressed confidence that God was preparing the South to show the world the superiority of slavery as a social institution that reconciled the interests of labor and capital . . . but to enjoy God's favor, Southerners must demonstrate, "a proper understanding and regard for the rights of both master and slave."[24]

Methodist Bishop George Foster Pierce, echoed Tichenor's understanding that God was simply testing the resolve of southern whites. Unlike Tichenor, however, Pierce cited denying slaves the opportunity to read, particularly the Bible, as the slavocracy's biggest sin. If, he taunted, the Bible sanctions slavery, then slaveholders should want a Bible in every slave cabin in the South.[25] Pierce is indirectly making the claim that God demands slavery of blacks by whites but only wants whites to show more compassion to the slave but not end the institution itself.

And on the same theme, Presbyterian minister Reverend James A. Lyon of Columbia, Mississippi, saw the events of the war as a sign by God to southern white leaders to completely overhaul the slave codes. He too was adamant about the treatment of slaves but completely sold on the salvific value of the slavocracy. In fact, for Lyon, the salvation of all humans was predicated on the existence of slavery and was necessary to bring all of God's children under the behavioral domain of divine morality.

> As to the lawfulness of the institution slavery in itself considered, disconnected from its abuses, we scarcely deem it necessary to discuss it. Like the existence of God, it is taken for granted from the beginning to the end of the Bible. It [slavery] has existed in all past ages, and will continue to exist for ages yet to come. It is incidental to a state of sin and depravity . . . it will continue to be necessary, until Christianity gain such ascendancy over the minds and hearts and lives of men (humans) — all men (humans) — as to bring the entire race under the absolute and delightful control of the principles of the Gospel. Then, slavery will, as a natural result, cease.[26]

Although we see in Lyon's assessment, in contrast to Tichenor and Pierce, a provision that could possibly at some point in human history end the slavocracy, we also see an unrequited comfortability with its existence theologically. In this regard, he is very much in sync with Tichenor and Pierce.

In the final analysis, while we see white clergy in sync theologically about the virtues of slavery, their ultimate ideological commitment is to black dehumanization in human history. Whether God is White Supremacist or Sovereign Lord, God still condones black subordination. Even under the typology of Sovereign Lord, a more humane slavocracy is still a slavocracy and a way of life that sought incessantly to establish black oppression as the norm in daily life. Hence, the significance and power of theological language becomes evident in convincing not only whites but blacks themselves of the "natural" disposition of their inferiority. This has been and continues to be an acute internal struggle for black self-identity and self-image. Whether God is White Supremacist or Sovereign Lord, blacks have been made to struggle with the transgenerational nature of slavery, segregation and contemporary racial struggles as the historical backdrop for attempting to answer humanist philosopher William R. Jones' question, Is God a White Racist?[27] Black people have been put into a theological matrix in proclaiming the power of a God who has brought them out of slavery and legal segregation confessionally, while struggling with why we were/are made to endure those incomparable hardships theologically. That is, if whites are the superiors and blacks the subordinates, then maybe God is a white racist or one who is for all people but appointed whites to be rulers over all other humans. If nothing else, the facts of history seem to validate this notion! This becomes a particularly intense theological struggle for a healthy black self-image, when, throughout American history, white standards of beauty have been established as the norm and, more important, the Son of God has been imaged as a Caucasian man!

Notes

1. Lester Scherer, *Slavery and the Churches in Early America: 1619-1819*. Grand Rapids: Eerdman's Publishing Company, 1975, 98.
2. Ibid., 98-99.
3. Na'im Akbar, *Chains and Images of Psychological Slavery*. Jersey City, New Jersey: New Mind Productions, 1984, 21.
4. Joel Kovel, *White Racism: A Psychohistory*. New York: Columbia University Press, 1984, 225.
5. Joseph T. Leonard, *Theology and Race Relations*. Milwaukee: Bruce Publishing Company, 1963, 26.
6. George S. Sawyer, *Southern Institutes: or an Inquiry into the Origin and Early Prevalence of Slavery and the Slave-Trade*. Philadelphia: J. B. Lippincott & Company, 1858. Taken from Ibid., 27.
7. Ibid.
8. Sawyer, *Southern Institutes*. Taken from Ibid., 28.
9. *Dark Symbols, Obscure Signs: God, Self & Community in the Slave Mind*. New York: Orbis Books, 1993, 18.
10. Ibid.
11. Ibid.
12. Ibid.
13. Forrest G. Wood, *The Arrogance of Faith: Christianity and Race in America from the Colonial Era to the Twentieth Century*. Boston: Northeastern University Press, 1990, 67.
14. Taken from Ibid., 72.
15. Scherer, *Slavery and the Churches*, 95-96.
16. Ibid., 96.
17. Leonard, *Theology and Race Relations*, 23.
18. James Cone, *A Black Theology of Liberation (Twentieth Anniversary Edition)*. New York: Orbis Books, 1990, 63.
19. George M. Fredrickson, *White Supremacy: A Comparative Study in America and South African History*. New York: Oxford University Press, 1981, 141.
20. Taken from Ibid.
21. Columbus Salley, Ronald Behm, *What Color Is Your God? Black Consciousness and the Christian Faith*. New York: Citadel Press, 1988, 109.
22. Wood, *The Arrogance of Faith*, 63.
23. Ibid., 67.
24. Eugene Genovese, *A Consuming Fire: The Fall of the Confederacy in the Mind of the White Christian South*. Athens: University of Georgia Press, 1998, 58.
25. Ibid.
26. Ibid., 59.
27. Boston: Beacon Press, 1998. Originally published in 1973.

6

The Divinity of Whiteness Revealed

Not only Christian asceticism but Christian theology became infected. Since light is white, the divine *Logos* itself, incarnate in the Christ, must also be white or else it could not conquer the darkness that engulfs both the world and the soul in its redemptive mission. . . . White and black, therefore, were elevated to the status of ontological as well as moral designations, and the character of all subsequent Christian thought was firmly set in this intellectual mould. As long as Christian theology was written by white theologians, that is to say, virtually until the present day, this pattern was not seen as tainted by racial assumptions.
Alan Davies, *Infected Christianity*

Arguably, no other image has had as much of a devastating impact on the emergence of a healthy black self-image than the presentation to blacks of a white-imaged Jesus. This has been the case principally for two reasons. First, given that blacks have imaged Christian faith itself (like most Christian adherents) as a thoroughgoingly positive phenomenon, the reception of a Christ in any image could only bring positive benefits. Moreover, given that Christian pedagogy is understood to be from God through revelation and is therefore not to be questioned, no atmosphere existed with which to address the gradual damaging effects of a white Jesus on black self-image or for that matter produced an analytical conscience for understanding that black self-image was being dealt a tremendous blow. Hence, even for the black people who saw an acute incongruence between the will of God and their enslavement, they were for the most part praying to a God whose son embodied the very will that was responsible for their enslavement. In this regard, a dreadful dichotomy was being created in the slave's mind between a single Caucasian male image that at one and the same time, sought its eternal enslavement and its eternal salvation. How then, was the slave to work through this dichotomy between a cruel master and a loving God? Second, and most devastating, was ironically Christian theology itself. Through the theological category of the incarnation, Christian faith is the only religion to maintain that God became a man in Jesus of Nazareth. While this no doubt calls Christians to a higher responsibility in my judgment relative to its work in the world for a more liberated humanity, this was certainly not the intent of white clergy and theologians during the slavocracy. Taking seriously Jesus proclamation that, "When you see me, you see the Father," the intent was clearly to establish the will of the white male mind with that of God and subsequently Jesus. Thus, Jesus' words to be a "light to the nations" based on one's actions was effectively usurped by an example based on one's race in general and one's whiteness in particular. Thus, in a very deceptive way, the incarnation served as a negative category of theological reflection in American history for blacks insofar as white clergy and theologians were able to effectively "sell" a racist hermeneutic of divine will based on the image of Jesus as a Caucasian male and reinforced it by their control of the social, economic, and political processes in American life. But more important, because the treatment of the incarnation by white clergy and theologians strongly equated whiteness with divinity, it allowed slaveholders to unequivocally assert the divinity of the slave codes as well. In this regard, slaves were put into an almost impossible dilemma. While still "intuiting" freedom from the slavocracy as God's will, slaves were faced with the acceptance of the treatment of the incarnation by white clergy and theologians and wait for freedom until the eschaton (i.e., assume a docile disposition throughout the slavocracy) or strive for freedom in history and possibly offend the only God and Jesus that many of them had known — a white God, a white Jesus. In sum, the intent of white clergy and theologians was to sell divinity as a white male way of life and to further solidify that blackness was either demonic or at the very least ungodly. As such, the ultimate intent was to thoroughly convince slaves that their thoughts of earthly freedom were anti-Christian and that their only chance of salvation lay in a lifetime of service to a white God, a white Jesus, and a white male overseer. That lifetime of service, to be sure, meant that the slave was to see the incarnation as that which required of her, not surprisingly: 1) an unshakable faith in a Jesus that possessed the power to save her because of his whiteness, and 2) a resigned docility to her earthly status. This chapter examines both demands in greater detail.

Whiteness Is Next to Godliness

As we saw in the last chapter, every attempt was made by white clergy and theologians to equate white supremacy with the will of God. This was the case either in shameless intentionality (God as White Supremacist) or ultimate benevolence (God as Sovereign Lord). The selling point, of course, was that the white race's possession of social, economic, and political power meant that God had intentionally ordained that placement by virtue of God's own whiteness. Thus, white clergy and theologians had, at the very least, the structure theologically that equated divine will with white privilege.

Yet because Christian faith maintains that God became a man in Jesus, white clergy and theologians now had the conduit necessary to create a divine face of white supremacy for the world. In particular, given so many biblical references of Jesus as both the son of God and later in Christian theology as the second person of the Trinity, and more important Jesus' proclamation that, "I and the Father (God) are one," white clergy and theologians saw in this structure the opportunity to put a white face on the mind of God. That is to say, white supremacy had an ideological face but it did not yet have an aesthetic face. In order to solidify the supremacy of whiteness and the dehumanization of blackness as divine will in both history and eternity, Jesus of necessity had to be white. With God now in the world in human form, the presentation of Jesus had to reflect not only the thinking of white men but the image of white men as well. This meant that Christian theology was now being done in America such that whiteness was the ontological gauge out of which all authentic Christian activity was measured. In imaging Jesus as white and male, it meant that white males were the standard bearers of divine will. In so doing, it served as the perfect complement to the "stations in life" hermeneutic and racial stratification that had come to characterize European life and, thereafter, life in the colonies and America. Thus, while ultimate salvation through God for all Christians had not changed, the whiteness and maleness of Jesus did imply that God required of all people of color and women, an unquestioned deference to white males as a requirement for salvation. It also implied the permanence of white male rule in human history insofar as God had ordained it not only on moral grounds but seemingly on aesthetic grounds as well.

To be sure, this created a tremendous theological struggle for both women and black people in America. In particular, both were faced with the task of deciphering how righteousness was possible for them given that divinity and righteousness had been measured by whiteness. How were, put another way, blacks and women to adjudge their standing with a white God when they were not white? What did it mean to have Jesus when that Jesus is seemingly identified with the goals and aspirations of the very people who were responsible for their oppression? What did it mean for people of color and women to love God with all one's heart, mind, and soul when that same God became Jesus in the image of the very people that had defined love in such dehumanizing terms? James Cone articulates that struggle as a black theologian in an America of immense white privilege:

> The task of explicating the meaning of Jesus Christ for blacks is not easy in a white society that uses Christianity as an instrument of oppression. White conservatives and liberals alike present images of a white Jesus that are completely

alien to the liberation of the black community. Their Jesus is a mild, easy-going white American who can afford to mouth the luxuries of "love," "mercy," "long-suffering," and other white irrelevancies, because he has a multi-billion dollar military force to protect him from the encroachments of the ghetto and the "communist conspiracy." But black existence is existence in a hostile world without the protection of the law.[1]

Cone articulates the immense interconnection between the ideology of white racial superiority and Christian imagery. But more important, he exposes white racial superiority as an ideological distortion of the gospel insofar as its chief aim is to concretize relationships of human inequality and to equate white "law and order" with the laws of the gospel. By imaging Jesus as white, the connection between white thinking and divine being were ideologically wed. In contrast, by imaging Jesus as white and the demonic as black, divinity and blackness were understood to be cosmic polar opposites whose twains were incapable of ever meeting. We have stated earlier how this cosmic interrelatedness between divinity and whiteness uplifted many whites and provided them with the assurance of superior thoughts of their humanity. So much so that it created a people who were convinced they were of God in a way that no other race was/is. So much so that they became intoxicated on the idea of their superiority and have unleashed an historical fury on the humanity of black people that is incomparable in the annals of human relationships. This newfound sense of divine ontology robs whites, for Akbar, of the self-corrective imperative necessary for future survival.

> The European world is on the verge of self-destruction because it no longer has the capacity to correct itself. It has somehow gotten consumed by its own consumption because it cannot naturally correct and regulate itself. It has made itself hated by nations around the world because it cannot naturally correct its addiction to excess. They are drunk on the idea of being like the image that they portrayed as God.[2]

That drunkenness has produced untold amounts of wealth off the backs of free slave labor of African people and has created the enduring problem of black self-respect and healthy self-image.

As children of the devil, the inescapability of their blackness has caused many blacks to search for a substantive identity by adopting European values for affirmation as human beings. Moreover, because the character of God is revealed through the lens of whiteness, black people have also sought to reconfigure their complexion and features such that their appearance takes on more of a European look. This is as a direct result of blackness being imaged in dirty, inferior and demonic terms in American history. Given that whiteness then, in contrast, was next to godliness, and given that black people, like any other people of faith, wanted to get as close to divinity as possible, many black people sought as much as possible a white identity as the only means to fellowship with God.

Thus, white clergy and theologians major goal was accomplished: equate true character with racial embodiment and make the race most closely resembling the mind and will of God as white. In treating the incarnation in white racial terms, white clergy and theologians used Christian theology to "reveal" to whites their greatness, and to blacks their inferiority. The "fact" that the messiah was white could only mean one thing: God's will for the human situation is made known through Jesus Christ in biblical history and through white people in American history.

Salley and Behm are not wrong in their assessment of the relationship between divine character and the incarnation when they stated that, "The character of God as revealed in the earthly life of the God-Man, Jesus Christ, displays qualities which speak to the modern tensions existing between Blacks and Whites. Jesus revealed the character of God by word and deed."[3] Indeed, Jesus did reveal the character of God by word and deed but that is not the history we have inherited theologically. Rather, word and deed have been successfully co-opted by white clergy and theologians to be wrapped around a thin veneer of white racial privilege by linking the character of God to the character of white males in America. That is to say, Jesus did in fact reveal the character of God by word and deed but the white supremacist mind re-revealed Jesus aesthetically as the quintessential white racist and in so doing made image a fundamental dimension of the revelatory process alongside word and deed.

Over time the image dimension of God's revelation in Jesus became so codified in American Christian theology that the distinction became blurred between objective revelation and subjective construction. That is to say, Jesus whiteness came to take on not only the same significance as his words and deeds but actually came to take on even greater significance in American history. Jesus' image insidiously overtook his words and deeds such that they became recognizable by his image. In sum, white clergy and theologians had so successfully incorporated Jesus' image into American life that the words and deeds of white men became comparable to the words and deeds of Jesus because they now shared the same image! The white Jesus became such a staple part of American Christian life that its authenticity was rarely questioned. As such, particularly for whites, subjective theological construction became objective revelation. For instance, in his fanatical condemnation of slavery, racist minister Josiah Priest insisted . . . that God preferred a white complexion or else he would not have given Jesus light hair and blue eyes.[4] And for French sociologist Roger Bastide, who rightfully argued that, "it was Christianity that first introduced the black/white color code into Western thought," that the spirit of the Enlightenment in daring humans to think for themselves, "had [so] replaced the 'old Christian code of ethics,' that the association [between Jesus and whiteness] was so universal that its, 'symbolism had become secularized.'"[5]

This becomes particularly problematic when prior to the Middle Ages, blackness was imaged positively. One is able to see both Jesus and Mary as black. The latter, referred to as the Black Madonna, had graced the canvases of many artists as a loving, caring and quintessential symbol of Christian motherhood in both the Mediterranean and Africa. However, the Middle Ages became literally the age of whiteness and the European man began his transgenerational assault on black culture, intelligence, and aesthetic qualities. Black culture had been reduced to tribalism, black intelligence had been relegated to the Dark Ages, and black aesthetic qualities became the constant target of white ridicule, scorn, and mockery. With the advent of the Middle Ages, The Dark Ages became The Unenlightened Age and enlightenment became more than a newfound intellectual disposition. The Middle Ages had now become literally the age of enlightened people (racially speaking, that is) i.e., European people.

> In the Middle Ages the Black Madonna, or the Black Virgin, was a sorceress to be feared rather than a Loving Mother to be adored. . . . Of course, graphic portrayals of Christ had to be "as far removed as possible from anything that could suggest darkness or blackness." The result was a Renaissance image of Christ that recorded the transmogrification from Semitic to Aryan, his dark hair and beard evolving into "the color of sunshine" and his dark eyes magically taking on the "color of the sky from which he descended and to which he returned."[6]

Indeed, the age of Enlightenment, both racially and philosophically, found no social phenomenon, including religion, as immune from its ubiquitous presence in European life. The world was now to be seen through a white lens and even Christian theology itself had effectively incorporated anti-black sentiment into two of its most significant categories of theological reflection — the Incarnation and the Parousia!

In particular, it was the Incarnation and the Parousia that white clergy and theologians concentrated most. The reasoning was quite transparent. In focusing on the Incarnation and the Parousia, it kept Christological discourse centered squarely on the being of Jesus and not the ministry of Jesus. The impact of Jesus on the people's lives in whom he had contact was purposely given minimal significance in slaveholding theology. By centering theological discourse on the being of Jesus rather than Jesus' ministry, white clergy and theologians were able to racialize Jesus as white with far greater ease. If they were to focus on Jesus ministry it could lead black people into believing they had the same human worth as whites! Moreover, people of color could conclude that they could establish a personal relationship with Jesus independent of whites and, in so doing, possibly create a much better self-image. That clearly was not the intent of white clergy and theologians. It was certainly not the intent of slaveholders. In dealing, however, with the Christ-event through the Incarnation and the Parousia, and by establishing Jesus' being as white racially, it rendered Jesus' ministry superfluous as a means of growing in relationship with him. It sent the debilitating blow to black self-image that no matter the level of devotion to Jesus' life in word and deed, blackness makes it ontologically impossible to have any substantive fellowship with him. Fellowship was possible only through a total capitulation to those in whose image Jesus shares — white males! Thus, Jesus image in white as a medium of black dehumanization lies in the notion that the righteousness of God exists in word in deed only because they are housed in the body of a white male. Put another way, the authenticity of the God of Christian faith is revealed in Jesus' words and deeds only insofar as that authenticity is preceded by his whiteness. For Kelly Brown Douglas, this aspect of slaveholding theology was the linchpin in the creation of the white Christ:

> In general, the interpretation of Christianity that focuses on God coming from heaven and becoming incarnate in Jesus, while sacrificing Jesus' ministry, unleashes the possibility for the emergence of the White Christ. Undergirded with such an understanding of Christianity, slaveholders were free to develop a notion of Christ that justified the enslavement of Africans. . . . It was the White Christ, as the center of slaveholding Christianity, that allowed White slaveholders to engage in Black slavery with religious impunity.[7]

In fact, not only did the White Christ allow slaveholders to engage in Black slavery with religious impunity but pushed slaveholders to engage in black slavery as a religious mandate. Given slavery's existence and seeming approval by Jesus and Paul in biblical history and given the enormous benefits to be derived, salvifically, by bringing heathen Africans into civilization, there were no negative and every positive reason for black enslavement. The justification for black slavery, i.e., Jesus never publicly condemning slavery, ceased being a justification and became codified in the life of the slaveholding community as a natural way of life that was not to be questioned just as any other confessional commitment. The White Christ is, thus, predicated upon an understanding of Jesus that disregards what he did do — that is, minister to the poor and the oppressed — yet accents what he did not — that is, speak directly against slavery.[8]

To be sure, the creation of the White Christ was intended to make a socially engineered black inferiority appear as if it were a divinely ordained black inferiority. The result was two highly contrasting racial internalizations. Whites internalized the cultural, intellectual, and social privileges that came in being the racial descendents of the White Christ while blacks internalized the cultural, intellectual, and social indignities that came in being the Christological stepchildren of Christian faith. Whites internalized all the adulations and racial privilege that came from being the same race as Jesus while blacks internalized all the condemnations that came with their non-white aesthetic features. Whites internalized grandiose conceptions of their whiteness and basked in the glow of their "divinely revealed superiority," while blacks struggled daily for a healthy self-image internalizing the goodness of a white Jesus while possessing a black body. So if you have internalized the view of the deity and the Creator as being in flesh, having a nationality and physical characteristics different from yourself, then you automatically assume that you are inferior in your own characteristics.[9]

These internalizations strike at the very heart of racial self-perception and ultimately the realm of possibility for the achievement of human aspiration. Further, it also goes a long way in determining what is reasonable for one to aspire to racially. One not only begins to believe that one is capable of accomplishing less because of one's non-whiteness, "but you begin to believe that you have less human potential than one who looks like the image."[10] Indeed, blacks began to internalize the notion that they have less human worth than whites and to act out of their inferiority that had been socially engineered.

By the mid-seventeenth century, blackness, racially and symbolically, had effectively been removed from the realm of aesthetic virtue. In fact, black people's historic significance, beyond cheap slave labor, only lay in its paradoxical import in providing the European man with a distinctly visible contrast with which to assert his superiority. Thus, black people, while shorn of ontological worth, possessed a distorted historical worth (and still do!) as commodities of a free market society in both labor and non-white skin hue. Hence, blacks are to see their dehumanization (read exposure to white civilization) as a salvific possibility not in spite of their blackness but because of their blackness!

More practically, churches, homes, and businesses of black people are and have been "graced" with the presence of a white Jesus on their walls solidifying God's presence and favor on their endeavors. In fact, any suggestion that this white Jesus is historically baseless and is an invention of the mind of white racists would surely make one the object of a vicious diatribe from many black Christians! Unfortunately those suggestions have been few in the history of America not just because of the fear of ostracism but because the white image of Jesus has become so ingrained in the minds of black people that its existence seems natural. Further complicating the issue is the notion that it is sinful to question the faith community in any significant theological adoptions. As a result, for many black Christians, the image of a white Jesus does not register in the religious consciousness as a source of unhealthy self-image. Even though the image is white, it is still an image of Jesus and, as such, must yield salvific power. It is a common understanding among many black Christians that criticizing this image as a product of unhealthy black self-image may compromise one's eternal bliss and/or have one labeled demon-possessed! In establishing the link between graciously accepting one's earthly lot and one's heavenly ascension the intent of white clergy and theologians has been fulfilled — blur the distinction between social construction and divine revelation. Many black Christians of all professions and socio-economic status have internalized the notion that the incarnation is not only one of deed and word but of image as well. Even black people who are conscious of racial realities in "secular" areas are not able to make the connection between these racial realities and a white-imaged Jesus. Akbar comments on the psychologically destructive affect this socialization has had on the lives of black people.

The compelling evidence that the Caucasian image problem is so serious is that of all the things that were identified as leading to this negative self-image, almost no one dealt with the most obvious factor, that the highest power of all was represented in Caucasian flesh. They objected to Santa Claus; they objected to the Dick and Jane characters with no Black playmates; they objected to the fact that there were no lawyers, no doctors, no nurses, no professional people on the television. They objected to all these things, but they did not object to the fact that their children were sitting down at two years old (and younger) being taught: "this man with blond hair, blue eyes, pale skin, is the Savior of the world, who died for your sins, and he is your God."[11]

The comfortability of black people with both its enslaver and savior being of the same image stems directly from the inordinate dependence that blacks were made to have on whites for survival. Given that enslavement was styled by slaveholders as the only road to being saved, this did not seem like a far stretch socially. Yet, psychologically, this dichotomy would adversely affect black people's understanding of its own humanity in acutely self-deprecating ways. Deeply entrenched in the slavocracy and perpetuating itself into contemporary times, Akbar struggles with the fact that this dichotomy between a white enslaver and savior has affected even socially conscious blacks who have been able to identify their excessive dependence on whites socially and economically but have not linked this dependence to salvific dependence on a white Jesus. By virtue of religious expression being off limits as a source of constructive criticism and its transformation being a non-issue given its "revealed" perfection, the road to a sterling black self-image is dead-ended by a rigid religious orthodoxy intentionally intertwined with white privilege. The corollary of this rigid orthodoxy was the creation of a black theological conscious that was either unaware that Christian faith in America is a racial problem or that the religious life does not deal with racial transformation. As Akbar points out, the unconscious affect of white images of divinity on blacks is no respecter of professional or academic attainment.

> Perhaps the most disturbing fact is that this Caucasian image of Divinity has become an unconsciously controlling factor in the psychology of African-Americans. Brilliant scholars of the mind, usually so perceptive, were unable to see this influence. Their fear of accepting it even after it was pointed out, demonstrated the presence of a mental barrier to addressing this issue. Some of the most verbal critics of racism and its consequences have been thoroughly incapable of addressing this issue. The evidence of the potency of the effect is in the inability of even the most militant thinkers to openly challenge what they had come to believe unconsciously was actually the image of God.[12]

As a result of not being able to challenge Jesus whiteness, many blacks capitulated to the demands of church structure while challenging its legitimacy in other realms. In fact, Christian faith in American history required not only total allegiance to white superiority in all its historical applications but demanded of the slave a docile disposition as a prototypical expression of Jesus himself.

Docility is next to Godliness

While it is true that white Christian leadership demanded Jesus be imaged as white and male, it is even truer that a certain disposition was demanded of the slave in light of that image. For while Jesus' image was a crucial spoke in the wheel in white superiority, of equal significance was Jesus behavioral traits as well. Styled as a meek, mild, soft-spoken, and consummate humanitarian, white clergy and theologians were seeking to accomplish two crucial objectives. First, presenting Jesus in a meek and pious way provided the necessary contrast to the hostility of slaveholders in plantation life. In so doing, it presented white males as capable of a compassionate disposition. This was important in establishing the necessary interrelationship between the immediate hardship of the slave at the hands of the white male slaveholder and the ultimate salvation of the slave in the hands of the white male Jesus. In this regard, white maleness is presented to the slave as possessing total control of the slave's life. The intent was, of course, to establish in the mind of the slave a sense of complete dependence on the master. The sinister nature of such an approach is that only one presentation of the white male can be historically verified — that of the rogue slaveholder concerned with the slave's productivity in history. The extent to which the slaveholder was concerned with the slave's destiny beyond human history was the extent to which he was concerned with its theological effectiveness in convincing the slave that her salvation hinged on her productivity in history. Thus, the white-imaged Jesus becomes the selling point to the slave to be industrious as a requirement for salvation with no definitive knowledge that such an outcome is even a possibility let alone a reality. Second, in presenting Jesus as white and meek, it was intended as a clear suggestion by white clergy and theologians that the slave's emulation of what a meek Jesus implied was necessary for salvation as well. Hence, not only then was whiteness next to godliness but docility was next to godliness as well!

A white Jesus not only demanded imperturbable faith but a mild disposition as a necessary virtue for true Christian living. The problem with that approach was and continues to be a moral juggernaut for black people. How then is one to be black and Christian seeking a life of eternal bliss when it required a status quo-seeking disposition in regard to encroachments on black humanity? How is a black person to love Jesus and hate slavery and its dehumanizing affects at the same time? What was one to conclude about a God who required a lifetime of black dehumanization as the price for eternal bliss? These questions became particularly crucial for black people who were not able to emulate Jesus' whiteness racially. The only other arena for getting closer to Christ was to emulate Jesus behaviorally.

Thus began the process of convincing the slaves that Jesus demanded an unconditional love that meant nonresistance to their own dehumanization. While styled in most literature as a purely social phenomenon, unconditional love in the form of loyalty to the white way of life in American history has profound Christian underpinnings. Its creation and deep entrenchment in church life became a fait accompli. Even up to the present time, taking public stands on unpopular issues, particularly in regard to race and gender has one branded by conservative Christians as ungodly, anti-Christian, and an abandonment of faith. To be sure, there was an effective collaboration between church leaders and slaveholders to proverbially wrap Christian faith around black docility. Jesus was portrayed as a savior who cares for all human beings but who was/is also given over to a stations-in-life hermeneutic for Christian living. This meant that slaves should accept their subordinate status and see Jesus as a "friend" no matter the horrific circumstances of their existence. For Clayton Sullivan, this sentimentalization of Jesus in both art and deed as every Christian's heavenly buddy has been a potent force in the perpetuation of relationships of human inequality:

> By sentimentalization, I am referring to the tendency of some Christians to view Jesus in an overly personal or maudlin or sugary manner. This sentimentalizing proclivity is exhibited in automobile stickers that read "Jesus is my buddy" and T-shirts that declare "Jesus is a pal." Perhaps the most recognized sentimental portrait of Jesus is Warner Sallman's *Head of Christ,* and Sallman's associated paintings, such as *Christ at Heart's Door, The Lord is my Shepherd,* and *He Careth For You.* These pictures have been described accurately as Protestant icons, for they adorn Sunday school classrooms and sanctuaries and provide the image of Jesus with which most Protestant Christians identify. Sallman's art portrays Jesus as "everyone's friend."[13]

To be sure, this was no ordinary friendship. Although, its intent was to form lifetime interaction between master and slave, it was by no means designed to establish an interaction of mutual sharing and human equality. Rather, the intent was to legitimate a "divinely" created plan for a superior-subordinate relationship between slaveholders and slaves. But more important, it was to instill in the mind of the slave that Jesus has her ultimate well-being at heart precisely because his benevolence could not be divorced from his whiteness. In short, Jesus is benevolent because he is white!

Under normal circumstances this would seem a social and intellectual impossibility. But Jesus imaged in white racially and benevolent morally made for a most effective sell to the slave regarding the superiority of whiteness. The pervasive existence of hymns in Christian teaching emphasizing Jesus' benevolence affirms this presentation. Hymns such as, "Jesus Is The Sweetest Name I Know," or "Jesus Loves Me," or "Oh, How I Love Jesus," not only makes Jesus a sentimental, mild-mannered, approachable savior but a caring God in human form who loves humankind and asks nothing more in return than that the love

God so graciously gives to humanity be reciprocated. The problem with such an Christological approach is that it is not only an inaccurate depiction of the New Testament Jesus but it is an ideological distortion of the gospel. The Jesus of the gospels is not always mild-mannered and, in fact, develops antagonistic relationships with religious and political authorities in first century Palestine that were committed to Jewish oppression. Sullivan has similar concerns with this approach given that Christianity is the only religious faith that pursues such a depiction of its central figure:

> Others religions do not have this sugary portrayal of the heroes of their faith. I have never heard a Jew sing, "Oh, how I love Abraham" or "Oh, how I love Moses," I have never heard a Jew sing, "Moses is the sweetest name I know." Nor have I heard a Buddhist sing, "Siddhartha Gautama is the sweetest name I know." Nor have I heard a Zoroastrian sing, "Zarathustra is the sweetest name I know." Reflective reading of the New Testament gospels suggests Jesus was not a "sweet" person (nor was Moses or Muhammad). A "sweet" Jesus would not have antagonized the Jewish religious leaders of his day. Nor would a "sweet" Jesus advocating intimate friendship have incurred the wrath of the Roman authorities.[14]

Sullivan reminds us as to how far we have deviated from the Jesus of the Synoptics in American Christian history and how effective Christological treatments of Jesus as white, divine, and ultimately friendly have religiously solidified whiteness as a normative way of being in the world.

The foundation had been laid for an Christological affirmation of the stations-in-life hermeneutic by none other than the consummate friend of black people — a white Jesus! Moreover, the smooth transition in American Christian theology to the worship of Jesus from God placed even more emphasis on the whiteness of Jesus as that which gives him the power to reconcile God and humanity. The reconciler being imaged in white form implicitly suggested white males have an insight into the mind of God that no other race had. It equated the worship of Jesus with the worship of white males. Sullivan not only sees the worship of Jesus as cultural convenience but also as the attempt to subvert Christian faith into cultist doldrums:

> In some places, the Christian faith has been transformed into a self-serving Jesus cult. Jesusolatry, the worship of Jesus, has supplanted the worship of God the creator and sustainer of life. It is possible for Jesus cultists to oversell Jesus by presenting him as a genie who exists to do the will of those who call upon him as his disciples.[15]

While Sullivan highlights a most insightful understanding of Jesus in Christian history, to white clergy and theologians in America, Jesus could never be oversold because of his whiteness! The intent by white clergy and theologians was to co-opt the God as sovereign Lord typology, transfer it to Jesus as reconciler, and then to whiteness racially to confirm Jesus' ontological identification with white values. This becomes particularly evident when examining the frequent singing of such hymns as, "My Jesus, I Love Thee," and, "Jesus Is All The World To Me." Not only then was the slave to understand that Jesus required a reciprocal love from Christians but more important, every opportunity was taken by white clergy and theologians to instill in the mind of the slave that God (read white Jesus) demanded of them a nonresistant obedience to the slavocracy insofar as it is an ordained institution in God's sovereign plan for all humanity. Thus, it was not the slaveholders but God, as white ontologically and intellectually, that had ordained their bondage as a prerequisite for eternal bliss. Therefore, the slave was to understand that rebelling against the institution of slavery was the biggest sin and that eternal damnation was the non-negotiable price for such activity. The slave was to learn to faithfully respect temporal authority and see it as a manifestation of God's mind regardless of natural intuitions to the sinfulness of those institutions regarding black suffering. Thus, for the slave, it was not cleanliness that was next to godliness, and certainly not a revolutionary spirit that was next to godliness, but rather it was docility that was next to godliness.

What we have here is a virulent and oppressive approach to Christian theology crafted by white clergy and theologians that minimized human responsibility in the salvation/liberation process. This not only went a long way in exempting slaveholders from possible damnation if it were to miraculously be the case that slavery was a sinful institution but it also went a long way in minimizing the salvific significance of slave strivings for freedom. Hence, Jesus was to be seen mainly as an object of worship for salvation. Such an Christological understanding continually reaffirmed the presupposition that Jesus' image was more significant than his ministry by emphasizing the superiority of whiteness racially and Jesus as the sole guarantor of salvation because of that whiteness. But more important, it severed any theological understanding between the Christ-event and human responsibility in the transformation of oppressive human relationships. That is to say, such an Christological understanding allotted for being a Christian and a proponent of slavery at the same time with no divine consequences for slavery's creation and perpetuation.

> Little is required of humans [in slaveholding theology] in order to receive salvation. Christians are the passive recipients of God's grace. If persons believe that God has become "human" in Jesus, and thus Jesus is Christ, then they do not have to be anxious about their salvation. To believe God's act in Jesus is to become convinced that through that act salvation has been secured. With salvation guaranteed through belief, White people could be slaveholders *and* Christian without the guilt or fear about the state of their soul.[16]

Douglas is affirming two very important dimensions in slaveholding theology necessary for its effectiveness. The first is that we are not saved by our actions in any way (a significant Reformation theme racially co-opted!) but through

God's grace alone. In this regard, passivity as normative behavior for a Christian is not only a theological suggestion but the very foundation on which one's salvation depends. One need not *work* one's way into heaven; it only suffices that one *believe* one's way into heaven! The second dimension is that one could still be a slaveholder and be righteous in God's sight. For either slavery is ordained of God and whites are simply carrying out their duty to God as an earthly manifestation of their divinely selected salvation (Calvin co-opted) or slavery is sinful but not a death sentence on salvation given that human acts are minimized as a criterion (Luther co-opted).

To that end, if slavery was a sin in any way, whites were convinced that their enslavement of heathen Africans was a devout gesture and, dare I say, "atoned," for their transgressions. The proselytizing of blacks was considered a necessary endeavor to expose a group of non-Christians to the faith. Their dehumanization into docility was a necessary endeavor to get them to accept a way of life that would realize an eternal bliss that their heathenism prevented them from realizing. This is why, for Douglas,

> In order for humans to benefit from God's saving act, they must have knowledge of Jesus as the divine/human encounter. Slavery supposedly provided the opportunity for Africans to attain this salvific knowledge. Apparently, to the minds of many slaveholders, enslavement was the only means Africans had for learning anything about Jesus.[17]

Douglas is raising the fundamental problem of Christian theology in American history. Its racist salvific scheme has been used to convince slaves that their bondage is either ordained of God (and thus theologically affirming white racial superiority) or that human actions are not a part of the salvation process (save for black docility in the slavocracy!).

Theologian James Cone has been insistent throughout his career that the failure to make the biblical witness of Jesus' concern for the oppressed central to the black-white relationship in American history has made the white theological enterprise exactly what Christian faith was never intended to be — an unashamed supporter of the status quo!

> Theologians and churchmen (clergy) have been of little help in this matter because much of their intellectualizing has gone into analyzing the idea of God's righteousness in a fashion far removed from the daily experiences of men (humans). They fail to give proper emphasis to another equally if not more important concern, namely, the biblical idea of God's righteousness as the divine decision to vindicate the poor, the needy, and the helpless in society. It seems that much of this abstract disputation and speculation — the favorite pastime for many theological societies – serves as a substitute for relevant involvement in a world where men (humans) die for a lack of political justice.[18]

Indeed, white theologians and clergy have been of little help because their intent
was never to make the gospel relevant to the liberation of black people. Rather,
the intent was the creation of a highly unequal relationship of white privilege
and black dehumanization. Christian theology in American history's point of
departure was/is whites being the sole beneficiaries of earthly freedom and
blacks serving as quintessential pawns, serving whites without envy and anx-
iously awaiting their salvation in the hereafter. Thus, the biblical witness that
Cone speaks of that demands the uprooting of human injustice has been distorted by white clergy and theologians to be understood as God's favor on black
dehumanization. But more sinister, blacks were to accept that dehumanization as
a theological condition for salvation.

Paulo Freire expands our analysis and argues in his classic, *Pedagogy of the
Oppressed*, that this conditioned docility as God's will is endemic to most
oppressor-oppressed relationships.

> Fatalism in the guise of docility is the fruit of an historical and sociological
> situation, not an essential characteristic of a people's behavior. It almost always
> is related to the power of destiny or fate or fortune — inevitable forces — or to
> a distorted view of God. Under the sway of magic and myth, the oppressed . . .
> see their suffering, the fruit of exploitation, as the will of God – as if God were
> the creator of this "organized disorder."[19]

It becomes a deeply entrenched fatalism insofar as over time and after several
generations of indoctrination we have seen many black people come to internalize much of the theology given to them by white Christian leaders. Not only has
it created in black people tremendous problems with self-image and range of
achievement but has also resigned many blacks to the conclusion that full freedom must wait until the eschaton and must be realized by God and God alone.
The unfortunate result of such an understanding of God by blacks is that the
interests of white supremacy are unwittingly accommodated and black people
unknowingly become participants in its own oppression. The predicted result
has been an intra-racial nihilism.

> Submerged in reality, the oppressed cannot perceive clearly the "order" which
> serves the interests of the oppressors whose image they have internalized. Chaf-
> ing under the restrictions of this order, they often manifest a type of horizontal
> violence, striking out at their own comrades for the pettiest reasons.[20]

Freire has touched on the crux of the black struggle for self-affirmation in
America. A Christian theological approach that has placed primary emphasis on
Jesus in white image has not only has served effectively as a means of social
control of black people but has also served the dual purpose of nihilism making
difficult efforts to free themselves and construct a better self-image.

Finally, as stated in the previous chapter, as a white-imaged Jesus and black obedience to a white-ruled nation became codified as orthodoxy in the American Christian tradition, efforts to secure a better self-image and freedom by black people were deemed ungodly rather than godly. The further consequence is that this understanding of black humanity has also made its way into black Christian thinking no matter how sincere black Christian religious leadership has been historically in its attempt to forward a healthy black self-image. That attempt has been sought under the canopy of a white-imaged Jesus which in itself truncates efforts for total freedom both socially and psychologically from whiteness. However sincere black Christian leadership has been in America, the uncritical acceptance of a rigid Christian orthodoxy that places more emphasis on individual morality than socio-political transformation represents a disingenuous approach to religious faith in a context of racial and gender domination. Thus, the call to the ministry of Jesus Christ has been the call for many black ministers in America to the sacred canopy of white divinity. That has historically meant either a capitulation to the theology of white supremacy and black dehumanization until the eschaton, i.e., Let the Lord handle it, or a surrender of the black liberation struggle to the civil rights and black power communities, i.e., I was called only to save souls and not deal with that black stuff! This is because the structure of black ministers thinking is prescribed even before entering the ministry through the inheritance of several generations of uncritically accepted white Christianity. Hence, religious and intellectual institutions in America have been imprinted with the stamp of white privilege by creating "substantive" theoretical systems that are either irrelevant to or condones black suffering.

> It is almost as if a man with African features cannot be an authority unless he has been authenticated and credentialed by the highest European and Caucasian authorities. . . . The only exception to this rule is the situation of the fundamentalist minister whose claim to authority is that he "has been called." With such legitimization, he is often given unbridled authority, even when he may not represent the self interest of the people he is leading. [But] because he has been "called" by a figure from the Caucasian imagery of Divinity, his word becomes law. The point is the same, whether one is authorized by Harvard or a "call," the source of legitimization is identical.[21]

Akbar reminds us of the depth of black internalization of white images of divinity and the impact it has had on the religious expression of black people as it relates to the pursuit of freedom in America. Thus, Christian pedagogy has been a mixed blessing at best for black people in America — a pedagogy that is hammered into the religious conscience of black people institutionally on a weekly basis and that has unwittingly contributed to black oppression. That institution, the church, arguably then, becomes the most significant institution in American life.

Notes

1. James Cone, *A Black Theology of Liberation*. New York: Orbis Books, 1990, 111. First published in 1970.
2. Na'im Akbar, *Chains and Images of Psychological Slavery*. Jersey City, New Jersey: New Mind Productions, 1984, 44-45.
3. Columbus Salley, and Ronald Behm, *What Color Is Your God: Black Consciousness and the Christian Faith*. New York: Citadel Press, 1988, 94.
4. Forrest G. Wood, *The Arrogance of Faith: Christianity and Race in America from the Colonial Era to the Twentieth Century*. Boston: Northeastern University Press, 51.
5. Ibid.
6. Ibid.
7. Kelly Brown Douglas, *The Black Christ*. New York: Orbis Books, 1994, 14.
8. Ibid., 15.
9. Akbar, *Chains and Images*, 47.
10. Ibid.
11. Ibid., 49.
12. Ibid., 50.
13. Clayton Sullivan, *Rescuing Jesus from the Christians*. Harrisburg, Pennsylvania: Trinity Press International, 2002, 97.
14. Ibid., 99.
15. Ibid., 100.
16. Douglas, *The Black Christ*, 13.
17. Ibid., 13-14.
18. James H. Cone, *Black Theology and Black Power*. New York: The Seabury Press, 1969, 43.
19. New York: The Continuum Publishing Company, 1992 (First published in 1970), 48.
20. Ibid.
21. Akbar, *Chains and Images*, 55-56.

7

The Christian Institutionalization of Black Dehumanization

> If it is to the established church we look to for rescue, we will not be especially cheered by its accomplishments to date, for the American church has consistently failed to take to heart the ancient indictment that racism is a corruption and a denial of those immutable values which are critical to human dignity. More than that, it has been reluctant to resist with the vigor of conviction the contemporary onslaught of narcissistic hedonism, in a variety of guises, which further jeopardizes that dignity by idolizing the individual self as the center of all values, and demanding that all other values be bent into conformance.
> C. Eric Lincoln, *Race, Religion, and the Continuing American Dilemma*

The white-imaged Jesus that solidified the superiority of whiteness in American society received its institutional legitimacy in the church. It became the face, literally, of Christianity in America governing this country's understanding in regard to race and gender. Given the church's unquestionable legitimacy in being the source of revelation from God to humanity, its significance in the life of any Christian nation can never be underestimated, the least of these being America and its national affirmation of the indispensability of a life of faith. Thus, "it cannot be too strongly emphasized that Christianity as an institution (regardless of theological refinements and denominational distinctions) is the major force in undergirding and approving the values of the socio-political and economic institutions of America."[1] More to the point, the institutionalization of black dehumanization owes itself to the teachings of the church becoming codified as sacred and mediated from parents to children who become steeped not only in the

pedagogy itself but in its sacred designation and thus its unquestioned acceptance. Such a pedagogical structure becomes particularly attractive when one
seeks a Christian interpretation of life that is characterized by racial and gender
stratification and by huge variances in wealth along those racial and gender
lines.

Hence, the image of Jesus as white and male has served white males well in
American history. It has served as the linchpin of an unquestioned American
way of life that has legitimated white male superiority as the point of departure
for substantive Christian theology and subsequently black dehumanization as a
necessary process in the perpetuation of a divinely decreed relationship between
the races. Yet, such pedagogy could never find divine legitimacy apart from its
being institutionalized. That is to say, an approach to human relationships that
favors one group of humans over another, even as a so-called divine decree,
could not have been cemented into the faculties of either the superior or inferior
designated group by any exclusively social institution. The church's claim, however, that it is not a purely social institution but distinguishes itself as the *only*
institution in the world in which one can find God's intention for all humanity
can make what might be rejected by humans in a purely social institution become wholly acceptable in the name of Christian obedience. In this regard, an
institution touted as holding the keys to the kingdom for slaveholder and slave
alike and white male clergy being the primary advocates in light of a white-
imaged Jesus made the church as it developed in American history an irrefutably
potent force in theologically synthesizing white supremacy with divine will.

In this light, Berger's notion of, "world historical maintenance," is particularly useful for our discussion. White clergy were "constructing a world" in
which both whites and blacks were to be heirs to a superior-subordinate relationship wherein Jesus' whiteness and maleness would serve as the cornerstone of a
church pedagogy that inferred a reverential deference in all matters divine to
white males. But more important, such pedagogy was ultimately intended to
infer a reverential deference for white males in all America's social institutions
as well — including slavery! Given the aesthetic, and therefore divine, connection between Jesus and white males, it just made theological sense for white
males to be the arbiters of due process and the leaders of all America's religious
and social institutions. Thus, the white church from America's origins, set out to
eternalize a racial relationship of white privilege and black dehumanization as
divine wisdom and in so doing has made Christian faith in American history at
best a mixed blessing and at worse a theological fraud. Salley and Behm weigh
in:

> Just as the white church has supported and continues to support oppressive
> forces by both its action and inaction, we believe that the White church, recog-
> nizing its true identity as God's people who should function as a force for good,
> can generate and advance those values which liberate and promote justice for
> all Americans. The inability of the White Christian church to demonstrate val-

ues which oppose racist forces has made the church ineffective in aiding Black people (and others) in their quest for survival.[2]

Not only has the white church been ineffective in aiding Black people in their quest for survival/liberation but the church has been intentionally ineffective in this process and has, in contrast, been the single most effective weapon in perpetuating the dehumanization of black people in the history of America. Let us take a closer look.

An Ecclesiology of Black Dehumanization: Initial Considerations

It does seem a rather harsh indictment, given the altruistic way in which we as confessing Christians have been taught to view the church, to depart from the assertion that it has been the most effective weapon in legitimating black oppression but it is a much deserving one. In fact, it may seem unashamedly blasphemous to those of extreme Christian devotion. Yet, even a cursory look at the white church in American history reveals an institution unashamedly committed to black dehumanization with no significant "racial soul-searching" in an examination of that commitment. Beyond the profound economic benefits that whites procured through an enslaved and dehumanized black humanity, what was at stake here was a morality of human decency in the effort to establish black oppression as consistent with the gospel of Jesus Christ. That moral framework had to revolve around what constitutes proper treatment to a people that were not human on the level of that of white humans. Ideologically, what was at stake was not just what white people wanted economically for themselves, *but what God wanted for both races in history and eternity!* In light of this, the church throughout Christian and American history has always had to navigate its way through the thicket of distinguishing between God's will and humanity's will.

Yet, history is not kind in this sense given that Christian leaders have done a poor job of separating the two. Christian leaders have throughout the history of the faith, been given over to the demands of so-called secular leaders and have tended to do Christian theology from the standpoint of the wealthy and not the poor. This owes itself in large part to the fact that many of them inherited a social existence of wealth with either little regard given to the poor or had no misgivings about an approach to religious life that rendered God's blessing on their wealth and more important the coercive ways in which they attained that wealth. Thus, one could argue that Christian history has been predominantly concerned with making sure that the wealthy are assuaged of their guilty conscience in the creation of the poor for their own wealth attainment and the exclusionary social practices like segregation in America that has served as a necessary concomitant. Hence, if one wants to witness a quintessential hatchet job being done on poor people, one can find it, ironically, in the church!

The problem becomes quite apparent theologically. Even though Jesus has been imaged in American history as white and male for the purpose of divinely legitimating white wealth attainment at the expense of black people, no one can deny the synoptic portrayal of Jesus as someone who is eternally concerned about the poor. I use eternally insofar as Jesus is portrayed by the Synoptic writers as not only someone who is concerned about economic systems that create poverty but also as someone who makes the poor the beneficiaries of the kingdom in eternity. This discrepancy between Jesus favor on the poor and white Christian leader's portrayal of Jesus as someone who condones racial oppression has been the theological conundrum that white clergy and theologians have not been able to convincingly resolve. But to the extent that they have, countless numbers of lives have been destroyed and many poor people have remained poor from cradle to grave in the name of God and Jesus. And unfortunately it has been the church that has perpetuated the, "You are poor because you want to be," syndrome throughout most of American history while conveniently ignoring the economic structures that create poverty!

In this regard, the Church in American history has constructed a Christian tradition that many may find surprising. It has given itself over to the legitimacy of a superior-subordinate relationship racially and in so doing, has taught its parishioners that such a relationship is the very manifestation of divine will. In particular, it has unashamedly taught both white and black Christians that the superior-subordinate relationship between whites and blacks is not a manifestation of white greed but a manifestation of divine revelation. Thus, what may seem to be a complete disregard for the humanity of black people has been articulated as a divinely appointed assignment by God to white males to do what is necessary to maintain the status quo. Thus, with this theological understanding, one is not left to tarry with the proverbial notion of which came first, the chicken or the egg (i.e., white supremacy or divine will). Because white supremacy has been presented as divine will, white clergy in particular can present themselves as servants of God rather than racists. In this regard, white supremacy precedes divine will although it has been presented to both blacks and whites in the church as the converse.

Yet in the final analysis, despite its effectiveness in convincing both whites and many blacks of the legitimacy of white privilege, its Christian theological legitimacy searches frantically for a suitable foundation in regard to Jesus emphasis on the poor and his overarching theme that he is, "no respecter of persons." W. E. B. DuBois is poignant in his criticism of the white church:

> When the church meets the Negro problem, it writes itself down as a deliberate hypocrite and systematic liar. It does not say "Come unto me all ye that labor": it does not say "love its neighbor as itself": it does not welcome "Jew and Gentile, barbarian, Scythian, bond and free"; and yet it openly and blatantly pro-

fesses all this . . . the church has opposed every great modern social reform; it opposed the spread of democracy, universal education, trade unionism, the abolition of poverty, the emancipation of women . . . and the emancipation of the Negro slave.[3]

The white church has opposed every great modern social reform because it had no other choice. Once it had committed itself to a stratified understanding of human relationships, it was at the same time committing itself to the perpetuation of relationships of social, economic and political hegemony. In short, the white church was committing itself to the perpetuation of a white supremacist status quo. In practicality, it was affirming the dehumanization of black people as sacred duty.

The white church's biggest challenge, however, lay in the construction of an accompanying Christian theology that would normalize that status quo as a divine mandate. In order to accomplish this, Christian theology would need a teaching center with which to solidify the legitimacy of black dehumanization — that center would be the church. So successful would the teaching of Christian racism become over time, it became clear that most white Christians in the slavocracy saw no remote incompatibility between being Christians and slaveholders at the same time. Institutionally, white churches not only taught its parishioners of the eternal compatibility between slavery and divine will but also frequently reminded slaveholders that no amount of physical and/or mental abuse was excessive in maintaining control of the slaves and further that God's favor was in sync with that abuse. Lester Scherer makes clear the white church's systemic collusion with slaveholders in the process of black dehumanization:

> Not only on occasions of solemn oratory but in daily routine churches contributed to slave control. Christians along with others rode slave patrols, served as constables, administered the whippings, and generally maintained the private tyranny by which whites asserted their mastery.[4]

In this regard, the church served as the primary moral affirmer of white values relative to black dehumanization providing white males in particular with the religious validation necessary to ground their behavior, "in the wisdom of the creator." One then can conclude that this was the church's indirect participation, at the very least, in the historical maintenance of white supremacy.

However, the church was also directly involved in the process of black dehumanization. White clergy made catechisms that promoted slave docility and made complete obedience to slaveholders a central dimension of Christian pedagogy. Moreover, the theme of strict obedience to the slaveholder as strict obedience to God was frequently mentioned in their sermons even before slaves were allowed to attend worship services. And as Scherer reminds us, this was done not so much to dupe the slaves (at least at this point) as it was to remind whites of their duty to protect the slavocracy as true servants of God.

In some provinces, such as Maryland and Virginia, clergymen were required to read slave codes from the pulpit several times a year. This was not to cow the blacks, since usually few of them were in attendance, but to remind God's people of their obligations related to keeping peace and order in society.[5]

To be sure, that peace and order, it was thought by slaveholders, could not be destroyed more effectively by anyone better than the slaves. Thus, Christian teaching in the way of white privilege also lay in the fact that blacks were not capable of government or civilization and that to allow them to topple the slavocracy and to attain to such lofty heights would not only lead to anarchy but prevent the kingdom on earth from realizing itself. Thus, an aggressive campaign to instruct blacks in the "true" teachings of Christ trumped any other process in the life of the church — even conversion itself!

An Ecclesiology of Black Dehumanization: Stage 1 — Pedagogy Outside The Church

As the primary target of those slaveholders thought could topple the slavocracy, the slaves were always looked upon with extreme suspicion. As such, the slave's initial exposure to the church was not to its walls but rather to its pedagogy. Concerned that the presence in the church might imbue the slave with a higher self-image and make her "uppity," white clergy in collaboration with slaveholders thought it more prudent for purposes of social control to render the slave a theological apprenticeship prior to extending "full" fellowship to her. According to Winthrop Jordan, this became a staple part of the approach to the slaves by white Protestant churches:

> With all the Protestant sects, converting heathens required instructing them first. Especially during the early years of slavery's rapid growth in the eighteenth century, there were mountainous practical difficulties. An Anglican minister replied in 1724 to an official query concerning the "infidels" in his parish saying, "A great many Black bond men and women infidels that understand not our Language nor me theirs: not any free. The church is open to them; the word preached, and the Sacraments administered with circumspection."[6]

The church was indeed not only open to slaves but ultimately demanding of their presence insofar as its divine dimensions were the "hook" needed to create a racist theocracy.

The church was open to the slaves; the word was preach and the sacraments were administered but with circumspection. That is because Protestant Christian pedagogy as it developed in the slavocracy was never designed to make slaves equals to whites in society but to compel blacks to forfeit societal freedom in exchange for *Christian equality*. A Christian equality that made blacks and whites equal in eternity but not history. This was insisted upon by most Protestant white clergy. What better way to socially control slaves and coax them into accepting their earthly dehumanization than by teaching them that human equality is not an historical possibility but only an eternal possibility. All other teachings to slaves emerged out of this theological paradigm.

As slaves began to internalize this pedagogy, it did divert their energies from earth to heaven and from slaveholders to Jesus Christ. The freedom denied slaves physically in society was granted in a "spiritual" way in Jesus Christ. Protestantism's insistence on the equality of humans in eternity (but conveniently not in history) demonstrated the slave's desire for freedom but in the final analysis only called for a subjective freedom rather than an objective freedom. (The implications of such a paradigm are still prevalent in American churches today!) It was at this point that white clergy felt more comfortable turning over the reins of the preaching of the gospel to the slaves to black preachers — many of whom were illiterate and had no formal training. However, this became a positive development for white clergy who found untrained black ministers more "cooperative" and "easier to manipulate" than those who were literate. When this church increase in slaves was coupled with the Great Awakening of the 1740's and the emphasis placed on emotional fervor with the advent of the religious revival, it not only created the atmosphere for the establishment of Luther's notion of the priesthood of all believers on American soil but also made the unchanneled emotionalism that accompanied many of these observances an ideological ruse for diverting the slaves thoughts from earthly oppression. Thus, religious escapism became glorified as an authentic expression of Christian devotion.

> Almost by definition a religious revival was inclusive; itinerant preachers aimed at gathering every lost sheep, black as well as white. The revivals tended to break down the traditional structure of clerical control and emphasize once again the priesthood of all believers. Religious enthusiasm elbowed aside religious sophistication as the criterion of true piety.[7]

Yet whether it was religious enthusiasm or religious sophistication, both were equally damaging to the self-affirmation of black people. The former simply daubed (and continues to daub) the wounds of a people frantically searching for some semblance of exuberance and hope in a horrific existential situation. The latter was so consumed with the creation of an earthly kingdom rooted in racial hegemony that it set itself up as an historical adversary of true human equality. Rather, an ideological equality masqueraded as true equality. In so doing, Protestant principles were co-opted by white clergy and made a most worthy contribution to the perpetuation of black dehumanization in America. The equalitarian principles in Protestant Christianity were never more apparent; if it was difficult for Negroes to become men (women) of affairs in this world, it became increasingly easy, after the watershed of the Great Awakening, for them to become men (women) of God.[8]

Before the indoctrination of divine equality came a nicely packaged Christian pedagogy to slaves prior to their entering the church in large numbers. To be sure, this pedagogy had profound biblical sources and in so doing went a long way in sacralizing white superiority. Biblical foundations for black dehumanization begin with Pauline Literature. While there was considerable debate about Paul's ever condoning slavery and whether the Bible itself should be used as a justification for black dehumanization, there were certain passages used frequently with very little debate among white clergy. For instance, Titus 2:9-10 implores the slaveholding community to teach, "slaves to be subject to their masters in everything, to try to please them, not to talk back to them, and not to steal from them, but to show that they can be fully trusted, so that in every way they will make the teaching about God our Savior attractive." This passage not only emboldened white church leaders in promoting the virtues of slavery but to assume whatever posture pragmatically to produce a docile spirit in black slaves. Put another way, white ministers and theologians assured slaveholders that the process by which they created the "proper" spirit in slaves was trumped by any moral argument one could make as to slavery's violation of true human equality. But more important, slaveholders were assured that their role in creating an America of white privilege was indispensable in creating a racially stratified church!

As for the biblical pedagogy to the slaves, the book of Ephesians, in general, and chapter six in particular, was a staple part of white clergy and theologians teaching to establish the legitimacy of slavery to black people. For instance, verses 5-8 of chapter six read, "Slaves, obey your earthly master with respect and fear, and with sincerity of heart, *just as you would obey Christ.* Obey them not only to win their favor when their eye is on you, but like slaves of Christ, *doing the will of God from your heart.* Serve wholeheartedly, as if you were serving the Lord, not men (humans), because you know that the Lord will reward everyone for whatever good he (she) does, whether he (she) is slave or free."

The two italicized phrases of the passage go to the root of our discussion. First, it was imperative for white clergy to sell the slavocracy to slaves by equating obedience to the slaveholders with obedience to Christ. In so doing, it not only presented slaves with an understanding of Christian faith and the church that diverted their energies away from earthly freedom but also demanded of them a freedom-relinquishing disposition as an inescapable duty of a faithful Christian servant. Hence, it was the white church that was the most effective institutional medium in divinizing this teaching and thus making it more theologically palatable to the religious conscience of the slave. In short, the life of faith itself was being presented in such a way that the slave grows closer to Jesus through the assumption of a pious (read anti-revolutionary) approach to life.

Not only did this reinforce the link between the authority of Jesus and the authority of slaveholders but it also represented the initial exposure to a pedagogy that would create a dilemma in the slave regarding the inclination to earthly freedom on the one hand but Christian teaching to forsake that earthly freedom for Christ on the other hand.

The second italicized phrase, *doing the will of God from your heart*, is rooted in the notion that the person of sincere faith always wants to think that her approach to faith is consistent with the will of God. In most instances, our understanding of that will is mediated to us through the church. In that regard, the white church would not miss out on the opportunity to theologically reinforce a white supremacist way of life with the blessings of divinity. Hence, doing the will of God in a slavocracy meant that if one were white, one was to seek to maintain the institution at whatever cost and if one were black, one was to accept the terms of slave life unconditionally and abandon any notions of earthly freedom. Doing the will of God for slaves, in other words, meant doing the will of white slaveholders. No other alternatives existed.

Moreover, Peter's charge to slaves to totally submit themselves to their masters, particularly harsh ones, proved a valuable biblical source for the white church in its quest to legitimate slavery. In particular, I Peter 2:18-20 encouraged slaves to, "submit yourselves to your masters with all respect, not only to those who are good and considerate, but also to those who are harsh. For it is commendable if a man (slave) bears up under the pain of unjust suffering because he (she) is conscious of God. But how is it to your credit if you receive a beating for doing wrong and endure it? But if you suffer for doing good and you endure it, this is commendable before God."[9] Thus, black people were led to an understanding of faith that divinized their enslavement, i.e., concretized their submission to the slavocracy as non-negotiable demand of God. Conveniently, the master's disposition, whether considerate or harsh (or the perils of slavery itself!), was never an issue of substantive theological scrutiny.

Yet, given some of the slaves caution about southern clergy and slaveholder's instruction, northern white clergy and other slaves were brought in to reaffirm the "appropriateness" of Christian racism to the slaves. In [1835] [when] [Episcopal] Bishop [Nathaniel] Bowen sent out his letter regarding the suitability of black enslavement, nine other prominent ministers in the New England and New Hampshire conferences, growing anxious over the controversy created by some of their antislavery colleagues, cited I Timothy 6:1 – "Let as many servant as are under the yoke count their own masters as worthy of all honour" – "as an impregnable demonstration that slaveholding is not in all cases and invariably, sinful."[10] While never being able to provide a substantive rebuttal as to why it was not sinful, this God-sponsored black dehumanization would have a huge impact on the slaves who considered northern whites to be far more racially progressive than southern whites, particularly white northern clergy.

As for the use of other slaves that had thoroughly internalized Christian racism, two illustrations aptly suffice. First, to avoid joining a new master in Georgia, a slave named William Grimes actually believed that God wanted him to remain a slave when, after praying to break his own leg with an axe so he would be left behind, the leg wouldn't break and, "then [I] prayed to God that if it was his (God's) will that I should go, I might willingly."[11] Second, even famed abolitionist Frederick Douglass lamented that, "I have met many religious colored people at the South who are under the delusion that God requires them to submit to slavery and to wear chains with meekness and humility."[12] On this second point made by Douglass are poignant implications for the black church, particularly after Reconstruction and into the twentieth century which I will have more to say in the next chapter. But it suffices to say briefly here that the internalization of white precepts for being Christian by many black ministers has been the reason why the black church has not been, institutionally, at the forefront or even a dependable participant in the black freedom struggle in America. Only a few black pastors were empathetic and opened the doors of their sanctuaries for mass mobilization during the slavocracy and up to the civil rights movement. Most were not able to connect their understanding of faith with either a challenge to the white establishment in America or with so-called human solutions to global oppression. Rather, it sufficed that one should, "Let the Lord handle it." This was by no means an unashamed attempt to subvert the quest for black self-affirmation by many black ministers but rather a sincere understanding of faith inherited from the white church. But also it was a tacit admission, as Douglass points out above, that many black Christians labor under the delusion that they should accept their lot in life *until God changes it!* Otherwise, one could easily be found guilty of subverting God's plan for the black-white relationship and thus make oneself a candidate for divine retribution. In this regard, white Christian pedagogy had clearly done its job! The fear of God, one of the staple principles of Christian devotion, was ideologically co-opted to mean a fear of God as a fear of white males. The slave was to understand a merciless beating or being separated from one's family for being an "uppity nigger," as a sign of an angry God and not a hostile slaveholder. True Christian devotion to Jesus, for the slave, became inseparable from her own dehumanization. This was black people's initial exposure to Christian faith in America.

An Ecclesiology of Black Dehumanization: Stage 2 — Pedagogy Inside The Church

As a harbinger to segregation, blacks' initial presence in the church was one of separated demoralization. Blacks were seated in a separate area of the church, usually in the balcony. For that reason, most balconies in white churches were deemed *buzzard's roosts* with the clear intention to equate black people with a buzzard in both color and value. While white Christians clearly did not want blacks in their churches, they had become convinced of the virtues of social control through Christian faith. Further, many whites were convinced that no one in the community was better prepared to instruct slaves in the gospel than white clergy. Thus, the dilemma ensued not as to whether the slaves ought to be religiously instructed but whether they should be instructed with whites or separately. The Presbyterian Synod of South Carolina and Georgia in 1834 took the latter route:

> The gospel, as things are now, can never be preached to the two classes (whites and blacks) successfully in conjunction. The galleries or back seats on the lower floor of white churches are generally appropriated to the Negroes, when it can be done without inconvenience to the whites. When it cannot be done conveniently, the Negroes must catch the gospel as it escapes through the doors and windows. If the master is pious, the house servants alone attend family worship, and frequently few of them, while the field hands have no attention at all. So far as masters are engaged in the work [of religious instruction of slaves], an almost unbroken silence reigns on this vast field.[13]

Although extremely reluctant to instruct slaves beyond the church and to not have them worship with whites, most whites were convinced that this process was of benefit to both them and the slaves. Thoroughly given over to the notion of people of African descent's heathenism and, therefore, inferiority, whites were given over to the understanding that black people's slave and Christian statuses were far better for them than the African heathenism that characterized their pre-colonial existence. Pro-slavery advocate and white minister the Rev. C. C. Jones reflects on the late eighteenth-early nineteenth century white Christian impact on the African:

> It is not too much to say that the religious and physical condition of the Negroes were both improved during this period. Their increase was natural and regular, ranging every ten years between thirty-four and thirty-six percent. As the old stock from Africa died out of the country, the grosser customs, ignorance, and paganism of Africa died out with them. Their descendents, the country-born, were better looking, more intelligent, more civilized, *more susceptible of religious impressions.*[14]

This passage is quite revealing in that it brings to bear the slaveholding community's historical intent for African people. Not only was there an incessant effort to Christianize slaves as a means of social control but there was also an unashamed effort to sever any ties culturally the African had to her indigenous habitat. This was seen as crucial to white clergy and slaveholders in being able to induce in the slave a pious disposition. Godly slaves should also pray for their fellows and set good examples by "engaging in a regular, sober, modest, pious behavior.[15]

By this time, namely the mid-eighteenth century, slaves had become as indoctrinated in the rudiments of Christian racism as slaveholders and white clergy thought possible and the demand was placed on slaveholders by white clergy to bring their slaves to church as much as possible to institutionally confirm God's favor on a racial relationship of white superiority and black piety. Particularly, they should come to church as often as possible (assuming they have permission) and make good use of their leisure time.[16]

But it became more than clear at this point that the best use of the slave's time would be frequently attending the white church. Christian racism had moved into its second phase moving from the preliminary instruction to slaves outside the church to the pious indoctrination to slaves in the church. In this phase, the intent was to convince the slave once and for all that she should relinquish a life of freedom in this world and concentrate her energies on freedom in the hereafter. Put another way, every attempt was made to convince the slave that obedient toil on the plantation was a prerequisite to inheriting eternal life and that a life of freedom on earth was not a part of God's plan for black people. This was accomplished by teaching the slaves ironically, that they were equal to whites and all other races of humans at the end of the world but not in human history. Every religious ritual was employed by the white church with the common purpose of practically affirming these theological axioms. None moreso than baptism.

Francis LeJau's construction of a baptismal vow intended exclusively for slaves leaves little doubt as to white clergy's intent: You declare in the presence of God and before this congregation that you do not ask for the holy baptism out of any design to free yourself from the Duty and Obedience you owe to your Master while you live, but merely for the good of Your soul and to partake of the Graces and Blessings promised to the Members of the Church of Jesus Christ.[17] This was crucial for white clergy in the sense that baptism did convey a freeing from the forces of evil and oppression. Hence, it was the job of white clergy to convince the slave that whites were not their oppressors and that the freedom of which baptism implies is not one of a socio-political nature but exclusively one of a spiritual nature. This meant that spirituality itself had to be presented to the slave not as a holistic phenomenon concerned with the entire being of the person of faith but as the epitome of Christian piety, meekness and long-suffering. Spirituality, put more precisely, had been compromised by the white church such that it was divorced from the social plight of oppressed communities and to establish that is was ungodly to work for earthly freedom. Hence, spirituality had been co-opted and given to the slaves to control their "subversive" behavior. An ex-slave gives her impression of ecclesial life for the slaves and the hypocrisy laden therein from slaveholders who were also Christians:

White preacher he preach to de white fo'ks an'when git thu' wid dem he preach
some to de "Niggers." Tell'em to mind deir Marster and b'have deyself an'
dey'll go to Hebben when dey die. Dey come 'round an' tell us to pray, git
'ligion, dat wuz on Sun'dy, but dey'ed beat the life out'cha de next day ef ya
didn't walk de chalk line. Our white fo'ks made us go to church an' Sun'dy
School too. Dey made us read de Catechism. G'ess de re-son fo'dat wuz, dey
tho it made us min' dem bedder.[18]

To be sure, the exclusive reason for Christianizing the slave was to equate divine
will with the slave, "min'in dem [slaveholders] bedder." Walking the chalk line
was a common expression used by slaves to denote slaveholder's desire for them
to be pious and content with their slave lot. It was slaveholders interpretation of
the Bible's, "walking the straight and narrow path," when it comes to Christian
practice. This most assuredly meant a lifetime of laborious and productive industry and never participating in any insurrectionist activity! Thus, even the
biblical dictum of, "walking the straight and narrow path," had been co-opted by
white clergy and neatly fit into a white supremacist biblical hermeneutics. A
hermeneutics that deified whiteness dehumanized blackness and emanated from
the mind of God. This meant for white clergy that black dehumanization was
appropriate, sacred, and necessary for the salvation of both races.

But by far, one of the principal teachings of most white clergy to slaves was
that this "arrangement" between the races is far more beneficial for blacks. It
was impressed upon the slaves at every opportunity that they did not have the
responsibilities as slaveholders to be concerned with everyone's and the institution's well-being. That is to say, slaves had only to be responsible for being productive laborers but not with the business dimension of plantation life as slaveholders were. This represents yet another manifestation of the stations in life
hermeneutic we have established as one of the major selling points to the slaves
regarding the legitimacy of their bondage. But more important, this was intended to infer for white clergy that the attempt to subvert the slavocracy would
only yield for the slave divine chastisement.

The final cautions which follow end with a warning not to "fret or murmur,
grumble or repine, at your condition," since it will only yield present misery
and future punishment. God, after all, knows which condition is best for each
person. He (God) knows that riches and power would cause unhappiness for
some people, and in such cases he (God) mercifully withholds those burdens.
Thus slaves really have a great advantage over white people, who have to
worry not only about their daily labor (which is all that blacks need to be concerned about) but also providing for their families and servants both now and in
the future.[19]

Thus, what appears to be the ultimate in paternalism, actually served as an extremely valuable tool in sacralizing an America of white racial superiority.
Christianity in American history never had a chance to become an authentic

religious faith. From its inception on this soil, it was a source of white "world historical maintenance," conceiving of the church as an eternal institution committed to getting every individual and every race to their proper "station in life." The result: the transgenerational acceptance of a white supremacist doctrine for living the true life of faith for black and white Christians! Thus, the very institution that Jesus commissioned to Peter had/has become the most virulent institution in American history regarding the sacralizing of black oppression.

> Racism has been a part of the life of the Church for so long that it is virtually impossible for even the "good" members to recognize the bigotry perpetuated by the Church. Its morals are so immoral that even its most sensitive minds are unable to detect the inhumanity of the Church on the black people of America.[20]

Cone eloquently reminds us of the insidious nature of racism when it becomes codified in the life of an institution for so long that no one has the presence of mind to raise the question of its legitimacy.

This becomes particularly endemic to a religious institution that prides itself on the establishment of its core principles as "essential truths" to protect its parishioners from being swayed by the ill-informed prevarications of heretics! The problem with such an approach is the nature and content of the "truth" itself and its insistence on a racially stratified, stations in life hermeneutic. This has historically caused many church leaders and parishioners to look upon those few who have had the courage to question the church's teaching on black oppression with deep suspicion. More practically, the church has dismissed those concerns as theologically inappropriate or branded that person a servant of Satan! Or worst yet, those persons are killed in the name of God. This not only sent a message to anyone thinking about challenging the theology of white supremacy but also reaffirmed for white church leadership God's approval of the reign of white supremacy.

> It was the church that placed God's approval on slavery and today places his (God's) blessings on the racist structure of American society. As long as whites can be sure that God is on their side, there is potentially no limit to their violence against anyone who threatens the American racist way of life. Genocide is the logical conclusion of racism.[21]

Cone brings to bear the essential mission of the white supremacist mind: to create an eternal earthly reality of white privilege and black dehumanization and to employ all dimensions of thought, including religious symbols and theological treatises, to ethically and morally justify that reality. Whether directly or indirectly, most white clergy were involved in the divinization of black dehumanization. There was no medium too sacred or fell out of the bounds of appropriateness for white clergy and slaveholders to employ in the lexicon of black dehumanization. In fact, the designated sacredness of Christian symbols became the principal reason why they were incorporated into the lexicon of black dehumanization!

The logic, of course, is that the sacredness of Christian symbols would carry far greater gravity in the minds of black and white Christians in convincing both of the "natural" order of white superiority and black inferiority. After convincing both of the sacredness of religious pedagogy itself whatever was taught under that canopy became a mere formality in terms of its unquestioned acceptance. Hence, the teaching of white superiority was an immorality passed off as the pinnacle of morality. But more sinister, using the church with which to solidify that moral claim is far more immoral than the claim itself. Theologically interpreted, God demands black subordination to whites in history as a sacrifice for a life of eternal bliss after death. The result has been the painful reality that Christian faith in American history has never been authentic either structurally or theologically in the sense that it has wrapped black dehumanization around a pole of moral turpitude and in so doing has presented the highest immorality of human inequality as the highest morality.

> It is a history in which the church not only compromised its ethic to the mood and practice of the time but was itself actively unethical, sanctioning the enslavement of human beings, producing the patterns of segregation, urging upon the oppressed Negro the extracted sedatives of the Gospel, and promulgating a doctrine of interracial morality which is itself immoral.[22]

Haselden's analysis reminds us of the extent to which our cultural values shape the way we appropriate religious faith. Thus, if one is given over to the normalcy of a racially stratified society that understanding of human relationships will ultimately make its way into that community's religious institutions. Long seen as an institution that has the power to lift us out of our unrighteous behavior and lead us to a more mature way of being Christians, the white church has been led rather than leading. That is to say, we have shaped the church more with our understanding of human relationships than the church has shaped us in leading us to a more egalitarian understanding of human relationships in the way of a man who said he was, "no respecter of persons." In short, America has taught us the art of glorifying selfish individualism as ambition and the wealth of a few at the expense of the masses as the essence of Christian faith when the central figure of that faith dedicated his life to the destruction of both. This is why Cone termed the white church in America more of the Antichrist than the true church of Christ!

This church-sanctioned drive for individual success and human "commodification" of people of color has in no small way brought the church down as opposing every major reform movement in American history. The white church doggedly resisted slave emancipation and every other movement designed to bring about human equality. White clergy used their highly respected status to ardently defend the doctrine of white superiority as the only understanding of Christian faith both in the pulpit and in the community. In the pulpit, he affirmed the merits of an emotionally thrilling, other-worldly (read socially irrelevant) worship service and beyond the pulpit insisted on deep involvement in the "activities" that would preserve white privilege. Swedish sociologist Gunnar Myrdal, in his classic, *An American Dilemma*, renders his interpretation of Christian life in America's South through the actions of both the lay and clergy white man in the late nineteenth, early twentieth century:

> It would seem that the Southern white man, especially in the lower classes, goes to church more to get an emotional thrill than to get an intellectual framework into which to put his daily problems. . . . In spite of his other-worldliness in church, the Southern preacher is often interested in power. Until recently he was often quite important in local politics: during the 1920's clergymen may almost be said to have dominated the South. They were a potent force behind the resuscitation of the Ku Klux Klan. They backed the "Blue Laws." They dominated many universities. The Dayton trial, which was fought over the question of teaching of evolution in Tennessee, was only the most spectacular manifestation of the general power of the fundamentalist clergy.[23]

Myrdal's insight, when combined with that of DuBois's earlier in the chapter, exposes white clergy in the slavocracy and beyond as not only not supporting movements that promote human equality but duplicitous in publicly advocating ideologies and organizations that perpetuated black dehumanization. In short, Christian faith was co-opted by the leadership of the white church such that it made the church a moral and ethical affirmer of white privilege. In so doing, the church was also made then to affirm any actions and public stands taken by white clergy to maintain that privilege. With white superior ideology firmly solidified as the "way" of Jesus and subsequently the church, Christian orthodoxy came to be measured by ritualistic adherence and not liberating activity. Frequent church attendance, frequent bible reading, tithes paying, highly emotional worship services and the internalization of racial stratification as divine sovereignty became the practical norm for expressing Christian faith. As impositional in slavery as it has been subtle beyond slavery, the notion that only divine intervention changes human relationships gave white clergy the perfect theological structure to establish that human efforts at eradicating relationships of inequality are ungodly acts of Christians who lack faith in God's omnipotence and wisdom! (This is why, in large measure, black and women Christian activists in American history have always been perceived in a suspicious manner by many ministers and laypersons who have questioned their faith in God's omnipotence in light of their public stands for black and women's equality.) When asocial piety, as I have termed it, is combined with emotional gratification it is little wonder that the white church has been historically successful in creating "Christian warriors" poised to defend a Christian orthodoxy of social detachment and otherworldliness. Besides absolving Christians of any responsibility in the salvation/liberation process beyond ritualistic expression, white clergy could affirm the omnipotence and wisdom of God as the only entity capable of realizing human liberation. In the final analysis though, it served only as a clever ruse with which to extend white supremacy in human history.

Although phase two of Christian pedagogy required slaves to enter the white church for instruction and worship, whites made no pretense as to their minimal desire to worship with blacks. As such, the time had come for the third and final phase in the establishment of a racist theocracy in American history — setting the slaves up in their own congregations.

Notes

1.   Columbus Salley, Ronald Behm, *What Color Is Your God: Black Consciousness & The Christian Faith*. New York: Citadel Press, 1988, 100.

2.   Ibid.

3.   Phil Zuckerman, ed., *DuBois on Religion*. Lanham, Maryland: Rowman & Littlefield Publishers, 2000, 11.

4.   Lester B. Scherer, *Slavery and the Churches in Early America: 1619-1819*. Grand Rapids: Eerdman's Publishing Company, 1975, 66.

5.   Ibid., 67.

6.   Winthrop Jordan, *The White Man's Burden: Historical Origins of Racism in the United States*. New York: Oxford Press, 1974, 96-97.

7.   Ibid., 97.

8.   Ibid., 97-98.

9.   For a more exhaustive treatment of the bible's use in justifying black dehumanization, see Chapter Two, in particular, of Forrest Wood's, *The Arrogance of Faith: Christianity & Race in America from the Colonial Era to the Twentieth Century*.

10.   H. Shelton Smith, *In His Image But...Racism In Southern Religion, 1780-1910*. Durham: Duke University Press, 1972. Taken from Ibid., 69.

11.   William Grimes, *Life of William Grimes, the Runaway Slave, Brought Down to the Present Time*. New Haven, Connecticut, 1855. Taken from Ibid.

12.   Charles H. Nichols, *Many Thousand Gone: The Ex-Slaves' Account of Their Bondage and Freedom*. Leiden, Netherlands, 1963. Taken from Ibid.

13.   W. E. B. DuBois, "Religion in the South." Taken from Phil Zuckerman, ed., *DuBois on Religion*, 72.

14.   Ibid., 72-73.

15.   Scherer, *Slavery and the Churches in America*, 99.

16.   Ibid.

17.   Ibid., 96.

18.   John W. Blassingame, ed., *Slave Testimony: Two Centuries of Letters, Speeches, Interviews, and Autobiographies*. Baton Rouge, Louisiana, 1977. Taken from Wood, *The Arrogance of Faith*, 73.

19.   Scherer, *Slavery and the Churches in America*, 99-100.

20.   James H. Cone, *Black Theology and Black Power*. New York: Seabury Press, 1969, 72.

21.   Ibid., 75.

22.   Kyle Haselden, *The Racial Problem in Christian Perspective*. Taken from Ibid., 78.

23.   Gunnar Myrdal, *An American Dilemma* (Two Volumes). New York: McGraw-Hill Book Company, 1964, 458. Originally published in 1944.

8

White Religion and the "Independent" Black Church

The Black Church has no challenger as the cultural womb of the black community. Not only did it give birth to new institutions such as schools, banks, insurance companies, and low income housing, it also provided an academy and an arena for political activities, and it nurtured young talent for musical, dramatic, and artistic development. E. Franklin Frazier's apt descriptive phrase, "nation within a nation," pointed to these multifarious levels of community involvement found in the Black Church, in addition to the traditional concerns of worship, moral nurture, education, *and social control.*
C. Eric Lincoln, Lawrence H. Mamiya, *The Black Church in the African American Experience*

Now that white clergy and slaveholders were pleased with their indoctrination of slaves in the pedagogy of Christian racism, the time had come for the last phase in the creation of a racist theocracy — setting black people up in their own churches. In so doing, it ushered into existence one of the most paradoxical and complex situations in the history of America.

Termed independent black churches, religious historians are universally agreed that these congregations were anything but independent. In fact, the increasing concern slaveholders and white clergy had for slaves plotting insurrection in their Brush Arbor religious meetings made this transition anything but a done deal. Adding to the trepidation of white clergy and slaveholders was the increasing anti-slavery stances taken by their white Christian brethren in many northern cities on the heels of the colonies revolution against Britain for its own independence. Hence, the spirit of independence celebrated publicly by slaveholders and white clergy did not extend to slaves. In fact, the promise of black independence was little more than a front for tempering black fervor for freedom in general and for keeping a more watchful eye on black "rabble-rousers" in particular. Thus, one should not be historically and religiously naïve and conclude that black independent congregations meant black independence from white dominance. Nor did it mean institutional freedom for slaves in the life of the church itself. To be sure, white clergy and slaveholders were still convinced of the divine nature of slavery and had no inclination of freeing slaves even as they were on the cusp of their own freedom from England and, ironically, about to draft a declaration of independence.

Independent black congregations meant for whites a much welcomed separation from "mixed worship," but more important, they meant a major milestone in Christian pedagogy regarding the social control of slaves. That milestone was rooted in the conclusion that slaves had been thoroughly indoctrinated into a slaveholder-friendly Christian faith and would pose no significant threat to the slavocracy. This meant that, *independent black churches were not created to make black people independent, free, or righteous.* Rather, the intent of independent black churches was to complete the last phase of a racist theocracy. It was to create in the mind of the slave an easy affinity between Christian institutional life and social control. With that assertion serving as the theological foundation for black congregations, we see the establishment of the first "independent" black church in Mecklenburg, Virginia in 1758 and the first "independent" southern black church in Silver Bluff, South Carolina between 1773 and 1775. Both were founded on plantations at the consent and encouragement of the owners of those plantations.[1] That milestone also meant for white clergy that slaves had been thoroughly indoctrinated into a Christian pedagogy that, among other things, placed ultimate emphasis on the religious individual, made otherworldliness the primary locus of Christian reward, divorced the life of faith from earthly freedom, and made white privilege and black dehumanization God's desire for race relations on earth. This implied more than anything else that the slave demonstrate ultimate obedience to God and Jesus by comfortably accepting her earthly lot from cradle to grave not only for herself but her posterity as well. As stated earlier, her salvation depended on it — no other alternative existed!

The slave community's response to this Christian pedagogy has been one of constant paradox since the independent black church's establishment. To be sure, also as stated earlier, the slave's response to her slave condition and Christian pedagogy was wrought with internal struggle. On the one hand, slaves intuited that their destiny was not eternal enslavement but on the other hand both their condition and their religious indoctrination contradicted that intuition. Thus the hope that Christian faith promises vacillated in the slave mind between God rewarding her with a life of eternal bliss after death for respecting the slavocracy as white clergy preached on the one hand and God being with her as a co-partner in the destruction of the slavocracy as she intuited on the other hand. The Du-Boisian "double consciousness" of two warring souls between being both a Negro and an American not only characterized the historical reality of black people but being both a Christian and a slave also produced two warring souls in the theological consciousness of blacks as they "transitioned" from the white church to the black church. This vacillation has been by no means easy for the black Christian community and has by and large been the reason that no historian of religion has been able to truly get an analytical grip on the complexity of the black church.

In this regard, C. Eric Lincoln maintains that any true analysis of the black church must remain clearly within a dialectical framework of vacillating poles lest we run the risk of engaging in oversimplification of what the black church has meant, and what it has not meant, to both the black and the American experience.[2] Yet, as association breeds assimilation in varying degrees in any social endeavor, a more direct analysis of the black church's origins is operative beyond Lincoln's dialectical framework to determine what impact white Christian pedagogy has had (and continues to have!) on black people's understanding of themselves and their relationship with God and how they have sought to express that understanding in such an acutely horrific national life. The concern of oversimplification must be taken into consideration but must be trumped by a poignant treatment of the black church at its raison d'etre in Lincoln's own assessment — social control.

White Christian Pedagogy as a Medium of Direct Social Control

Although being placed in independent congregations served as a profound sense of progress for many slaves, the black church was not created to serve the liberative interests of black people. White clergy and slaveholders were convinced that through their Christian pedagogy to slaves in the white church they would be able to exert enough control over the thinking of slaves to socially control them. For white clergy, that Christian pedagogy as provided in the Bible sanctioned slavery as a divine institution not only in biblical history but in contemporary history as well. In particular, white clergy were convinced of the direct references to slaveholding in the Bible concerning African enslavement. The Christian affirmation of African slavery was to be understood as the essence of the gospel.

As for the Old Testament, white clergy were steadfastly sold on the biblical narrative of the so-called curse on Ham as direct proof of African slavery. Referred to formally as the Hamitic Hypothesis, the narrative supposedly sentences the descendents of Ham, the father of Canaan and whose posterity settled in Africa, to eternal bondage to the descendents of his brothers, Shem and Japheth, whose posterity settled in Europe, for Ham mocking his father Noah in his drunkenness. (Gen. 9:18-27) Upon learning of his son Ham's mocking him after awakening from his stupor, Noah said, "Cursed be Canaan; a servant of servants shall he be to his brothers."[3] (v. 25) Though no references are made to Africa or Europe (and certainly not America) and though the narrative is understood by most Old Testament scholars to have been fulfilled when the Israelites entered the Promised Land and defeated the Canaanites, it nevertheless served as the primary Old Testament foundation for white clergy's biblical justification for African enslavement. In framing Christian theology in this way to the slave, the intent was to instill in the mind of the slave that this was an extension of the mind of God and not white men. Despite the fact that Noah was scarcely sober and obviously reacted in a fit of rage, a prominent minister of the Methodist Protestant Church claimed that, "he spoke under the impulse and dictation of Heaven. . . . His words were the words of God himself (Godself), and by them was slavery ordained."[4]

In addition, by connecting Ham's descendents to Africa, white clergy were able to connect biblical history to American history by maintaining that the Hamitic Hypothesis was not an interpretation of a biblical narrative but rather a contemporary manifestation of God's activity in the world. In this regard, white clergy were conveniently seeking to establish that *God not only condones human enslavement in principle but also condones African enslavement to whites in American history.* This is why a South Carolina preacher and slaveholder emphatically proclaimed, "that the Africans or Negroes, are the descendants of Ham; and it is by no means improbable that the very name Ham, which signifies burnt or black, was given to him prophetically, on account of the countries that his posterity were destined to inhabit. The judicial curse of Noah upon the posterity of Ham seems yet to rest upon them."[5]

While still considered a direct means of social control, white clergy had a more difficult time demonstrating to slaves the New Testament references to African slavery. Yet it proved more effective than the Old Testament insofar as there were more references to the issue of slavery in the New Testament particularly in the letters of Paul. In addition, white clergy went to great lengths to point out that despite the existence of servanthood in first century Palestine, Jesus makes no direct references to slavery's immoral existence in principle. In so doing, it lead South Carolina Baptist preacher Richard Fuller to declare to his good friend Francis Wayland, then President of Brown University, "What God sanctioned in the Old Testament and permitted in the New, cannot be sin."[6] Hence, for Fuller and many other proslavery theologians of his time, silence on the part of Jesus was tantamount to sanction. When combined with the fact that white clergy had convinced most slaves of the unquestioned authority of the bible in all matters divine, its impact on the shaping of a black church "orthodoxy" cannot be underestimated.

White clergy found in the letters of Paul a fertile source for advancing an agenda of slavery to black people. Beyond the fact that many of the Pauline letters made direct reference to the proper structure of the master-slave relationship, thus implying its legitimacy, Paul's admonition, particularly, to Onesimus, a runaway slave of Philemon to return to his master fortified the sacred nature of the master-slave relationship for white clergy. (Yet they conveniently omitted from that narrative that Paul also implores Philemon to accept Onesimus as a full brother in Christ!) Further, proslavery advocates point to the fact that slaveholders in biblical times were devout Christians and members of churches including Philemon himself at the church at Colossae. This meant that for most southern white clergy and slaveholders that the slavocracy was not only not sinful but actually represented one of the most esteemed virtues of human expression.

> To the religious leaders of the South, this fact demonstrated that the early church did not consider slaveholding sinful per se. They were the more certain of this, because applicants for admission to the primitive churches and to the sacraments were subjected to the most rigorous examination with respect to their spiritual qualifications for these privileges.[7]

On these two premises, one from each biblical testament, white clergy hung their biblical hermeneutical hats.

Hence, the origins of the "independent" black church was rooted in encouraging slaves to equate salvation with earthly obedience to slavery in general and white rule in particular. In sacralizing the slavocracy white clergy were imposing on slaves an understanding of their humanity that placed God's direct approval on their oppression. When combined with the fact that slaveholders prevented Africans from transmitting their African roots to their posterity, it left the slave in the institutional church with the task of constructing a meaningful approach to faith that resonated with their unique condition as Christians and slaves.

> From the moment the Africans lost the social basis of their religious community life, their religion itself had to disintegrate as a coherent system of belief. From the moment they arrived in America and began to toil as slaves, they could not help absorbing the religion of the master class. But the conditions of their new social life forced them to combine their African inheritance with the dominant power they confronted to shape a religion of their own.[8]

In the early shaping of that religion the slaves were not deeply persuaded by the theological axioms of direct social control by white clergy. In this regard, slaveholder's fears that white Christian pedagogy may not be controlling enough to keep slaves content were confirmed.

Slaves could not and did not accept derogatory understandings of their humanity from a Christian theological standpoint. They were of the belief that one cannot legitimately establish a paradox of Christian fulfillment and incessant hostility from whites regarding the valuation of their humanity. They were able to deduce that derogatory labels such as nigger, shine, hambone, or coon did not emanate from the mind of God. For most slaves, Christian faith did not irrefutably confirm their eternal enslavement despite the so-called airtight sophistry of the Hamitic Hypothesis. Hence, from the origins of the independent black church, resistance to black dehumanization was the top priority for the slaves. From its inception, the independent black church mounted aggressive public campaigns against egregious characterizations of black character, intelligence, and aesthetic features and at least, in this regard, experienced very little angst in expressing their understanding of Christian faith to whites. This was no small task given the proclivity of slaveholders to punish slaves for defiant behavior. This affirmation of black humanity by slaves was also discouraging for many white clergy who had spent considerable hours "preparing" black ministers for independent worship with a cornucopia of biblical passages designed to create pious black congregations with an inferior understanding of their own humanity and serving whites well in the slavocracy. Yet slaves were clearly interested in the creation of a new religious tradition that affirmed fidelity to Christian faith and fidelity to black freedom as well.

> The religious tradition to which the Afro-American slaves fell heir and to which they contributed more than has yet been generally recognized by no means unambiguously inspired docility and bland submission. Many of the white preachers to the slaves sought to sterilize the message, but they were condemned to eventual defeat. Too many carriers of the Word were themselves black men who interpreted in their own way. The Word transmitted itself, for some slaves and free Negroes in touch with slaves could read the Bible and counter the special pleading of the white preachers.[9]

In fact, what was at work was more than slaves that were happy to be in independent congregations. What was transpiring was the spirit of God yearning for freedom for slaves from the Brush Arbors to the black church. That is to say, the call for black self-affirmation transitioned from a private venue to a public venue. While the venue for black communication with God changed, its unrelenting demand for human self-respect remained the same.

> And the black community in slavery, oppressed and degraded as it was, summoned up too much spirit and inner resourcefulness to be denied. In their own way the slaves demonstrated that, whatever the full truth or falsity of Christianity, it spoke for all humanity when it proclaimed the freedom and inviolability of the human soul.[10]

The genius of black people is that they were able to recognize that they were creating themselves again in another context. A huge part of that creation for the slaves was re-making themselves morally and ethically in connection with a Christian faith that had been imposed on them by white clergy. Thus, while they understood themselves to be theological works in progress, they were clear that, fundamentally, Christian faith affirmed that their humanity was just as valued by God as any other race of people, including whites. But more important, the gospel insisted that they demonstrate that value in their interactions with whites despite their slave status. This is why Gayraud Wilmore maintained that, "these pioneers [black ministers] were not blind to the degradation of themselves and their people. They would never have been tolerated for long by the people if they had seemed to favor the masters over the demands of the gospel."[11]

Indeed, the inability of white clergy to win over black preachers to a slave-but-Christian doctrine ignited the spirit of freedom in the slave community. The tables had been, for the most part, turned on white clergy and slaveholders in presenting the illiterate black preacher as the image of the "ideal negro" for lay black Christians to emulate. For that reason, white clergy and slaveholders kept a "watchful eye" on black worship services to either disrupt any insurrectionist activity or to preempt any uprising plans by the black church community. For Wilmore, the reasons were clear:

> Shame and guilt made whites want to silence the black preacher even when the danger of insurrection was remote. They knew that the argument that God had ordained the enslavement of the African was a lie. And they knew too that whatever could be done by black preachers to hasten the demise of slavery — whether from the open pulpit or in secret — was a part of their commitment to the ministry.[12]

Thus, the early black church equated Christian faith with freedom from the slavocracy and was convinced that God was with them in their struggle for racial emancipation.

The origins of the black church movement for freedom actually began with the Awakenings of the mid-eighteenth centuries. Particularly in the North, interracial worship that was highly enthusiastic laid the foundation for an understanding of the spirit of the divine that is still with us today. It placed emphasis not on the education attainment or wealth of the believer but simply her sincerity in affirming the benevolent and omnipotent power of God to usher the kingdom into reality. The Awakenings, while branding slavery a moral evil that should be abolished, placed ultimate emphasis on institutional worship, prayer, the religious individual and unbridled enthusiasm in the adoration of God. Thus, contrary to popular belief, emotionally charged worship services did not begin with the independent black church but was rather deeply influenced by the worship style of the Awakenings. This owed itself in large part to the fact that most black ministers were not formally trained and many were functionally illiterate. In this regard, an approach to faith was ignited by the Awakenings that provided a place for those that were not members of the intelligentsia.

Yet even in the midst of this hopeful expression of faith regarding black humanity, the notion that slaves were equal to all other races in God's sight was mostly held by Northern whites. White Southerners were not budging on the question of slavery and actually co-opted the Awakenings by keeping the concept of emotionally ecstatic worship and combining it with a potent dose of individuality and other-worldliness that most aptly reflected their primary concern with social control. This, in turn, gave birth to the age religious conservatism or the notion that Christian faith demands a radical obedience to the "fundamental truths" of faith. The commonality of those "fundamental truths" is that they divorced Christianity from social change and theologically maneuvered America into issues of sexual morality and institutional maintenance.

> The Baptists and Methodists who carried much of the new religious drive often expressed hostility toward slavery and a hope that it would vanish. Throughout the Upper South the spirit of the revivals manifested itself in demand, often backed by administrative measures within the churches, for humane treatment of the slaves and for recognition that they were brothers in Christ. The inclusion of blacks and indeed the religious Awakening itself did not, however, extend much below Virginia; South Carolina, even then, stood as a bulwark of conservatism in religion as in most else.[13]

This brings us to the complexity of racial bigotry and Christian faith in American history. It also brings us to the theological morass with which the independent black church and its leadership had to contend. On the one hand, blacks had to deal with the fact that although many Northern whites spoke of ending slavery, they by no means considered the slaves of equal human worth. On the other hand, black religious leadership had to determine what would serve as their theological platform to imbue the slaves with a sense of racial cohesion and hope for the future they knew was in direct contradiction to the intent of white clergy and slaveholders. For instance, the, "brothers in Christ," in the quote above for Northern whites meant spiritual (read asocial) equality with blacks in the name of Jesus but not an America of equal opportunity and human worth. Thus, beyond their disagreement on slavery, Northern whites were in agreement with Southern whites concerning the "place" of black people in the church and society. In short, interracial worship was encouraged by Northern whites but social equality was not. It is into that backdrop that black religious leadership had to fashion a liberative approach to Christian faith.

Yet, even that interracial fellowship had limits in Northern churches. It should be noted that the origins of the Free African Society and the African Methodist Episcopal Church began with blacks walking out of the white Methodist Church because Absalom Jones (or any other black person) was not allow to pray at its altar in Philadelphia — a Northern city! Thus, while Northern and Southern whites differed on the slave status of blacks, they were in one accord that, at the very least, social equality was not in the offing in American life and that Christian faith, no less, demanded this relationship of racial stratification despite the theological implications of the Great Awakenings. This meant that black religious leadership had to struggle with the fact that the church itself, whether the white church or the "independent" black church, was little more than an institutional creation of a racist mind designed to perpetuate black oppression. As such, Christian symbols and racial superiority were wed at the altar of black degradation.

> It meant that the one institution which was at all prepared to accept the Negro as an equal was shattered — completely, as it turned out. The new Negro churches were equal but separate, prototypes of "separate but equal." When Christian equalitarianism ran head on into racial mores the result was, institutionally and in the public mind, gradual separation along racial lines.[14]

That separation along racial lines also had to be recognized by black religious leadership as beginning in the white southern church given the lack of desire of whites to worship with blacks. White clergy were calling for spiritual equality with all God's children, including blacks, but were also setting up "independent" black churches to separate themselves institutionally from blacks. This meant that black religious leadership had to reckon with the huge ideological chasm that existed between spiritual equality before God and racial equality in American life. This chasm is one in which black religious leadership and black people in general have been able to recognize as white racial hypocrisy and as a pretext for black dehumanization. Regardless of a lack of formal academic training, black religious leadership had the capacity for discerning blatant expressions of racial bigotry even when wrapped around a thin veneer of Christian faith. The tougher nut to proverbially crack for independent black churches, and a harbinger of things to come in Christian life in America, has been the seemingly sincere expressions (seeming nonracial) of Christian faith wrapped around a thin veneer of racial bigotry.

White Christian Pedagogy as a Medium of Indirect Social Control

As the Awakenings and the sense of freedom permeating the colonies during the soon-to-be-realized victory against Britain began to establish themselves, the question on what to do with the slaves remained the same — continue to subjugate them. At the core of this subjugation was still the paramount significance of Christian faith. The intent of white clergy was still the same but a newly independent Christian America transitioned into a more subtle methodology of indoctrinating slaves into a more pious (read docile) way of faith expression.

Beginning in the late eighteenth century, many white clergy who had been so intrusive in black worship services before the revolution were now willing to be around less provided black preachers give themselves over to certain theological presuppositions in their sermons. Presuppositions that have tremendous import in the way both black and white Christians had expressed faith earlier in the century. Black preachers for the most part yielded to such demands in the hopes of realizing a more authentic ecclesial independence that would parlay into black freedom in history. However, as time progressed and freedom in history did not occur (the Emancipation Proclamation was not drafted until eighty-seven years after the American Revolution) the slaves, except for a few prophetic voices, began to redirect its theological energies back into white Christian orthodoxy. This meant, most significantly, conceiving of freedom in purely spiritual terms and branding human strivings for freedom as religiously inappropriate. Historian of religion Gayraud Wilmore refers to this era as "the deradicalization of the black church."[15]

The deradicalization of the black church, for Wilmore, refers to the point in which the black church relinquished its quest for racial freedom on earth and turned its attention to other-worldliness, and to issues of sexual morality and institutional maintenance. While Wilmore and I are in agreement that a ubiquitous deradicalization of the black church took place, we differ as to when it began. Wilmore cites the devastation of black people psychically following the Plessy vs Ferguson decision by the Supreme Court in 1896 as the beginnings of black church deradicalization. Yet, I consider the end of the eighteenth century the era when black church deradicalization began to blossom. The process had already begun, in my judgment, in the post-revolutionary war period in the late eighteenth century with the devastation the slaves experienced when they were not beneficiaries of America's independence from Britain.

It is in the post-revolutionary era where we begin to see the black church incorporate the intense emotional enthusiasm and preoccupation with the religious individual from the Awakenings and reduce the emphasis given to the themes of justice and prophetic denunciations of unjust kingdoms by the Old Testament prophets. More important, we begin to see a definitive theology of the black church emerging that came to closely mirror the understanding of Christian faith of their white counterparts. This theology of the black church was coupled with the transition to a more subtle theological approach by white clergy wherein derogatory references to black people's humanity would be minimized and replaced with "universal truths" that every Christian, regardless of race, should adhere. These "universal truths" frowned on social reform movements as ungodly, particularly movements of racial reform in American history. The result is that it placed some black churches and its leadership in direct opposition to those movements as Christians and has gone a long way in attenuating the revolutionary fervor of black people. Put another way, black church leadership was faced with the complex dilemma of condemning movements of social reform as a sign of Christian obedience when those same movements have been the vehicles to black advancement in American life. This dilemma has and continues to make black people choose between Christian obedience and racial affirmation. This is why I refer to the "universal truths" that have given birth to this dilemma as mediums of indirect social control. A more elaborate examination of these "universal truths" is in order.

The first of these universal truths is that Christian faith mandates no linkage between religion and politics. The meaning of politics here is not just electoral party politics but social issues of collective human domination. Using the, "render unto God what is God, and unto Caesar what is Caesar's," biblical dictum, slaves were taught by white clergy that the affairs of the nation were not issues of concern for the true Christian insofar as she is bound by a higher law. Hence, the carrying out of God's will meant non-engagement with forces of earthly oppression regardless of one's lot in life. As such, movements of social reform came to be regarded as ungodly. Christianity, it was taught by white clergy, meant that we serve two kingdoms — one on earth and one in heaven. The former demands only that we respect its laws and pay its taxes for citizenship and of which we should only be temporarily concerned. The latter demands our ultimate allegiance and of which we are ultimately striving. In other words, radical obedience to God meant something of a totally different nature than radical obedience to sustained racial struggle as children of God. With racial advancement omitted from the criteria of salvation, Christian faith was coming to be understood as race-neutral and heaven-centered in a nation that possessed huge problems racially.

To be sure, the no faith and politics "truth" did not originate in American history. Augustine and later Luther crafted the duty of the Christian in society within this framework and is in many ways why Luther's denunciation of the Peasant's Revolt was so strong. In this context, the intent was the same — to fashion in both black and white Christians the understanding of socio-political reform as ungodly as a means of perpetuating white privilege in American life. Christian faith, then, became a medium for teaching slaves to have reverence for American law and order. That reverence came to be measured by the extent to which one divorced oneself from socio-political reform activity — even if one lived a socio-politically oppressive existence!

Yet because religion is a phenomenon that seeks to give its adherents a framework by which one discerns what is right and wrong, its moral and ethical significance not only lies in the ecclesiastical domain but the social domain as well. Even, "rendering unto Caesar what is his," is suggestive of some type of engagement with the world and one's relationship with God. But more important, such an approach to Christian faith does not take into account the instances in biblical history where God is commissioning a servant to socially engage oppressive structures. Whether it is Moses taking the Israelites out of Egyptian slavery, Samson and his confrontations with the Philistines, the Israelites entering into the Promised Land, Daniel and his condemnation of an unjust kingdom and the sudden end to a Belshazzar's rule, the Hebrew Boys being placed in the fiery furnace for not bowing down to an idol god and Jesus' liberating mission and his radical engagement with the forces of oppression in first century Palestine, Christian faith has demanded a radical engagement with forces of socio-political oppression *in this world* for the liberation of the oppressed *in this world*.

> The philosophical problem of religion, its truth and falsehood represents a domain only partially separate from that of politics. Since religion expresses the antagonisms between the life of the individual and that of society and between the life of civil society and that of political society, it cannot escape being profoundly political…In either case, religion makes statements about man (humanity) in his (her) world — about his (her) moral and social relationships — even when it makes statements about his (her) relationship to God.[16]

Genovese is establishing the inescapability of socio-political engagement in the salvation process and further as a mandate for salvation.

At stake was the legitimacy of a way of life that desired a racially stratified relationship between blacks and whites as the norm in American and Christian life. Sitting at the core of this relationship was a group of slaves that did not intuit their enslavement as eternal but that had also given themselves over to a Christian worldview. Thus began their journey to find a religious expression that would emphasize the virtues of a self-determined black humanity that would also be pleasing to the God of Jesus Christ. Put another way, the slaves sought a religious expression that honored ritual but denounced human oppression. This meant that for both races Christianity was the common denominator in shaping the image of black humanity making its appropriation crucial to both communities:

> Even when a man's (human's) adherence to a religion is purely formal or ritualistic, essential elements of his (her) politics are thereby exposed, for participation in rites normally means participation in social acts that precede, rather than follow, individual emotional response. He (she) enters usually as a child, into a pattern of socially directed behavior that conditions his (her) subsequent emotional development and that, from the beginning, presupposes a community and a sense of common interest. For good reason the whites of the Old South tried to shape the religious life of their slaves, and the slaves overtly, covertly, and even intuitively fought to shape it themselves.[17]

The result of these competing forces for the theological minds of black people regarding their humanity has resulted in a synthesis of each force. As stated earlier, association at some point breeds some type of assimilation. What would develop is a theological paradigm in the black Christian community that would place institutional emphasis on ritual and otherworldliness but that would also tacitly approve efforts in the slave community for freedom. As it relates specifically to our discussion, we begin to see in the late eighteenth century an institutional moving away of the independent black church from active engagement in the black freedom movement but a solid affirmation of slave insurrections. We further begin to see in the black church the planting of the seeds that would come to relish a separation between religion and politics broadly conceived and then about another half century for many black churches to openly oppose social reform movements and give themselves over to a neo-theistic theological outlook, i.e., a God will do everything for us approach to social transformation.

The second universal truth, God's omnipotence in all human affairs, became both a blessing and a hindrance for black people. On the one hand, it gave the slaves hope to know that God was concerned about their freedom and was more powerful than the historical power of white people. The slave was convinced that biblical revelation confirms God's intervention on behalf of the oppressed. On the other hand, belief in an omnipotent God also tended to place too much emphasis on God's intervention in history and not compel slaves to fight for their freedom in the name of God. To be sure, the severity of the punishment from masters for trying to run away from the plantation or to incite insurrection produced enough fear in slaves to serve as an effective deterrent. Yet the historical impact of a completely sovereign conception of God on an enslaved people with an unhealthy self-image has not surprisingly laid the foundation for a, "Let the Lord handle it," mentality in the life of the black church. It conveniently absolves the religious individual of personal responsibility in the process of human transformation and yields that responsibility to an omnipotent God who will liberate the oppressed. Hence, a sovereign God in an historical relationship of racial stratification becomes both a solution and a problem. It becomes a solution in the sense that it points God's moral compass toward human liberation in history. (Given the heavy emphasis on otherworldliness by white clergy, this is a major theological coup indeed!) It becomes a problem in the sense that in conceiving of the process of human liberation being carried out solely by God, Christian theology descends into ideology by affirming that the devoted Christian need only engage in institutional rituals to be an authentic servant of God. In so doing, it reaffirmed the paradoxical struggle for the slave community between doing the will of their earthly master and doing the will of their heavenly master.

> If [Christianity] calls for political submission to the powers that be, it also calls for militant defense of the freedom of the spirit and the autonomy of the personality. But the master-slave relationship rests, psychologically as well as ideologically, on the transformation of the will of the slave into an extension of the will of the master. Thus, no matter how obedient — how Uncle Tomish — Christianity made the slave, it also drove deep into his soul an awareness of the moral limits of submission, for it placed the master above his own master and thereby dissolved the moral and ideological ground on which the very principle of absolute human lordship must rest.[18]

Thus, the slave constantly found herself warring between submission to white supremacy and devotion to God. But given that the understanding of devotion to God itself had been deeply influenced by white Christian pedagogy, the dividing line between the two became more and more blurred over time. None moreso was the case than the slave's penchant for frequent prayer. While it imbued the slave with a more kindred relationship with God, it also was accepted by white clergy as a safe expression of the religious life because, short of the insurrections, it was rarely followed by a direct engagement with the forces of white supremacy. In this regard, theology became ideology — a meaningful engagement in religious expression that did not directly challenge an America of acute racial stratification. James Cone points out both the ideological intent and the authentic meaning of prayer:

> Praying is not kneeling morning, noon, and evening. This is a tradition that is characteristic of whites; they used it to reinforce the rightness of their destruction of blacks. Prayer is the spirit that is evident in all oppressed communities when they know that they have a job to do. It is the communication with the divine that makes them know that they have very little to lose in the fight against evil and a lot to gain. We can only lose our physical lives but can gain what the writer of the Fourth Gospel calls eternal life and what blacks call blackness.[19]

Cone rightly reminds us that prayer is not in and of itself a solution to human oppression but must be a precursor to liberating activity. If not, Christian theology serves the interests of racial bigotry and not of human emancipation. To be sure, the completely sovereign conception of God owes itself to the Reformation tradition and Calvin's adaptation of Luther's conception of the righteousness of God in saving the Christian by grace alone and not human works. Calvin's theological determinism minimized human works to its lowest point and elevated God's righteousness to its highest degree. What, as pointed out earlier, logically ensues from such a theological construction is that human works are not important either historically or salvifically. As such, it made for a fertile theological source of co-opting by white clergy in affirming a Christian faith that places human strivings for historical change in the category of sinfulness for not having true faith in God's sovereignty. Obviously, this further perpetuated the dilemma in the mind of many slaves between being enslaved and saved on the one hand and being free and sinful on the other hand.

The third and one of the most uncritical adoptions of "universal truths" by the "independent" black church was/is the subordination of women in both the church and society. So effective has this indoctrination been, even many women in the church who accepted their inferior status were/are biblically convinced of their submissive status in their interactions with men. Paul's dictum for women to be "silent" in the church, that women should inquire about matters theological to their husbands only at home, and that it is "disgraceful" for women to speak in the church (I Corinthians 14:34-35), was hammered home with great frequency by white clergy and uncritically adopted by many black ministers. This dimension of white Christian pedagogy was/is particularly formidable given that it did not entail racial subordination (thus allowing black men to experience a privileged status in an historical relationship) and that there were biblical passages that speak directly to ecclesiastical and social relationships between men and women. This represented for many black men/ministers a newfound sense of empowerment and prestige, however distorted, to know that God had ordained a superior relationship for them even as slaves.

White women, in many ways, gladly accepted their subordinate status particularly considering the fact that they were the wives of powerful, extremely wealthy white men. Thus, whatever indignities they suffered in daily plantation life from their husbands were at least materially compensated for by the marital benefits of being the wives of slaveholders. Moreover, white women were treated with the utmost respect for a woman insofar as standards of beauty, proper behavior, soft voice inflections, and a quiet gentility all came to be associated with "classy" womanhood. Her bright skin, long-flowing straight hair, and petite frame, as well as her exemption from physical labor and membership in bridge club societies all bespoke a woman who represented the epitome of the finer things in life and became the envy of other women and the object of desire for other men. But with that lofty status also came a secondary status in American life and the creation of the trophy syndrome i.e., being prized for her aesthetic qualities and not her ability to forward substantive intellectual thoughts.

Yet arguably, no other race and gender has been affected more by white Christian pedagogy than black women. The reason is clear: white Christian pedagogy has not only been racist but sexist as well. As such, black women have been two-fold recipients of white supremacist doctrine. When the dimension of class is added, plantation life is the ground with which black women's subordination became triple jeopardy (to borrow Teresa Hoover's term) — race, sex, and class. Further exacerbating the issue for black women was not only that she was locked in conflict with white men in regard to race and gender but that she was also in conflict with her own black man in regard to gender. She was expected to join with black men in the struggle for racial equality in her expected supportive role but was unable to get black men to see the unique struggles of black women in the society and the church. Black men were less willing to see the unique plight of black women given that for most black men, including black ministers, racial emancipation parlayed into gender emancipation. That is to say, for most black men, black women were oppressed not because they were women but because they were black. Thus, the key to liberating black women, for black men, was to liberate the entire race from white racism. This also meant that for most black men that black women's claims of unique suffering were highly overblown and represented faulty analysis of the racial situation in plantation life.

But more important, black ministers had begun to internalize the teaching of white Christian pedagogy that upheld the subordination of women. Thus, while black ministers were ambivalent on the question as to whether white Christian pedagogy was accurate in God ordaining racial subordination, they were reso lute on the question of God ordaining women's subordination. Black women, themselves, must realize that black men may disagree with and fight white men over racism, but far too many black men and white men (preachers included) are thoroughly bonded in their affirmation of the subordination of women.[20] Black women's subordination even applies to celebrated religious and social leaders concerning racial advancement. For instance, even Richard Allen, founder of the African Methodist Episcopal Church (AME) and who was with Absalom Jones that day in the white Methodist church in 1787 that would not allow Jones to pray at the altar, vehemently refused to allow the ordination of Jarena Lee, a member of the church that had professed a call to the ministry.

> I went to see the preacher in charge of the African society . . . the Rev. Richard Allen . . . to tell him that I felt it my duty to preach the gospel. . . . He then replied, that a Mrs. Cook, a Methodist lady, had also some time before requested the same privilege. . . . But as to preaching, he said that our Discipline knew nothing at all about it – that it did not call for women preachers.[21]

In this regard, black ministers were not able to see that they were becoming what they found to be abhorrent in white males.

Even W. E. B. DuBois in the early twentieth century echoed the sexist sentiment that had become characteristic of most black men when he maintained that, "Men are primary wage-earners and women are mothers and keepers of home," and that black people will never become a formidable race until its women, "are prepared to assume the responsibility of healthy families, of two or three children."[22] Thus, even a visionary like DuBois possessed no double consciousness in this regard clearly demonstrating that he had uncritically given himself over to a misogynist understanding of women that was a direct result of white Christian pedagogy.

The resultant paradox for black women was and still is finding a way in which to engage black men in the community and church that at one and the same time allies themselves with black men in the struggle for racial equality while at the same time not alienating black men in compelling other black women to see the divine necessity of women's freedom in the quest for a full human emancipation. When black women accept the realization that far too many black men and white men in power agree on the subordination of black women, perhaps they will begin to realize a serious women's movement within the denominational churches — a movement to free women's minds and lives of the androcentric indoctrination and the exploitive emotional commitments that cause many women to be tools of their own oppression and that of other women.[23]

Finally, indirect social control had/has fundamentally to do with the presentation and theological disposition of the black minister. In particular, this had to do with both the public posture and the theological emphasis of black ministers in their churches. This was crucial for white clergy. Most were of the thinking that if they could establish in the black minister a pious, socially detached theological disposition, black parishioners would follow suit. The image of the black minister white clergy was seeking to fashion was that of a materialistic, self-absorbed pietist that was content with his lot and that sought to convince black parishioners of the same. In short, the goal of white clergy was to create a pimp image in the black minister that was illiterate, colorful, loud, easily manipulated and generally someone who would not be taken seriously outside the black community. This became particularly crucial given the trust that both black and white laypersons were taught to have for their ministers in all matters divine. If white clergy were successful in selling this image of black ministers to black laypersons then it could go a long way in creating a content, docile spirit among black people that serves the interests of the white establishment. Not surprisingly, the black minister found himself yielding to some of white clergy's "suggestions" and at other times not given over to those "suggestions." In many ways, in the late eighteenth century, black people had begun their distorted adoration with white culture and it was important for the burgeoning leaders of the black community to be well accepted by the white establishment. Yet, at the same time, it was important for the black minister that he not completely lose his respected status in the black community. Then, as now, the black minister's dilemma has not changed.

> It cannot be denied that the black preacher is often identified as an "Uncle Tom," a collaborator. He is seen as a traitor to the best interests of his people. This is not a role which the black minister consciously assumed. Like the modern black middle class, he is torn with conflicting loyalties, sometimes drawn to his own people, sometimes drawn to the "foreign" rulers. The minister, in accepting Christianity, also in some degree identified with the major moral values and institutions of white society.[24]

Hence, we have reaffirmed our central contention: the acceptance of Christian faith itself as taught to black people by white clergy during the slavocracy has been at the same time the acceptance of an unconscious identification with the moral values of white society.

While black people have been able to snuff out direct denunciations of black humanity by white clergy, they have not been as effective in snuffing out the "neutral" theological assertions and their ultimate impact on black people's advancement. As such, black ministers, unwittingly given over to racist Christian pedagogy, have been the most ardent advocates of defending the "values" of American society — in some cases even better than whites.

> In general, the black community experiences little difficulty in seeing white so-called morality for the hypocrisy and cant that it is. Yet the black middle class, of which the black preacher is only the most conspicuous part, as the artificially created stepchildren of white society, acts as though it is driven to uphold that society's values and attitudes — even when whites fail to do so themselves.[25]

In light of this development, black people with a revolutionary conscience began to have less faith in the church to challenge the status quo leading to the establishment of the black prophetic radical tradition in the early nineteenth century and civil rights and black power organizations in the early twentieth century. The black minister was highly praised for doing ministry comfortably within the traditional ritualistic expressions that have now become characteristic of the black church experience but was roundly criticized for absolving himself and the church of direct engagement with the forces of black oppression. In so doing, he became the most visible symbol of white control. The manipulation of black ministers in the independent black church would serve as a precursor to how the white power structure rewarded blacks who compromised the aspirations of black people.

> The black minister became a most devoted "Uncle Tom," the transmitter of white wishes, the admonisher of obedience to the caste system. He was the liaison man between the white power structure and the oppressed blacks, serving the dual function of assuring whites that all is well among his people. More than any other one person in the black community, the black minister perpetuated the white system of black dehumanization.[26]

Of course, the most celebrated black ministers hand-picked by white clergy to lead "independent" black churches were those that demonstrated a deep piety and a nonthreatening disposition to white privilege. Most White churches will pick and support black-skinned individuals (Negroes) who are the least threatening to the church's real position on issues relative to race.[27] White clergy were always looking to "recruit" black ministers that were young, charismatic, handsome, functionally illiterate and highly emotional in their preaching. This approach to ministry had the best chance to instill in black congregants an escapist understanding of Christian faith in the hopes of diverting black people's thoughts away from earthly freedom. The most effective means of accomplishing this was/is to prepare black ministers to entertain their congregants until judgment. In sum, indirect social control through a sophisticated Christian orthodoxy that frowned on social engagement, smiled on other-worldliness, and celebrated the religious individual has proved to be the most formidable obstacle to overcome in the quest for a fully liberated black humanity.

Notes

1.   See Chapter Five of Gayraud Wilmore's, *Black Religion and Black Radicalism: An Interpretation of the Religious History of African Americans.* 3/e. New York: Orbis Books, 1998. Originally published in 1973.

2.   In this regard, Lincoln constructs six dialectical categories for examining the black church: 1) priestly versus prophetic; 2) other-worldly versus this-worldly; 3) universalism versus particularize; 4) communal versus privatistic; 5) charismatic versus bureaucratic; and 6) resistance versus accommodation. See his, *Black Church in the African American Experience*, Durham, North Carolina: Duke University Press, 1990, 12ff.

3.   For an excellent account of this narrative and its impact on Christian faith in American history see Stephen R. Haynes, *Noah's Curse: The Biblical Justification of American Slavery.* New York: Oxford University Press, 2002.

4.   Taken from H. Shelton Smith, *In His Image But...Racism in Southern Religion: 1780-1910.* Durham: Duke University Press, 1972, 130.

5.   Ibid., 130-31.

6.   Ibid., 133.

7.   Ibid., 135.

8.   Eugene D. Genovese, *Roll, Jordan, Roll: The World the Slaves Made.* New York: Vintage Books, 1972, 184.

9.   Ibid., 166-67.

10.   Ibid., 167.

11.   Wilmore, *Black Religion and Black Radicalism*, 103.

12.   Ibid.

13.   Genovese, *Roll, Jordan, Roll*, 185.

14.   Winthrop Jordan, *The White Man's Burden: Historical Origins of Racism in the United States.* New York: Oxford University Press, 1974, 160-61.

15.   See Chapter Seven of *Black Religion and Black Radicalism.*

16.   Genovese, *Roll, Jordan, Roll*, 162.

17.   Ibid.

18.   Ibid., 165.

19.   James Cone, *A Black Theology of Liberation.* (Twentieth Anniversary Edition) New York: Orbis Books, 1990, 133.

20.   Taken from Delores S. Williams, *Sisters in the Wilderness: The Challenge of Womanist God-Talk.* New York: Orbis Books, 1993, 214.

21.   Ibid., 41-42.

22.   Taken from Ibid., 214.

23.   Ibid., 214-15.

24.   Robert L. Allen, *Black Awakening in Capitalist America.* Trenton, New Jersey: Africa World Press, 1990, 12.

25.   Ibid., 12-13.

26.   James Cone, *Black Theology and Black Power.* New York: Seabury Press, 1969, 105-06.

27.   Columbus Salley, Ronald Behm, *What Color Is your God: Black Consciousness and the Christian Faith.* New York: Citadel Press, 1988. 110.

9

The Last Things and the Black Things

When I faced a congregation, it began to take all the strength I had not to stammer, not to curse, not to tell them to throw away their Bibles and get off their knees and go home and organize, for example, a rent strike. When I watched all the children, their copper, beige, and brown faces staring up at me as I taught Sunday school, I felt that I was committing a crime in talking about the gentle Jesus, in telling them to reconcile themselves to their misery on earth in order to gain the crown of eternal life. Were only Negroes to gain this crown? Was Heaven, then, merely to be another ghetto?
James Baldwin, *The Fire Next Time*

No other doctrine in Christian theological reflection has descended into ideology more than that of eschatology. That has mainly to do with my contention that no other Christian theological doctrine is capable of descending into ideology more than eschatology. By ideology I mean the treatment by white theologians of the doctrine of eschatology, in this case, such that it places God's approval on black dehumanization and white privilege as a pretext for economic prosperity.

Meaning literally in English, the study of the last things, eschatology, in Christian tradition, maintains that when conceived in our mother's womb we are on an inescapable journey to either a life of eternal bliss (heaven) or eternal damnation (hell) after death. The two mediums by which eternal bliss is achieved in Christian history has primarily been through either justification by faith in God's grace in the atoning work of the Christ-event (Protestantism) or by good works in service to other humans and the church (Catholicism). To be sure, we have witnessed theological treatments that have sought a synthesis between these two mediums (of which the author advocates) but in both cases, the notion that there is "something" beyond the realm of human history and that this "something" consists of the extremes of wrath or reward is one of the more universally accepted understandings of Christian faith.

Yet, the dimension of eschatology that makes it such an easy target for ideology is that it is rooted more in a hope that physical death is not the end of life rather than its empirical affirmation through spatial concreteness. Put more simply, our assertions about what happens beyond physical death cannot be empirically verified and as the old saying goes, no one comes back from the dead to reveal to the living whether heaven and hell as we have conceived them actually exist. Precisely because it deals primarily with the metaphysical dimension of human existence, eschatology has been the most potent doctrine in convincing black people to accept their earthly lot in lieu of "the divine promise," of eternal bliss. With the goal by whites to make a life of earthly privilege by eternally subjugating black people, the use of Christian eschatology to "assure" eternal bliss for black people in exchange for a life of inhumane labor has indeed been an intelligent misuse of Christian faith. After all, what could be theologically more reasonable than to teach slaves that an inversely proportional relationship exists between the level of their earthly misery and the level of their heavenly reward. In this sense, white clergy and theologians were more readily able to place God's favor on black suffering in history by connecting it to God's ultimate design beyond history.

If social gospeler Walter Rauschenbusch is correct in his contention that any true eschatology must raise the two questions: 1) What is the future of the individual after his (her) brief span of years on this earth is over?; and 2) What is to be the ultimate destiny of the human race?[1] then white clergy and theologians constructed a viable eschatology of white supremacy. However oppressive, it satisfied both criteria. But precisely because white Christian eschatology was rooted in the oppression of black people as a legitimate dimension in the ultimate destiny of the human race, it undermines the notion that God is, "no respecter of persons," and affirms an eternity of earthly misery for black people.

To be sure, this eschatological approach was intimately connected with Christian piety and the religious exuberance of "knowing" one's ultimate destiny if one behaved properly. For slaves, this meant a religious exuberance demonstrated in not rebelling against the slavocracy and accepting one's dehumanized earthly lot as a just duty for entry into the kingdom of heaven. Indeed, religious exuberance came to be understood as an ecclesiastical expression of the assuredness by the slave that her ultimate destiny would be one of eternal bliss.

Moreover, the model for this disposition was Jesus himself. We have already discussed the ideological ramifications of a white-imaged Jesus on the psyche of the slaves, but added to this presentation of Jesus by white clergy and theologians was Jesus' disposition as well. That disposition, then and now, presents Jesus mainly as a mild-mannered, soft-spoken, passive, and, in some instances even, effeminate man who had very little regard for the transformation of human relationships and even less regard for oppressed people. Thus, the central figure of the faith was presented to slaves as the prototypical Christian whose behavior they should emulate without question if heaven was to be obtained. The fact that Jesus knew nothing of what we today call Christianity did not matter. The theory that Jesus was inaugurating a Christian worldview rooted in black obedience to its own dehumanization is what ultimately mattered. The Prince of Peace became literally an eschatological tranquilizer in making black dehumanization in service to white domination on earth a non-negotiable demand for a life of eternal bliss.

It is the height of irony that this was all white clergy and theologians could possibly offer slaves. Given that the slavocracy was to be an eternal earthly phenomenon, the reward for the slave for a lifetime of misery in the building of a white heaven on earth could only be a reward that transcended history. This fit the existential scheme of slaveholders well for a dead slave could no longer contribute to the slavocracy and could not, more important, come back to tell the slaves if the divine promise of heaven was fulfilled. Hence, slaveholding theology's insistence on the primacy of otherworldliness became the presupposition out of which a virulent eschatological treatment for black people was fashioned and established as orthodoxy in the life of the church.

Eschatology, Theology, and Black Dehumanization

Eschatology as a promised future reward for the individual has its origins in Greek culture. Greeks were deeply concerned about what they considered the disheartening inevitabilities of human existence. In particular, seemingly incessant conflicts between individuals and nations, living inescapably under the canopy of universal sin, and reckoning with one's own immortality produced an overwhelming sense of pessimism for earthly life. This made the eschatological dimension in Christian faith of acute import for the Greek worldview. The esoteric dimension of Greek religion regarding keys to better living, which was more prominent than Christian eschatology, provided a temporary fix to their existential angst. But this understanding of human destiny proved to be inadequate and soon gave way to the far more reasonable explanation as to why earthly life is filled with so much tragedy — the life of unrequited joy after physical death provided by Christian eschatology.

> Greek religion was characterized by a profound desire for immortality and an equally deep sense of the sin and sadness of this earthly life. The "mysteries" ministered to this desire; Christianity did it more effectively. In turn, these religious desires brought out and strengthened those eschatological facts and ideas in Christianity which could serve them. Here we have one chief cause for the increasing other-worldliness of Christianity.[2]

Greek religious leaders saw in this otherworldly eschatology literally a new lease on life and used their influence to promulgate its enhanced understanding of human destiny to the world.

Yet the most consistent commonality in the pursuit of an otherworldly approach to eschatology has, not surprisingly, emerged in the context of a people collectively enduring tremendous persecution. The Roman Empire's compromising of the Greek government, and its thorough oppressive hold on the dispensation of social, economic, and political justice created an existence of acute misery for its working class. A flight to a better life beyond a world of tremendous subjugation and socially accepted imperialism after death provided the only hope in what appeared to be a one-time life of human degradation.

> If we imagine a single empire today permanently holding the seas and continents in its grip, and enriching its aristocracy from the industry of others, with every way of escape barred, we shall understand the apathy of men (people) under the Roman Empire. The escape into immortality was the only way to freedom left to all.[3]

This persecution in the Roman Empire also extended to the early church until the conversion of Constantine further solidifying the significance of otherworldly eschatology for early Christians. Further, the tremendous persecution of the Jews in both biblical and contemporary history also contributed to increasing acceptability of an otherworldly eschatology. As Rauschenbusch reminds us, the common characteristic connecting these flights to heavenly bliss is not necessarily its reality but the social context of human oppression that left no hope for freedom in this world.

> Thus, eschatology has all along been influenced by social causes while keeping on its own conservative path of tradition. The Jewish people under social and political oppression and the primitive Church under persecution wept and prayed our eschatology into existence. Our Apocalypse is wet with human tears and must be read that way.[4]

The identification of an otherworldly eschatology for a persecuted community as a means of dealing with its unfavorable context provides us with a solid foundation with which to address the emergence of Christian eschatology in the colonies and America.

With precedence in Christian and Jewish history, it was not a far stretch for white clergy and theologians looking for an otherworldly eschatology to custom make such an eschatological treatment for African slaves. However, it did differ on two fronts from its predecessors. First, Christian faith itself was, in this context, more impositional than indigenous. Certainly, Christianity existed in Africa prior to European colonization but was not very prevalent in West Africa. Thus the exposure to Christian faith in America for the slaves was not only novel but oppressive in its intent. That is to say, Christianity was not chosen by slaves as a viable faith emerging out its cultural experience but was imposed on them by white clergy and theologians more interested in social control than with a genuine encounter with Jesus Christ. Second, given that Christian faith in this context was more impositional, white clergy and theologians were more intentional as to how they wanted their eschatological treatment to be understood by slaves. More particularly, white clergy and theologians wanted themselves and slaveholders to be looked upon by slaves as benevolent servants carrying out their mission to God rather than ruthless dictators. In the previous contexts, the concerns from the power elites in the Roman Empire and early Palestine had little regard as to how they wanted their dispossessed class to conceive of them or how the suffering of the dispossessed would parlay into eternal bliss in the world beyond. So, whether it was the New Jerusalem coming down from above or Apocalyptic visions of the destruction of the children of Satan and the, "last finally becoming the first," the dispossessed were free to construct their own theological visions of God's millennial activity both here and beyond.

Christianization of the slaves in America, however, was of a different breed. Given that the rationale for exposing slaves to Christian faith was for the slaveholding community to carry out what it understood to be the divine mandate for, "converting all souls to Christ," it was imperative that white clergy and theologians depict both history and beyond as part of God's eschatological reign. This meant, therefore, that eschatology's historical application should not be questioned by slaves despite the acute suffering they were enduring. It also meant that slaves should see slaveholders as benevolent human beings deeply concerned about their ultimate destiny. Paul's admonition that, "I consider that our present sufferings are not worth comparing with the glory that will be revealed in us," (Rom. 8:18) represented one of the main passages that gave white clergy and theologians the biblical foundation to convince slaves that they were only looking out for their eternal well-being and as such were the "good guys." It also made the construction of an eschatological model of otherworldliness a logical extension of biblical revelation — or at least appear that way!

Yet the pinnacle of otherworldly eschatology's usefulness for slaveholders had far more to do with this world than the next. For in conceiving of the millennial task in this way, white clergy and theologians were proverbially able to, "kill two birds with one stone," insofar as it perpetuated the slavocracy and provided a positive outcome for slaves who demonstrated the piety necessary for entry into heaven. Thus, white clergy and theologians felt obligated to teach slaves of the joys of heaven as a criterion of their own Christian duty especially since that joy occurred only after physical death.

The point of departure for this otherworldly eschatology was the contention by many white theologians that the slaves were more enslaved internally than externally. Yeoman effort on the part of the white Christian community to rid the savage Africans of their own demons was expected of God-fearing white Christians. Cotton Mather, a well-known white clergyman, insisted to whites that blacks were brothers in Christ and that whites should see their (blacks) Christian instruction as the epitome of service to God. "How canst thou Love thy Negro, and be willing to see him (her) ly under the Rage of Sin, and the Wrath of God?" proclaimed Mather, given that the slaves, "were more Slaves to Satan than they are to You."[5] Mather also insisted that this duty be carried out by whites until slaves had been successfully converted to the faith and thus freed from their demons of lust and desires of earthly freedom.

In particular, white clergy wanted to be clear in asserting that the freedom God has ordained for the slaves could only come by otherworldliness. This was just as imperative to be taught to whites as it was to be taught to the slaves. Whites then were duty-bound to teach an eschatology of otherworldliness to the slaves on two fronts. First, one's otherworld destiny, either heaven or hell, was to be seen as a divine punishment or reward for Christian obedience or the lack thereof. This extended not only to slaves but to the slaveholding community if it did not make every opportunity to bring slaves into the Christian fold.

> These pleas for faithfulness and compassion were backed by reference to divine punishment and reward. How could people call themselves Christians if they refused to offer the means of salvation to the poor slaves? Their "stupid Carelessness about Religion" and about their own souls largely accounted for the spiritual neglect of slaves. Those who withheld the means of mercy from slaves might find God withholding mercy from them.[6]

The Christianization of slaves in an eschatology of otherworldliness provided a purposive pedagogical element for white Christians in its quest for righteousness. But because it taught slaves that devotion to Jesus was synonymous with devotion to the slavocracy, it represents one of the more sinister dimensions of slaveholding theology.

This leads to the second point. Those slaveholders who did have a little remorse for the slave life from cradle to grave certainly were huge proponents of connecting the divine reward of after life with the life of toil here on earth. That is to say, some slaveholders were convinced that the most effective eschatology was one that made entry into heaven after death synonymous with how well they labored for whites. In this way, those remorseful slaveholders could continue to get high worker productivity from the slaves and at the same time ease their conscious concerning the denial of basic services and full human participation in society to blacks. Bishop Edmund Gibson refers to this as *compensation for unrequited service* and provides further explanation:

> Since slaves are so unhappy in this world, "it would be the very highest cruelty in anyone to deny them the use of those means which might advance them to a State of Happiness in the other." Forcing them into maximum misery in the present world heightens the obligation "to put them into as advantageous situation as we are able with regard to another."[7]

In a twist of irony, slaveholder's penchant to want to compensate the slaves in some way for their unrecognized contribution to the economic prosperity of whites actually formed the seminal basis of otherworldly eschatology in the colonies and America. A sharing of the wealth produced by slaves during their earthly lives was certainly not an option! The much better route was to make the quality of work on earth as a slave a significant criterion for divine reward after physical death. In so doing, white clergy and slaveholders were able to perpetuate white privilege on earth and at the same time render slaves the ultimate reward – salvation in God's kingdom.

This understanding of eschatology quickly made its way into the fabric of American life. Slaves were reminded in all facets of American life that their destiny had long been determined by God to include an earthly reality of servanthood to whites. Further, slaves were also reminded that their lot was of the behest of God and therefore sinful to attempt to change through insurrection. For instance, the judge in the Denmark Vesey insurrection of 1822 sentenced Vesey to death for trying to undermine the, "divine influence of the Gospel," which was, "to reconcile us to our destinies on earth."[8] Further, in 1829 Charles Cotesworth Pinckney maintained in a speech that the slaves could endure hard work only if he (she) believes it is temporary and/or that good Christian behavior will guarantee, "superior rewards in that which is future and eternal."[9] As a significant corollary to this eschatology, slaveholders were then given a theological license by white clergy and theologians to work their slaves mercilessly "knowing" that God will grant slaves a life of eternal bliss when they were through with this world.

In a strong sense, white clergy and theologians' ability to sell this eschatological approach to the slave had to do with the level of misery on earth and its polar opposite — unrequited bliss in heaven after death. That is to say, the misery needed to subject the slaves to merciless toil to build a kingdom of heaven on earth for whites was the point of departure for convincing slaves that their heavenly reward would mirror the level of their earthly misery. Save for black revolutionaries in each generation, this made for a convincing theological sell to many slaves, and given the level of that human misery, slaves found themselves internalizing this eschatological approach for fear that it may be true and they did not want to miss out on heaven after death through a slothful work ethic or insurrectionist activity. Surely no God-fearing slave would want to jeopardize his (her) passage through the pearly gates to meet Sweet Jesus and to see his (her) loved one again.[10] This suffering on earth included not only "fair" punishment but unfair punishment for the slave as well.

In 1840, a white preacher named John Mason told a group of slaves that they should not complain if they were wrongly punished because God, "will reward you for it in heaven, and the punishment you suffer unjustly here, shall turn to your exceeding great joy, hereafter." Did not sweet Jesus himself say, "Blessed are they which are persecuted for righteousness' sake: for theirs is the kingdom of heaven?"[11]

Every effort was made by white ministers to convince slaves that there was actually something salvifically beneficial about their enslaved status. Referred to by Whitefield as the, "Sense of their natural misery," the implicit theological suggestion is that black people were actually made by God to be slaves and are best equipped to handle the physical and psychological rigors of slavery.

What was fundamentally at stake for both slaves and slaveholders was how Christian eschatology's provision for human freedom would be determined. Theologically and biblically, Christian faith had universally been interpreted in every generation of its existence as a faith of human freedom. What is still in debate even today is what Christian freedom looks like. Slaves were buoyed by the sense of liberty that Christian faith provided but were also dealing with a slaveholding community that had instructed them that the freedom that Christian faith promises is one of spiritual rather than physical freedom. This dichotomy in the way freedom is interpreted has been a theological source of huge debate in American life and the black Christian community. The hypocrisy is that there has always been public debate and in churches as it relates to black Christian freedom. White freedom was a theological and anthropological given.

On the one hand, some slaves interpreted Christian freedom as this-worldly as well as otherworldly. While they accepted Paul's dualistic theology between spirit and flesh, they were moved by the Old Testament prophetic books and Moses' heroic deed to liberate Israel from Egypt at the call of God. So, for some slaves, Christian freedom did entail some type of earthly freedom. On the other hand, the complexity of Christian freedom, particularly when coupled with the notion by white clergy that the attempt to free themselves from the slavocracy resulted in a rebuking of God's providence, provided the slave with an intense theological dilemma. The question was never whether Christian faith called for human freedom. The question has always been, does Christian freedom entail earthly freedom and if so, in what way? Is it then a violation of divine will for someone in human bondage to seek freedom from that bondage or is that bondage the bondage of responsibility to God that black people must all obey? In structuring the argument in this way, white clergy conveniently made the question of Christian obedience one of racial obedience as well.

What we have is a variation of the same theme. The root of American Christian theology is primarily concerned, ironically, with the earth and not heaven and is only concerned about the latter as an ideology for increasing slave productivity. As such, we have been governed theologically in American history by a Christian eschatology that Peter Berger has termed American religiosity. Its roots: Protestant theology.

We suspect that it is a theological task in our situation to elaborate the eschatological character of Christian faith against the this-worldliness of American religiosity, to set justification by faith against our pervasive legalism, to explain the meaning of the cross in a culture that glorifies success and happiness. And we would argue . . . that such an understanding of the Christian faith will of necessity lead at least to a measure of alienation from the culture.[12]

Berger highlights the two most significant components of Christian eschatology in American history: 1) it is the linchpin of a larger white Christian theology that was/is primarily concerned about this world and the economic prosperity of whites; and 2) it "demanded" that whites severely punish those who attempted to reform American life. Its effectiveness in the minds of slaves is evident in this testimony from John Atkinson who defied all odds and escaped from a Norfolk, Virginia plantation to freedom in Canada. Atkinson is poignant in his assessment when he declares that, "A man who has been in slavery and knows, and no one else can know, the yearnings to be free, and the fear of making the attempt. It is like trying to get religion, and not seeing the way to escape condemnation."[13] Hence, slaves who dared try to escape not only wrestled with the slaveholding posses that were trying to recapture them but also, because of white Christian pedagogy, wrestled with the inner demons that haunted their religious psyche regarding the possible breach of trust in God's providence.

Christian eschatology in American life created the desired struggle between the slave's outward and inward conditions placing ultimate emphasis on the slave's soul rather than her body. In so doing, Christian eschatology serves as one of the most virulent ideologies in American history in divorcing the slave's physical condition from her spiritual condition and placing ultimate emphasis publicly on otherworldliness while the intent was to fortify whites position as a superior race in this world.

In the realm of power, Christianity has operated with an unmitigated arrogance and cruelty — necessarily, since a religion ordinarily imposes on those who have discovered the true faith the spiritual duty of liberating the infidels. This particular true faith, moreover, is more deeply concerned about the soul than it is about the body, to which fact the flesh (and the corpses) of countless infidels bears witness.[14]

Baldwin is penetrating in his critique of the soul-flesh dialectic and its use in creating the so-called "true faith" to which all unenlightened "infidels" must submit in order to share in God's millennial reign.

In the final analysis, Christian eschatology in America was a most effective theological construction that has served Western European humanity well in its mission to subvert people of color and women in a racial and gender stratified society that sought control not only of bodies but of land as well. Land that was not flowing with milk and honey and the sprawling lawns of the banks of the Jordan River but the land of this world and control over its most precious resources. Thus, for all its emphasis on otherworldliness, the European conquest of people of color was a conquest of incomparable avarice and greed for the resources of this world that not only sought God's favor but, in borrowing from a prominent Reformation theme, confirmed God's favor on whiteness through the overwhelming success of the conquests.

> Priests and nuns and schoolteachers helped to protect and sanctify the power that was so ruthlessly being used by people who were indeed seeking a city, but not one in the heavens, and one to be made, very definitely, by captive hands. The Christian church itself — again, as distinguished from some of its ministers, sanctified and rejoiced at the conquests of the flag, and encouraged, if it did not formulate, the belief that conquest, with the resulting relative well-being of the Western populations, was proof of the favor of God.[15]

Christian eschatology in America cannot and should not be divorced from the this-worldliness of black dehumanization. Such an eschatological treatment served as a necessary process for whites to demonstrate their chosen status by God. Dominion and rule over the earth clearly meant white male racial dominion with the other races and women sharing the existential abyss of being higher than lower animals but certainly not higher than white males. The doctrine of the last things meant in American history the doctrine of the earthly dehumanization of black people who had been reduced to a subhuman status or "the black things." An examination of Christian eschatology's impact on the American church in the creation of, "the black things," is worth our attention.

Eschatology, The Church and Black Dehumanization

In the creation of any oppressive theocracy that is Christian-based, the church is needed to teach and to practically express the goals of that theocracy to its congregants and citizens. Not only did white clergy see no inherent moral contradiction between a church consisting of power elites and subjects, most maintained that it was precisely the job of the church to perpetuate this relationship between whites and blacks as the essence of divine activity.

Having transitioned the slaves from the white church to independent black churches, white clergy were concerned about whether black ministers would continue to espouse an otherworldly eschatology and to maintain the cleavage between the soul and the body. The dilemma this produced in slaves is, to the extent they could still remember their West African religious roots, no separation existed between the soul and the body or the natural and the supernatural.

> African religions know nothing of a rigid demarcation between the natural and the supernatural. All of life is permeated with forces or powers in some relationship to human weal or woe. Individuals are required, for their own sake and that of the community, to affirm this world of spirit the merges imperceptibly with the immediate, tangible environment. One enters into communion with this other reality in a prescribed way to receive its benefits and avoid its penalties.[16]

Although African religions subscribed to the notion of divine benefits and penalties, they also taught that we are already living in God's eschatological reign. That is to say, human life and everything in the universe are sacred in its divine construction. One need not wait on God's reward/punishment until death — one is already living in the midst of it.

Yet, when West African people's geographic location and social status changed, so would their eschatology. They became the principle subjects of an impositional Christian faith by white clergy and slaveholders that made them the lowest form of human being on earth, and whites the ideal form of humanity as exemplified in the whiteness of Jesus himself. Thus, religion became not a God thing but a white thing making whiteness the source of earthly dominion. When blacks were "independently" churched by white clergy, maintaining control over black people through religion was the linchpin in perpetuating a racist theocracy. This meant, for white clergy, making sure that the theological emphasis in worship services took on more of an otherworldly rather than this-worldly tenor. This made (and makes!), then, the eschatological dimension of Christian faith the most significant dimension in the life of the church. The logic is clear: if whites could keep blacks spied on heaven rather than earth, it would not only divert black people's attention away from its earthly oppression but it would go a long way in creating theological enmity between black preachers and insurrectionist leaders. Given the options of preaching this doctrine publicly to its congregations or not having "independent" churches, most black ministers, who not surprisingly were handpicked by white clergy, yielded to this understanding of eschatology. While some black ministers publicly preached this doctrine in the presence of white clergy with an understood double-meaning between him and his congregation of something more liberating, some black ministers also openly accepted it and preached it with all earnest. In so doing, it laid the foundation for a contemporary understanding of the church today regarding the enthusiastic response that otherworldly language receives. Targeting white missionaries as the primary culprits, James Cone puts it rather succinctly:

> The most corrupting influence among many black churches was their adoption of the "white lie" that Christianity is primarily concerned with otherworldly reality. White missionaries persuaded most black religious people that life on earth was insignificant because obedient servants of God could expect a "reward" in heaven after death. As one might expect, obedience meant adherence to the laws of white masters. Most black people accepted the white interpretation of Christianity, which divested them of the concern they might have had about their freedom in the present.[17]

With the next world established as the primary concern for black Christians, slaveholders and white clergy were well on their way to establishing a racist theocracy and black acceptance of it as a requirement for divine communion with God. This, no doubt, had a tremendous affect on the black church's understanding of earthly reality and certainly many black ministers joining with white clergy in condemning acts of black racial advancement as un-Christian.

The eschatological theme of otherworldliness became a major tenet of Christian orthodoxy particularly at the end of the nineteenth century and into the era of the black church's deradicalization according to Wilmore. The significance of this development lies in the realization that even though the institution of slavery had been abolished, black people were still living under the auspices of a racist theocracy in American life. So prominent was the otherworldly tenor of black worship and overall worldview that it caught the attention of Swiss sociologist Gunnar Myrdal. He perceptibly observed the tenor and language of black churches while at the same time recognized its potential to be a powerful force for black liberation:

> Potentially, the Negro church is undoubtedly a power institution. It has the Negro masses organized and, if the church bodies decided to do so, they could line up the Negroes behind a program. Actually, the Negro church is, on the whole, passive in the field of intercaste power relations. It generally provides meeting halls and encourages church members to attend when other organizations want to influence the Negroes. But viewed as an instrument of collective action to improve the Negroes' position in American society, the church has been relatively inefficient and uninfluential.[18]

That inefficiency and lack of influence has not been realized by chance. The primary, if not sole reason, for introducing slaves to Christian faith and Christian eschatology in particular by white clergy was to produce this type of theological conscience in the black church community. Hence, the call to Christian faith for blacks was also the call to social control. Many black ministers were convinced that their duty as a servant of Christ no longer entailed the socio-political liberation of black people but simply the saving of the black person's soul. Otherworldliness and the soul of the religious individual now trumped the slave's body and the larger community's struggle for racial emancipation and made the black minister one of the most outspoken opponents of black progress in America. Myrdal sees this more as an ideologically falling off rather than an ideological difference:

> The Negro church has been lagging ideologically, too. While for a long time the protest has been rising in the Negro community, the church has, on the whole, remained conservative and accommodating. Its traditions from slavery help to explain this. Its other-worldly outlook is itself an expression of political fatalism.[19]

Myrdal rightly identifies an otherworldly eschatology as the defining criterion that has made the black church an historical opponent of black social progress on two fronts: 1) if heaven is where our ultimate gift from God lies, then why seek social reform on earth; and 2) God has given black Christians the duty of impressing upon other blacks that efforts at social reform may land one in hell rather than heaven. Thus, outside of a few committed churches in each generation, the black church's theological conservatism, an intentional creation by the white Christian establishment, has proudly placed itself on the periphery of racial advancement in America or has incorporated black freedom into its theological outlook but maintains that it is a process in which, "we should let the Lord handle." On this point, Myrdal rightly recognizes black flight to heaven in its religious expression as a major contributor to unprogressive piety. But more important, he locates the establishment of an otherworldly ethos in the church as a representative theological understanding of the black community over the whole.

> When discussing the Negro church as it is and as it might come to be, it must never be forgotten that *the Negro church fundamentally is an expression of the Negro community itself.* If the church has been other-worldly in outlook and indulged in emotional ecstasy, it is primarily because the downtrodden Negroes have craved religious escape from poverty and other tribulations. If the preachers have been timid and pussyfooting, it is because Negroes in general have condoned such a policy and would have feared radical leaders.[20]

Moreover, the language produced in the pulpit to reinforce this thinking also became the orthodox thought of blacks who did not attend church regularly but who may have grown up in the church and uncritically accepted its orthodox teachings.

Myrdal's analysis, however accurate, did not go far enough in recognizing the power of orthodoxy itself in fashioning the religious conscience of a community. Black ministers did not resist black reform movements because they were trying to be an irritant to black leaders. They were doing it for the most part because it was/is a manifestation of their religious sincerity. They uncritically inherited a theological tradition that frowned on movements of human transformation from white ministers as the only true way of being Christian in the world. Most were truly convinced of this not only because of the mothers and fathers of the church who taught them this but also that the conservative nature of Christian pedagogy itself was such that one should never question what is being taught. As stated earlier, the white church was highly influential in making sure that the earthly emphasis of both churches, despite a higher emotional exuberance in black churches, reflected individualism, material success, sexual (but not racial!) morality, and a deep mistrust for progressive movements and organizations. When combined with black people's growing admiration of white culture from the mid-nineteenth century onwards, the black church began to define its success in terms of how well it could imitate the social customs and styles of the white churches, particularly as it relates to joining a church with a prominent pastor known more for his affiliations with safe charities rather than his courageous activism. It is difficult to know which has priority (social class or which church one attends) but from what is known about the white church's distrust of social radicalism, it should not surprise us that orthodox Christianity played some role in pacifying black Christians when their churches were trying to imitate the theology and lifestyle of the mainline white denominations.[21] This orthodox Christian mentality stems directly from the conservative nature of Christian theological reflection itself in the colonies and then America and the otherworldly emphasis of Christian eschatology in particular. This is why the call to Christian faith in American history was never a call to genuine righteousness. It certainly was never a legitimate call to a life of eternal bliss given its inability to be verified empirically. The call to Christian faith was, both in intent and effect, a call to black quietism in the name of God and Jesus. The intent was never to make black people true human beings but to maintain an earthly reality of white racial privilege and make black people comfortable with their dehumanized status. The sojourn of black people in America has brought about death and death more abundantly rather than life and life more abundantly and white Christian eschatology sits at the core of one of the most sinister theological treatments in human history. It has made many a black Christian comfortable with the quid pro quo of earthly misery for heavenly reward.

The name of Jesus itself became a source of comfort for many black Christians rather than a model of earthly change. This has in large part to do with Jesus being presented to black Christians as a *socially unconcerned pietist*. As such, white Christian eschatology had accomplished its task with many black Christians using Jesus' name as a source of emotional ecstasy to get through a life of earthly misery in patient wait for the eschaton:

> The contrast between white treatment of black people as things and God's view of them as persons is so great that it is easy for blacks to think that God has withdrawn from history and the "devil" has taken over. Black people begin to affirm that if one has "Jesus," it does not matter whether there is injustice, brutality, and suffering. Jesus thus becomes a magical name which gives the people a distorted hope in another life. Through identification with a name, unbearable suffering becomes bearable.[22]

Through the ideological treatment of Christian eschatology, a genuine approach to Christian eternity serves as a front for black people's acceptance of its earthly lot, particularly as it relates to the teaching that participation in movements to improve black status in America is ungodly. This is why the black church has historically been an opponent rather than a proponent of black earthly change. Whether it was because the notion of earthly change was not a God-desired goal for blacks or whether it was that God would bring about that change Godself, the notion of sustained human involvement in social reform has never really made its way into either white or black churches in American history. Given the way Christian faith has been taught in American history, this should come as no surprise. But more important, this should come as no surprise because of the way Christian eschatology has been taught in American history. Cone again explains:

> Instead of seeking to change the earthly state, they focus their hopes on the next life in heaven. In reality, this is not the perspective of the biblical faith but, rather, an expression of a hopeless faith which cannot come to terms with the reality of this world.[23]

An expression of this hopeless faith provides two examples. Henry Atkinson, a slave voiced the sentiment of many slaves when he proclaimed: "I was a member of the First Baptist Church, I heard the white minister preach, and I thought within myself, I will seek a better world — here I am in bondage, and if there is a better world above, where I shall not be pulled and hauled about and tormented, as I am in this [world], I will seek it."[24] Moreover, a former slave during an interview reflecting on his life made this admission: "As I look back over it now, I don't wonder that I felt as I did. I just gave up all earthly hopes and thought all the time about the next life."[25] While Raboteau points out the complexity of black religious belief in the slavocracy and the ways in which black people dealt with an earthly reality of such acute misery, one has also to register the large accommodationist leaning through the slave experience and Christian eschatology as a major influence in shaping black people's views of this world.

Yet, Professor Cone has touched on the fact above that this is not biblical faith but white supremacist ideology masquerading as Christian faith. The biblical faith is affirmative of abundant life in this world and not just the next world. It depicts Jesus as a liberator, not just one who tolerates earthly injustice. It depicts Jesus as one who comes, "to make the first, last and the last, first." In that regard the eschaton is inclusive of human history and not just one's otherworldly destiny. An eschatological treatment true to its nature is inclusive of both body and soul, earth and heaven. It does not frown on socio-political transformation but encourages it through the life of Jesus himself. The biblical revelation gives us a Jesus who was not mild-mannered and pious. Rather, a Jesus is revealed who is primarily concerned about the poor, the plight of his people, and exposing human inequities in first century Palestine. This is why for Cone:

> An eschatological perspective that does not challenge the present order is faulty. If contemplation about the future distorts the present reality of injustice and reconciles the oppressed to unjust treatment committed against them, then it is unchristian and thus has nothing whatsoever to do with the Christ who came to liberate us. It is this that renders white talk about heaven and life after death fruitless for blacks.[26]

It makes life after death fruitless for blacks because it robs many blacks of a more humane treatment of Christian faith relative to its own death-like existence and puts the black church at odds with black leadership championing the cause of black freedom. More important, it makes a mockery of Christian faith by placing its efficacy exclusively in the realm of the unknown rather than the known existence in which we currently reside. As such, an otherworldly eschatology divides the church community from efforts for socio-political freedom in this world by glorifying a "wait on the Lord," ethic and placing all of black people's eggs in the basket of the final judgment.

> Eschatology has been interpreted as a reward to those who remain obedient. In this view, the resurrection of Christ means that salvation is now completed, finished. This explains why the churches look at the world not as a place to die but to live piously and prudently in preparation for the future. If one thinks that Christ's work is finished, then there is nothing to do but wait for the Second Coming.[27]

This means that a true eschatology, for Cone, must also conceive of the Second Coming (Parousia) as being in process throughout human history rather than as a two-time historical event of resurrection and second coming. This point is crucial. By conceiving of eschatology in historical terms through oppressed peoples and not in ethereal terms through Christ alone, an exclusively otherworldly eschatology is made suspect at best and theologically damaging at worst. The latter model (ethereal through Christ alone), has been operative throughout American history, and has spiritually compromised whites and blacks by locking both into counterproductive expressions of humanity through the legitimation of racial caste. With this eschatological model, collective human sin as the eternalizing of black dehumanization emerges not because of human fallenness but because of divine will. In so doing, an exclusively otherworldly eschatology makes a cosmic liar out of not only whites obsessed with maintaining the status quo but also of Jesus and God. While it reaffirms that our theological concepts arise out of a limited and culturally conditioned history, it also represents the worst of the human spirit in not engaging in a critical assessment of those cultural precepts as it relates to human equality. But more important, it perpetuates the notion that humans must affirm their humanity in a superior way by making someone else different in aesthetic presentation, gender or religious persuasion inferior. Not only have avarice and greed won out over moral turpitude but even moral turpitude itself has come to be understood within the context of racial and gender superiority. Thus humans become dispensable to themselves across racial and gender lines in the drive for economic prosperity even petitioning God and Jesus as inaugurators of the reign of white racial stratification. In this regard, Christian faith in America has been the most prominent sponsor of the legitimacy of a racist theocracy.

Notes

1. *A Theology for the Social Gospel.* Nashville: Abingdon Press, 1990, 208. (Originally published in 1917)
2. Ibid., 212.
3. Ibid., 213.
4. Ibid., 215.
5. Lester Scherer, *Slavery and the Churches in Early America: 1619-1819.* Grand Rapids, Michigan: Eerdman's Publishing Company, 1975, 88.
6. Ibid.
7. Taken from Ibid., 89.
8. Taken from Forrest G. Wood, *The Arrogance of Faith: Christianity & Race in American from the Colonial Era to the Twentieth Century.* Boston: Northeastern University Press, 1990, 77.
9. Taken from Ibid.
10. Ibid., 81.
11. Ibid., 82-83.
12. Peter L. Berger, *The Noise of Solemn Assemblies: Christian Commitment and the Religious Establishment in America.* Garden City, New York: Doubleday & Company, Incorporated, 1961, 133.
13. Taken from Albert J. Raboteau, *Slave Religion: The Invisible Institution in the Antebellum South.* New York: Oxford University Press, 1978, 304-05.
14. James Baldwin, *The Fire Next Time.* New York: Dell Publishing Company, 1962, 65.
15. Ibid., 66.
16. Gayraud Wilmore, *Black Religion and Black Radicalism: An Interpretation of the Religious History of African Americans.* (3rd ed., rev., enl.). New York: Orbis Books, 1998, 37. (Originally published in 1973)
17. James Cone, *Black Theology & Black Power.* New York: Seabury Press, 1969, 121.
18. Gunnar Myrdal, *An American Dilemma: Volume Two.* New York: McGraw-Hill Book Company, 1964, 873. (Originally published in 1944)
19. Ibid., 876.
20. Ibid., 877.
21. Wilmore, *Black Religion and Black Radicalism,* 170.
22. Cone, *Black Theology & Black Power,* 122.
23. Ibid., 123.
24. Raboteau, *Slave Religion,* 303.
25. Ibid., 304.
26. Cone, *A Black Theology of Liberation.* (Twentieth Anniversary Edition). New York: Orbis Books, 1990, 137. (Originally published in 1970)
27. Ibid., 139.

10

The Twilight of a Racist Theocracy

Between the Christianity of this land, and the Christianity of Christ, *I recognize the widest possible difference* — so wide, that to receive the one as good, pure and holy, is of necessity to reject the other as bad, corrupt, and wicked. . . . I love the pure perceivable and impartial Christianity of Christ: I therefore hate the corrupt, slaveholding, women-whipping, cradle-plundering, partial and hypocritical Christianity of this land. Indeed, I can see no reason, but the most deceitful one, for calling the religion of this land Christianity. I look upon it as the climax of all misnomers, the boldest of all frauds, and the grossest of all libels.

Frederick Douglass, *Narrative of the Life of Frederick Douglass: An American Slave*

Douglass' rage concerning the black condition in America and the adverse effects slaveholding Christianity has had on the theological psyche of black people is a scathing but justified assessment of the way Christian faith has been practiced in American history. Christian faith has been anything but charitable to black people and, along with white supremacy, has been the hand-maiden of black dehumanization in American history. In short, Christian faith in American history has been demonic in both its intent and application. This is what led David Walker, in his classic, *The Appeal*, to raise the rhetorical question, Can anything be a greater mockery of religion than the way in which it is conducted by the Americans?[1]

Douglass' and Walker's disdain for the practice of Christian faith in American history is no doubt directed towards the unconscionable act of invoking the name of God as a means of establishing the dehumanization of black people as not only an American norm but a fundamental moral precept of Christian faith itself. By inference, then, white clergy and theologians were not only establishing Christian faith as conceiving of God's gratuitous love as white privilege in every arena of American life but were also establishing black dehumanization as a corollary of that love.

Far more incredulous was the notion that black people had been dealt this hand by God for acute sinfulness in Africa and were given this opportunity for redemption in American slavery if and only if they were obedient in their enslavement. Thus, God had given black people over to white enslavement for civilization and redemption. In linking the goals of white supremacy with the essence of divine activity, the foundation of a racist theocracy had been firmly established in American history.

As we have tried to establish with this work, the call to God and Christian faith in America for black people was never intended to be a call to authentic fellowship with God. It was designed to neutralize their revolutionary fervor for freedom from the slavocracy. This is why white clergyman Samuel Davies saw as imperative to the slavocracy's survival bringing slaves, "under the restraints of the *pacific* religion of Jesus."[2] Indeed, Christian faith in American history has been primarily concerned with instilling in black people a pacific disposition relative to slavery and more tragically getting the slave to understand this disposition as God ordained. As a result, Christian faith in America has been an inauthentic faith not in its universal legitimacy but in its historical application. Christian faith's appropriation in American history has been rooted in angst about black uprisings more than an authentic relationship with God and with other human beings. It has taken the, "all are one in Christ Jesus," proclamation of Paul and stood it on its head by glorifying racial and gender stratification and conceiving of God's favor on humans not because of their actions but because of their race. Hence, Christian faith's biggest contribution to America has been its ability to be a function of social control for black people by convincing a good number that Christian faith is primarily an otherworldly religion and that working for socio-political liberation is anathema to God.

In order to accomplish this task, white Christian leaders have been very intentional in constructing an approach to faith that divorces the life of faith from socio-political reform with great success. It has convinced many black and white Christians that the God of Christian faith has constructed the current society and is not interested in an America of racial and gender equality but interested in an America of white privilege. While one can see racial progress in America despite the advocacy of a racist theocracy, there still is yet another dimension to the perpetuation of a racist theocracy that still haunts American life. In conceiving of Christian faith as being divorced from socio-political change, and in the age of deradicalization (Wilmore), Christian faith in America continues to be uncommitted to true social change and continues to give more attention to issues of sexual morality, institutional maintenance, women's subordination in the church as well as society, and a deeply entrenched individualism. I intentionally structured the previous chapters on the slavocracy and its immediate aftermath to not only demonstrate to the reader how entangled Christian faith was with white supremacy but to also show that even from then to now the commitment to divorcing religion from the social terrain of American life (except to denounce social reform movements!) continues to be the de facto agenda of ecclesiastical life in America.

The twilight of a racist theocracy, then, is more a hope on my part rather than a reality. Yet a racist theocracy's existence and destruction begin necessarily with one's conception of God.

The God That Oppresses a Nation

A racist theocracy needs a God whose will is synonymous with national law and order. That not only means a God that sanctions the laws of that nation but a God who sanctions the punishment of those who violate those laws. That becomes particularly imperative in a nation that establishes a racially stratified order as its primary reason for existing and that constructs laws to maintain that order. A God is needed that is sovereign and whose will mirrors the laws of an oppressive nation. Given the understanding of divine wisdom as infinite and human wisdom as limited, most Christians have been taught, either directly or indirectly, to look upon American life, no matter the particulars of our lot, as God's purpose for us and that this purpose is eternally binding. For a racist theocracy in this country that has meant the establishment of divine favor on white authority.

After God had been "created" in the way of white racial privilege, Christian faith's primary function in American history has been to establish racial hegemony as divine wisdom. A nation that has publicly touted the virtues of democracy has been busy constructing laws that favored whites and that reduced black people to chattel. That this national way of life came to be characterized as a logical theological extension of the mind of God by white Christian leaders made it all the more diabolical (and believable!). Christian faith had come to serve the agenda of white racists and in so doing represented the diametric opposite of Jesus' concern for the poor. With God signed on to a white racial hierarchy, black dehumanization became the norm in both American daily life and in Christian theology. Peter Berger clearly identifies this ideological function of Christian theology in American history:

> Religion in itself is commonly an agency of social control, internalizing within the individual the norms of society, providing him (her) with the psychological mechanisms of guilt and repentance which enable society to get along with a minimal apparatus of external controls. Since our cultural religion ratifies and sanctions the general value system, it naturally has this function within itself as well.[3]

This represents a prime example as to how a community's cultural values shape that community's religious values. Berger is rightly establishing that the sin-redemption dialectic, so crucial to Christian theology in its ideologically co-opted form in American life, has produced a faith-oriented guilt in black people for challenging the legitimacy of oppressive laws that came to be equated with divine laws. In this way, Christian theology itself becomes the most potent ethical agent of black oppression aiding slaveholders with controlling slaves and after the slavocracy aiding America's law enforcement constituencies in the suppression of black self-determination.

More to the point, Christian leadership in America has been indoctrinated into an approach to faith that has served the interests of white power elites by serving the coercive function of black pacifism as divine mandate. By inference, then, the achievement of black humanity as the highest folly has served as the cornerstone of this racist theocracy. Berger puts it in more structural terms:

> It [cultural religion] reinforces and supports the coercive machinery of the state itself and, in turn, for specific ends, seeks to use this machinery for its own purposes. To put this in graphic picture — the same government budget that builds the walls of penitentiaries provides the salary of the prison chaplain. And, as any convict will tell you, the clergy are normally on the side of the cops — at least those of our middle-class Protestant churches.[4]

Berger makes clear the collusion that exists between American life and American religious life regarding the divine approval by white Christian leadership for black dehumanization. In other words, Christian faith in American history has been what racist power brokers have needed it to be — an ultimately meaningful phenomenon to Christians that either does not address issues of collective human domination or that condones collective human domination as divine will. In the first scenario, Christian faith becomes an agent of theological naiveté, keeping both black and white Christians in an individualistic, otherworldly box. In the second scenario, Christian faith becomes an agent of human repression, making the dehumanization of black people the norm in American life, sentencing black people to passive resignation concerning its lot in American life and making the eschaton the time for change. So it was that from the beginning the American nation under God showed no serious concern for either the spiritual or political needs of the black wards fetched from Africa.[5]

Now that God had been "created" as the Master Racist, a national daily life had to be created that reflected that nation's understanding of God. It began with the racial coloring of Calvin's notion of the elect of God. That is to say, Calvin's notion that an elect is chosen by God when one enters the womb of her mother was ideologically co-opted in American Christianity to mean that God had elected only white people for salvation. Further, Calvin's assertion that the elect exemplify that calling with the way they live their lives fit well with white people who seemingly had everything both materially and spiritually. This went a long way in convincing both blacks and whites that this was, in fact, God's plan for American life. The co-opting of Calvin's notion of the elect through a racial lens brought about a much-needed pretext for establishing white dominance as the norm in American life. It established a prototypical significance of whiteness racially and the perfect backdrop to the creation of a racially separated society for fear of being tainted by the black un-elected!

> In both America and South Africa, the epidermal evidence "spoke" with unam-biguous force. It enjoined social and psychological segregation. The elect sought to protect themselves against the possibility of perversion and pollution at every turn. At the same time, given Calvin's limitation of the precept of sal-vation to those who had some alliance or affinity with Christians, *white culture*, in effect, became identified with both the defense of faith and the demographics of health. It established the borderline of both spiritual and material certainty. Only within whiteness was one's existence secure.[6]

With that secure existence came the unquestioned right to create a worldview with the backing of Christian faith and God. But more important, that secure existence brought with it an unhindered authority to create a national religious approach that seeks to create meaning in faith that would not challenge that au-thority. Slave patrols and later law enforcement served as social and psychologi-cal reminders of the authority of whiteness for black "rabble-rousers" but Chris-tian faith by far was the most potent ideological weapon in providing a theologi-cal palliative for black social control. It created ultimate meaning in life while conveniently not addressing the very issues that kept black people in a state of subjugation. This allotted for the creation of Christians of "strong" faith that were both slaveholders and slaves without reconciling the apparent contradiction between Jesus' commitment to the destruction of human divisions of superior and inferior worth and being a follower of Jesus.

To be sure, this approach to Christian faith has easily detectable dimen-sions. Arguably, its most virulent dimension is that it placed primary emphasis on the religious individual. In so doing, both black and white Christians would come to understand the efficacy of faith manifesting itself only in the individual realm and not in the collective realm of human existence. While the significance of fellowship in a church community was certainly emphasized, personal rela-tionships with God were/are the norm for the Christian life. While the signifi-cance of the religious individual owes itself seminally to the Reformation tradi-tion, it also represents another ideological co-opting of a significant Reformation theme reinterpreted to protect white privilege. The logic is that it divorces God from the racial struggle of black affirmation insofar as God was only concerned about the religious individual within the context of a church community. When coupled with the idea of American democracy and the ability to accomplish any individual goal through hard work, both a political and theological foundation for individual achievement began to cement itself in American life. In particular,

the Awakenings of the mid-eighteenth century did more from a Christian standpoint to establish the significance of the religious individual than any other
movement in American history:

> In its "Great Awakenings," the emerging social order can be said to have be-
> come the "national" site of an increasingly localized quest for fulfillment.
> Those developments both fostered and furthered the narrowing of the scope of
> salvation to the individual. American frontier ideals of independence and self-
> sufficiency merely solemnized the shrinkage as "virtue."[7]

The shrinkage was indeed of paramount significance. What was sought by white
clergy and theologians was the establishment of a normative approach to faith
that produced ultimate satisfaction (particularly emotionally!) while maintaining
a theological cleavage between expression of faith and socio-political liberation.

In white Christianity's historic success, one is able to see clearly why many
Christians in American history, particularly Christian leaders, have been so
adamantly opposed to social reform movements. In this case, most Christians
are convinced that such movements are ungodly because it falls out of the realm
of religious concern and therefore are worthy of staunch criticism. But more
important, it is deemed demonic behavior insofar as black advancement falls out
of the realm of divine will as Christian faith has been historically taught. Thus
for all the theological reasons why social reform has taken an ideological beating in American Christianity, the root of that beating lies in the acutely anti-
black disposition of white power elites in American history. As such, Christian
faith in American history has also been a faith of the divine subordination of
black freedom. That is to say, divine subordination of black freedom presup-
poses not only a faith that depicts God as a racist but demands of Christians a
disdain for black freedom insofar as Christian faith is primarily concerned about
the religious individual and unconcerned with black liberation thus creating a
theological incompatibility.

> The need to work for social justice and social equality between the races is
> minimized, even dropped. If we are to focus on individuals only, then justice
> does not mean working against structures of inequality, but treating individuals
> as equals, regardless of the actual economic and political facts. Equality is
> spiritually and individually based, not temporally and socially based.[8]

The problem with equality being rooted in the spiritual and individual realm is
that racial inequality, of course, manifests itself in the historical and collective
realm of human relationships between blacks and whites. Yet, without a structural affirmation of the denunciation of racial inequality in Christian faith in
American history, white clergy and theologians were able to affirm the God of a
racist theocracy as a God of white power and individualism. Thus, the intent of
white clergy and theologians was never to conceive of faith as having racial ef-

ficacy for it would undermine the very purpose of exposing the slave to Christian faith. In order for white supremacy to flourish, every attempt was made to sever the connection between divine activity and human liberation. In this regard, far from being a contemporary phenomenon, the sin-salvation dialectic of Christian theology rooted in individual free will and accomplishment in American life regardless of race has been a clever ruse to divert, in particular, black people's attention away from the racial bigotry that has undermined the achievement of black humanity in American life in the name of God.

> Underlying traditional Christian thought is an image of man (woman) as a free actor, as essentially unfettered by social circumstances, free to choose and thus free to effect his (her) own salvation. This free-will conception of man (humanity) has been central to the doctrines of sin and salvation. For only if man (humanity) is totally free does it seem just to hold him (her) responsible for his (her) acts. . . . In short, Christian thought and thus Western civilization are permeated with the idea that men (humans) are individually in control of, and responsible for, their own destinies.[9]

This individual emphasis of Christian faith has had particularly devastating consequences on the quest for black self-determination. That quest has found an unfriendly home in both black and white churches throughout American history. In a real sense, the struggle for black liberation has not only been a racial struggle against the white power structure but also a theological struggle for the soul of America — a struggle for a soul that has been housed in the body of the God of a racist theocracy. What has instead happened is that committed black leaders, even some ministers, have forced America to deal with its virulent treatment of black humanity despite vehement protests from many black and white churches save for a few committed exceptions. The drive for African American equality has never had the support of the majority of white Americans; instead, racial progress has come in brief historical bursts, when a committed, militant minority — abolitionists, Radical Republicans, civil rights activists — stirred the nation, pressuring it to change.[10]

Save for such eruptions in a given era in American history, Christian faith in America not only taught its parishioners that there was no moral dilemma in putting individual interests above the achievement of black humanity but was diligent in establishing to the utmost degree the normative affirmation of the religious individual.

> A primary weakness of the religious establishment in America has been its apparent unwillingness to confront the exigencies of change with integrity. Time and time again the church has confused the people by looking the other way when personal interests have been measured against those values fundamental to faith. This has been especially true in racial matters.[11]

The church has looked the other way not only through the establishment of an individualistic paradigm, but has also prided itself on another significant dimension of a racist theocracy — universal language.

Universal Christian language holds that God does not see us as black and white, male and female, rich and poor. God, rather, sees us as one human family and therefore the language of Christian faith should reflect that oneness. While white clergy and theologians had to admit that differences in human characteristics and socio-economic status existed, they also concluded that *God wants the divisions to exist* — otherwise they would not. Thus, the extent to which white Christian leadership has felt comfortable in dialogue about matters beyond the religious individual has been the extent to which we universalize our common existence as wise creations of God. Yet the ideological hook to such an approach to faith is that it does not take into consideration the contradiction inherent in affirming the oneness of humanity in a nation of deep divisions nor does it allot for rigorous analysis regarding the interrelationship between racial bigotry and Christian faith in American life. The ideological hook serves, instead, as a moral and ethical escape for white Christian leadership bringing no reckoning to bear on them for the forwarding of a theological perspective that so comfortably weds divine will with black oppression. In this way, white clergy and theologians had no choice theologically. To establish a national life of acute white privilege and not connect it with the kingdom on earth and God's approval of it would allot for an approach to faith wherein God could be imaged as one who is intrinsically connected to the struggle for black self-determination. To allow such a theological development would be to forfeit the entire theological enterprise of white America. God had to be on the side of white racial stratification and not on the side of black liberation. To avoid dealing with the issue theologically but yet deal with the dimension of collective human destiny, white clergy and theologians were more comfortable dealing with a universal language of ultimate human destiny in the eschaton rather than the equality of opportunity for all human beings in American life. In this regard, universal language has always been ideological language in Christian tradition in America. What we were not in terms of equality in American life, we were in terms of our collective standing with God — sinners in need of being saved! Yet the disproportionate representation of anything valued in American life beyond a white male makes it clear that the pretensions of equality before God had/has little or no bearing on the will of white Christian leadership to realize that equality in American society.

> Certainly the character of the Divine and the divine intention for humanity are expressed quite clearly in the notion of a common father (God) in whose image all humanity is cast. This would seem to be an immutable value impossible of modification so long as God is God and man (humanity) comes in his (God's) likeness. And no less certain is the fact that racial preferment, however strongly it may be felt, is a derivative value, a *learned* response quite obviously at odds

with the notion of brotherhood (personhood) and the commandment to love. Hence, it can have no claim whatever to Divine approval or sanction. [12]

While Lincoln reminds us that both white supremacy and its concomitant theology are learned processes, precisely because of the ubiquitous power of white males in American history and the power of white religious leaders to shape common religious values, what they have taught has been of paramount significance in American history. The claim to divine approval has been established as the Christian theological norm in the United States. America itself has never been interested in the idea of human freedom for all her citizens but has established as existential and eschatological norm the notion of white racial superiority in all significant human endeavors and has enlisted the will of God as the ultimate affirmer of that norm.

Another significant dimension of God-talk in a racist theocracy is the frequent use of the satanic. The well-intentioned Christian seems to always be under attack by an unscrupulous, incessantly working devil who tries to take us off our goals, make us commit sinful acts like adultery and/or premarital sex, convinces us that we do not need a strong prayer life, tries to stop us from having spirited worship services, and keeps us from fellowship with God. In short, Satan is trying to ruin *our individual lives.* While this gives parishioners common purpose and provides them with a spiritual enemy to remind them of the inherent dangers of the Christian journey, it does not go a long way in producing a heightened Christian conscience regarding the socio-political transformation of black life in America. While it gives parishioners an opponent in regard to Christian obedience, the terms of that obedience itself are usually restricted to the ritualistic life of the Christian and not to the racial reality of the world. While making a, "liar out of the devil," may make one pray more, read the bible more, use profanity less, drink and smoke less and even come to church more frequently, seldom (if ever!) does that spiritual duel with Satan ever place in the socio-historical realm of human existence. In other words, making a, "liar out of the devil," never sends us to a more exhaustive knowledge of black and American history, or to the hegemonic history of the church, or to working for a liberated America, and, more particularly, to a theological exploration of the core of white America's values over and against its treatment of black people. Making a, "liar out of the devil," never compels us to raise critical questions about the nature of our religious indoctrination and who benefits most from it. More important, my point with this work has been to show that this understanding of Christian faith did not emerge by happenstance. It has been carefully thought out, constructed and implemented with the sole purpose of preserving white privilege in American life. In short, Christian faith's primary reason for being in American history has been to serve the role of social control of black people. The social irrelevance of the religious establishment is its functionality.[13]

The last dimension of the pedagogy of a racist theocracy is indoctrinating the Christian into *strong beliefs.* The strong belief posture has led in many instances to a rigid allegiance to Christian orthodoxy that often produces a blatant disrespect for other religions, a paternalistic view of those less fortunate and a highly emotional (and even pathological) defense of Christian tradition to those espousing an alternative expression of faith. But more dangerously, when strong belief is connected to a racial status quo, one's commitment to God becomes inextricably bound with maintaining that status quo. In short, strong belief in a racist theocracy makes racial bigotry a salvific function. The strong belief disposition encapsulates the religious norms of the community. Those norms are demonstrated daily *and are given Christian validity by God and Jesus in the life of the Church.* And in a nation of human inequality, the religious values of that nation will ultimately reflect the interests of those who benefit from that inequality.

> The religious do not hold values that are significantly different from those of others. But they hold to these values more strongly. Religion provides both social and individual integration of these values. The religious institution serves to "socialize" the individual in such a way that he (she) will conform to the norms of his (her) social group, regardless of what these norms are. Insofar as the norms include prejudice or anti-democratic values, religion serves to accentuate these as well.[14]

Thus the sacredness of religious pedagogy is not a manifestation of the mind of God, (even though it is presented as such) but of religious leaders who themselves are products of an unquestioned orthodoxy that has served the interests of white people in America well to the detriment of black people. This represents the power of theological tutelage, once accepted as orthodoxy, in the shaping of the theological conscience of both the oppressor and oppressed. When this happens, a nation becomes enslaved to itself at the risk of its own destruction.

> When particular understandings become rigidly fixed and uncritically appropriated as absolute truths, well-meaning people can and often do paint themselves into a corner from which they must assume a defensive or even offensive posture. With potentially destructive consequences, people presume to know God, abuse sacred texts, and propagate their particular versions of absolute truth.[15]

Kimball reminds us that religious leadership can be abused when particular approaches to faith masquerading as absolute truth are committed to the furtherance of oppressive human relationships. Moreover, he is also insightful in recognizing the hand-maiden of absolute truth — blind obedience. Once internalized as absolute truth, the parishioner finds herself in an unwitting predicament. Buoyed by the thinking that she is on the true path of God and Jesus, she often assumes a self-assured piety that compels her to revel in the "divine appropriateness" of the life of her church and its leadership, and to propagate that divine appropriateness to the public relative to its connection to American patriotism. In many ways, it never dawns on her to question the particulars of her Christian pedagogy and its historical collusion with white power elites regarding racial bigotry in American life. Not only does this not occur in many white churches in America but many black churches as well. When this happens, blind obedience begins to emerge, faith loses its critical edge, and divine will becomes a front for human oppression. For Kimball, this is the difference between authentic religion and corrupt religion:

> Authentic religion engages the intellect as people wrestle with the mystery of existence and the challenges of living in an imperfect world. Conversely, blind obedience is a sure sign of corrupt religion. Beware of any religious movement that seeks to limit the intellectual freedom and individual integrity of its adherents. When individual believers abdicate personal responsibility and yield to the authority of a charismatic leader or become enslaved to particular ideas or teachings, religion can easily become the framework for violence and destruction.[16]

This is how a nation could be so profoundly Christian, yet kidnap and make slaves of black people, go out on slave patrols after worship services, sell them off at auction, deny them the right to vote, deny them American citizenship, lynch, and castrate black men, falsely incarcerate them, rape black women, mock black people's aesthetic features and intellectual endowment, segregate them, discriminate against them in education, housing, and employment, and assassinate or compromise their leaders. This is how a nation could have a constitutional provision for freedom of assembly yet seek to compromise black mass mobilization for freedom at every turn; could have a constitutional provision for freedom of religion yet insists that the religious norm be socially conservative and individualistic; could have a pledge of allegiance to a flag that calls for one nation under God that is indivisible with liberty and justice for all but never has been one nation and certainly not indivisible; and scribes on its currency, "In God We Trust," but is seemingly content with that currency being concentrated in the hands of a few and centers the cause of one of the highest poverty rates in the world not on corporate greed and limited access to opportunity but rather to the lack of industry of black people. (Poverty, like crime, tends to wear a black face!) As such, when the cause of white superiority is intimately connected to God, the latter will invariably be depicted as one who is unconditionally given over to the creation and furtherance of that cause, i.e., a God that oppresses a nation.

The God That Liberates A Nation

The destruction of a racist theocracy calls for the destruction of a God that has given divine legitimacy to white supremacy. The God of a racist theocracy condones white racial privilege and mandates black dehumanization as a corollary of that privilege. That God also glorifies all the "inessentials" of the Christian life, to use Harry Emerson Fosdick's characterization. It glorifies an interior faith both anthropologically and ecclesiastically, divinizes the so-called chasm between the sacred and the secular, reduces religious efficacy to ritualism and minimizes the significance of oppressive human relationships on earth. In short, the God of a racist theocracy seeks to assuage the guilty conscience of white Christians regarding their treatment of black people and in the final analysis makes Christian cowards of us all! It ultimately glorifies individual accomplishment in the way of material abundance as a blessing from God. The problem is that this God does not compel the Christian to see that characterizing one's relationship with God as a blessing for material excess makes a mockery of the Christ-event. It does so in the sense that it does not compel most wealthy Christians to examine the process of exploitation of poor people by which their wealth was obtained. It further does not compel the wealthy Christian to explore as a staple part of faith how to eliminate poverty. In short, the historical intent of white clergy and theologians was to make Christian faith an oversimplified (and woefully insufficient) response to the social, economic, and political complexity that characterizes what our world has become. While I see this as a fundamental dimension in American Christianity in general, N. K. Clifford makes the same point focusing on Protestant Evangelicals:

> The Evangelical Protestant mind has never relished complexity. Indeed, its crusading genius, whether in religion and politics, has always tended to an oversimplification of issues and the substitution of inspiration and zeal for critical analysis and serious reflection.[17]

That oversimplification has been the historical foundation of Christian faith and affirmed by the God of a racist theocracy. This God has protected white interests (even whitened Jesus himself!), turned the church into a haven for escapism, and demonized any efforts at black self-determination.

While this goes a long way in making parishioners feel less overwhelmed by the complexities of life and provides a refuge from the trials of this world, it does not go a long way in preparing parishioners to live efficaciously in a highly complex world. Moreover, it does not cultivate a far-reaching theological maturity in conjunction with the life of Jesus compelling us rather to celebrate and, in many instances, feel relieved by Jesus' ultimate sacrifice at Calvary such that it absolves us of sustained activity in the process of human freedom. It leads the black and white Christian to the notion that the God-pleasing life is obtained through frequent bible reading, prayer, and church attendance, and the ceasing of smoking, drinking, sexual intercourse and profane language. Again, while this has its place in the life of faith, it conveniently does not lead the believer into a more soul-searching, intellectually accountable expression of faith that takes one to the intersection of the Christ-event and black dehumanization in American life.

Again, this is why movements to eradicate oppressive human relationships have been met with such stiff resistance by many black and white Christian leaders in American history. Insofar as Christian pedagogy in American history has been concerned primarily with the religious individual, black and white parishioners have been poised and ready to condemn such movements, given that such movements have been concerned with the social condition of oppressed humans and therefore fall out of the purview of orthodox Christian pedagogy. This is because Christian pedagogy in American life has been guided by the God of a racist theocracy. James Baldwin rightly sees the significance of one's understanding of God as the litmus test for determining a morally authentic person:

> It is not too much to say that whoever wishes to be a truly moral human being . . . must first divorce himself (herself) from all the prohibitions, crimes, and hypocrisies of the Christian church. If the concept of God has any validity or any use, it can only be to make us larger, freer, and more loving. If God cannot do this, it is time we got rid of Him (God).[18]

Baldwin is pointing us in the direction that we must travel theologically in order to make possible America's salvation. Divorcing oneself from the collective sins of the church will not be easy simply because the gatekeepers of Christian orthodoxy will resist mightily in their claim that the church does not need to purge itself of any sins. More important, church leadership has seen itself as anything other than the most potent ideological weapon in establishing black dehumanization as the norm in American life. It has rather seen itself as the salvation of individual believers from an admittedly wicked world but for the most part is doggedly insistent that it has not been the spiritual hand-maiden to white racial superiority. It has seen itself as an institution that has helped Christians and not oppressed them. Yet history suggests otherwise. Even a cursory analysis will lead one to the conclusion that while the church in American history has been concerned with the faith factor it has been more concerned with the black factor. That is to say, the church has been used by white power elites in conjunction with white Christian leaders as an institution not in service to Jesus Christ but in service to white privilege. In this regard, Baldwin is right: we need to get rid of that God! America needs to divorce herself from the God of a racist theocracy.

I suggest we replace the God of a racist theocracy with, say, *the God of egalitarian militancy*. This God will lay the foundation for an America that is in dire need of a theological renaissance. As egalitarian is suggestive of true equality and militancy has always been the disposition of the oppressed wherein movement toward human liberation is at its most effectiveness, a God who is possessed of both these attributes can ultimately be the saving grace of this nation.

If Jesus' proclamation that, "Do not think that I have come to abolish the Law or the Prophets; I have not come to abolish them but to fulfill them," (Matthew 5:17, NIV), and Paul's dictum that, "It is for freedom that Christ has set us free. Stand firm, then, and do not let yourselves be burdened again by a yoke of slavery," (Galatians 5:1, NIV), have any meaning for our time then the God of egalitarian militancy must be embodied in both passages.

In the first instance, Jesus' fulfillment of the Law frees us from preoccupations with rigid conformity to traditional rituals as a medium for salvation. The dread of the individual sinful life was replaced with the call to righteousness in the way of human relationships. While Jesus called us to the institution of the church, he commissioned that church to a rock that was not an actual rock but was Peter. The great commission by Jesus was not to institutional maintenance but to the primary significance of human freedom in an oppressive world. This means that the salvation for which Jesus died is promised us as we commit ourselves to the issues of humanity's inhumanity to humanity as Jesus did with his life. Hence, Jesus' fulfillment of the Law does not call us to the safe confines of elaborate buildings and individual comfort but to the highly discomforting task of human emancipation. In such a world, the flesh may be taken away but the spirit of human liberation will never be destroyed. This is the meaning of eternal life in an oppressive world. In addition to the fulfillment of the Law, Jesus' resurrection by the God of egalitarian militancy frees us from preoccupations with a plethora of moral proscriptions unrelated to human suffering. It also frees us from preoccupations with physical death itself and leads the mature thinking Christian to the quintessential moral responsibility of human freedom.

In the second instance, Paul's admonishment to the church at Galatia is just as relevant today as then. Although human liberation is the ultimate victory it still must be achieved. Paul admonished us that although we are free in Christ, we are not yet free in this world or within the world of human relationships. The God of egalitarian militancy sacrificed that God's only son to make clear to the world that being free in Jesus' resurrection was/is not God's ultimate goal. That freedom only laid the foundation for the pinnacle of human existence — a world of human freedom. Thus, Paul reminds us that the Christ-event has freed us not just to celebrate the life of Jesus but to secure human freedom as we live in global community with each other. The Christ-event calls us not just to emotional gratification upon hearing the name of Jesus but to the more protracted, and committed resistance to all forms of human oppression. This is the freedom for which Christ has set us free.

With that foundation, America's obsession with black dehumanization has been the crucible through which her moral compass has been constructed. That obsession with black oppression has been inextricably bound with the wealth attainment of whites and the notion of white superiority. But precisely because the God of egalitarian militancy has freed us from ideological treatments of Christian faith in American history, resistance to white supremacy in particular is no longer a theological afterthought or an historical issue that falls out of the purview of the Christ-event. Rather, resistance to all encroachments of white imposition becomes the crucible through which faith becomes authentic. As such, black people are able to affirm the God of egalitarian militancy as the God that frees us to challenge white supremacy with our total being insofar as the Christ-event has provided us with ultimate power over any oppressive earthly rule. We are free to pursue the kingdom of black liberation and to destroy the kingdom of white superiority knowing that the God of egalitarian militancy's moral compass points toward human emancipation. Thus, while the point of departure for the mature thinking Christian is still, "What shall I do to inherit eternal life?" its answer is now found in the penultimate question, "What shall I do to make the world freer?" It frees black people to see that their struggle is intrinsically connected to the kingdom itself and frees black people from the acceptance of all white impositions on their humanity. It is only in adopting the God of egalitarian militancy that Christian faith in America can no longer be employed as an instrument of black oppression but rather as an instrument of black liberation. Such a disposition is exemplified in James Cone's main theological question. He is now free theologically to begin not with a question about institutional maintenance or sexual morality but with a question about black suffering:

> The black community spends most of its time trying "to make a living" in a society labeled, "for whites only." Therefore, the central question for blacks is "How are we going to survive in a world which deems black humanity an illegitimate form of human existence?"[19]

Because the Christ-event has freed us to pursue freedom, direct inquiries into the condition of black oppression become the rubric out of which the God of egalitarian militancy reveals Godself. If we are freed for the pursuit of freedom by God's revelation in the Christ-event then the good news of the gospel is that the will of God is no longer enslaved to white supremacy but is freed in the black struggle for freedom from white supremacy.

> It [Black Theology] says that the God who was revealed in the life of oppressed Israel and who came to us in the incarnate Christ and is present today as the Holy Spirit has made a decision about the black condition. God has chosen to make the black condition *God's* condition. It is a continuation of the incarnation in twentieth-century America. God's righteousness will liberate the oppressed of this nation and "all flesh shall see it together." It is this certainty that makes physical life less than ultimate and thus enables blacks courageously to affirm blackness and its liberating power as ultimate.[20]

Laden in the power of Cone's theological affirmations about the Christ-event and the black condition in America is the freedom to start theologically with an oppressed context and to not be enslaved to the socially irrelevant universals of white Christianity. Framing Christian faith around the notion that, "We are all God's children," a prominent universal of white Christian pedagogy, fails to do justice to the disproportionate suffering of black people in America. The God of egalitarian militancy not only frees us to begin theologically with the particulars of black oppression but demands it of us insofar as Jesus' proclamation of his own ministry was to set at liberty those who are oppressed. (Luke 4:18) That can only be accomplished by the identification with the oppressed in one's context and devoting one's life to their liberation. Paulo Freire weighs in:

> Since it is in a concrete situation that the oppressor-oppressed contradiction is established, the resolution of this contradiction must be *objectively* verifiable. Hence the radical requirement — both for the man (woman) who discovers himself (herself) to be an oppressor and for the oppressed — that the concrete situation which begets oppression must be transformed.[21]

Hence, a new Christian paradigm must emerge in America that frees us from obsessing about rituals and piety and pushes us into the realm of contributory efforts to the eradication of human oppression. The grace that God gives in Jesus Christ must no longer be confined to the individual soul after death but to the opportunity that God gives us with our lives to render as a sacrifice in the struggle for full human emancipation. This is what Dietrich Bonhoeffer had in mind when he distinguished between "cheap grace" and "costly grace."[22] It is what Emerson and Smith had in mind when they distinguished between the Church of Meaning and Belonging, and the Church of Sacrifice for Meaning and Belonging:

> In trying to create meaning and belonging, even to teach religious truths and implications for social action, religious leaders must act within a limited range shaped by the social locations of their congregation. The congregation often looks to religion not as an external force that places radical demands on their lives, but rather as a way to fulfill their needs. Those who are successful in the world, those of adequate or abundant means, those in positions of power (whether they are aware of this power or not), rarely come to church to have their social and economic positions altered. If we accept the oftentimes reasonable proposition that most people seek the greatest benefit for the least cost, they will seek meaning and belonging with the least change possible. Thus, if they can go to either the Church of Meaning and Belonging, or the Church of Sacrifice for Meaning and Belonging, most people choose the former.[23]

Most Christians in American history have chosen the former because they have been guided theologically by the God of a racist theocracy. America's salvation lies in the abandoning of the God of a racist theocracy and the adoption of the God of egalitarian militancy. When this happens, we will no longer witness both black and white Christians in theological tandem condemning mass movements of social reform but actively participating in them as a standard part of faith expression. We will no longer witness churches that are more committed to Christian piety and institutional maintenance including the repression of women in the church especially those in ministry. We will instead see a church engaged in a "holy rage" concerning human exploitation in all forms and makes humanity's inhumanity to humanity the central reason for its existence. It is only in this context, under the reign of the God of egalitarian militancy, that America will truly become the nation she has always claimed constitutionally and has affirmed verbally. This is all predicated on the courage of the Church to shed itself of its historic ilk of Christian sponsored bigotry and usher into fruition an America that truly is, "no respecter of persons."

Notes

1.   Baltimore, Maryland: Black Classic Press, 1993, 63. (Originally published in 1830).

2.   Lester Scherer, *Slavery and the Churches in Early America: 1619-1819*. Grand Rapids, Michigan: Eerdman's Publishing Company, 1975, 94.

3.   *The Noise of Solemn Assemblies: Christian Commitment and the Religious Establishment in America*. Garden City, New York: Doubleday & Company, Incorporated, 1961, 72.

4.   Ibid.

5.   C. Eric Lincoln, *Race, Religion, and the Continuing American Dilemma*. New York: Hill and Wang Publishing, 1984, 44.

6.   James W. Perkinson, *White Theology: Outing Supremacy in Modernity*. New York: Palgrave-Macmillan Publishing, 2004, 59.

7.   Ibid., 63.

8.   Michael O. Emerson, and Christian Smith, *Divided by Faith: Evangelical Religion and the Problem of Race in America*. New York: Oxford University Press, 2000, 58.

9.   Rodney Stark, and Charles Y. Glock, "Prejudice and the Churches," in Charles Y. Glock and Ellen Siegelman, eds., *Prejudice U. S. A.* New York: Praeger Books, 1969. Taken from Ibid., 77.

10. Francis D. Adams, Barry Sanders, *Alienable Rights: The Exclusion of African Americans in a White Man's Land, 1619-2000*. New York: HarperCollins Publishers, 2003. 320.

11. Lincoln, *Continuing American Dilemma*, 16.

12. Ibid., 16-17.

13. Berger, *The Noise of Solemn Assemblies*, 103.

14. Ibid., 102.

15. Charles Kimball, *When Religion Becomes Evil*. New York: HarperCollins Publishers, 2002, 46.

16. Ibid., 72.

17. N. K. Clifford, "His Dominion: A Vision in Crisis." Sciences Religieuses/Studies In Religion, Volume 2. Taken from Emerson, Smith, *Divided by Faith*, 171.

18. *The Fire Next Time*. New York: Dell Publishing, 1962, 67.

19. James Cone, *A Black Theology of Liberation*. (Twentieth Anniversary Edition). New York: Orbis Books, 1990, 11. (Originally published in 1970).

20. Ibid., 12.

21. *Pedagogy of the Oppressed*. New York: Continuum Publishing, 1992, 35. (Originally published in 1970)

22. See his twentieth century classic, *The Cost of Discipleship*. New York: Macmillan Publishing Company, 1963. (Originally published in 1937)

23. Emerson, Smith, *Divided by Faith*, 164.

Bibliography

Adams, Francis D., and Barry Sanders, *Alienable Rights: The Exclusion of African Americans in a White Man's Land, 1619-2000*. New York: HarperCollins Publishers, 2003.

Akbar, Na'im, *Chains and Images of Psychological* Slavery. Jersey City, New Jersey: New Mind Productions, 1984.

Allen, Robert L., *Black Awakening in Capitalist America*. Trenton, New Jersey: Africa World Press, 1990.

Baldwin, James, *The Fire Next Time*. New York: Dell Publishing Company, 1962.

Bennett, Lerone, *Before the Mayflower*. Chicago: Johnson Publishing Company, 1964.

Berger, Peter L., *The Sacred Canopy*. New York: Doubleday and Company, Incorporated, 1967.

———. *The Noise of Solemn Assemblies: Christian Commitment and the Religious Establishment in America*. Garden City, New York: Doubleday & Company, Incorporated, 1961.

Berry, Mary Frances, and John W. Blassingame, *Long Memory: The Black Experience in America*. New York: Oxford University Press, 1982.

Bonhoeffer, Dietrich, *The Cost of Discipleship*. New York: Macmillan Publishing Company, 1963. (Originally published in 1937).

Buswell, James O., *Slavery, Segregation, and Scripture*. Grand Rapids: Eerdman's Publishing Company, 1964.

Cone, James H., *A Black Theology of Liberation (Twentieth Anniversary Edition)*. New York: Orbis Books, 1990.

———. *Black Theology and Black Power*. New York: The Seabury Press, 1969.

Davis, Angela Y., *Women, Race, and Class*. New York: Vintage Books, 1981.

Douglas, Kelly Brown, *Sexuality and the Black Church: A Womanist Perspective*. New York: Orbis Books, 1999.

———. *The Black Christ*. New York: Orbis Books, 1994.

Dussel, Enrique, *Philosophy of Liberation*. New York: Orbis Books, 1985.

Earl, Riggins R. Jr., *Dark Symbols, Obscure Signs: God, Self & Community in the Slave Mind*. New York: Orbis Books, 1993.

Emerson, Michael O., and Christian Smith, *Divided by Faith: Evangelical Religion and the Problem of Race in America*. New York: Oxford University Press, 2000.

Fredrickson, George M., *White Supremacy: A Comparative Study in America and South African History*. New York: Oxford University Press, 1981.

———. *The Black Image in the White Mind: A Debate on Afro-American Character and Destiny: 1817-1914*. New York: Harper & Row Publishers, 1971.

Freire, Paulo, *Pedagogy of the Oppressed*. New York: The Continuum Publishing Company, 1992. (Originally published in 1970).

Genovese, Eugene D., *A Consuming Fire: The Fall of the Confederacy in the Mind of the White Christian South*. Athens, Georgia: University of Georgia Press, 1998.

———. *Roll, Jordan, Roll: The World the Slaves Made*. New York: Vintage Books,1972.

Giddings, Paula, *When And Where I Enter: The Impact of Black Women on Race and Sex in America*. New York: Bantam Books, 1984.

Glock, Charles Y., and Ellen Siegelman, eds., *Prejudice U. S. A.* New York: Praeger Books, 1969.

Grant, Jacquelyn, *White Women's Christ and Black Women's Jesus: Feminist Christology and Womanist Response*. Atlanta: Scholar's Press, 1989.

Haynes, Stephen R., *Noah's Curse: The Biblical Justification of American Slavery*. New York: Oxford University Press, 2002.

hooks, bell, *Ain't I A Woman: Black Women and Feminism*. Boston: South End Press, 1981.

Jones, William R., *Is God A White Racist: A Preamble to Black Theology*. Boston: Beacon Press, 1998. (Originally published in 1973).

Jordan, Winthrop, *The White Man's Burden: The Historical Origins of Racism in the United States*. New York: Oxford University Press, 1974.

———. *White Over Black: American Attitudes Toward the Negro, 1550-1812*. New York: W. W. Norton & Company, 1968.

Kelsey, George, *Racism and the Christian Understanding of Man*. New York: Charles Scribner's Sons, 1965.

Kimball, Charles, *When Religion Becomes Evil*. New York: HarperCollins Publishers, 2002.

Kovel, Joel, *White Racism: A Psychohistory*. New York: Columbia University Press, 1984.

Leonard, Joseph T., *Theology and Race Relations*. Milwaukee: Bruce Publishing Company, 1963.

Lincoln, C. Eric, and Lawrence H. Mamiya, *The Black Church in the African American Experience*, Durham, North Carolina: Duke University Press, 1990.

Lincoln, C. Eric, *Race, Religion, and the Continuing American Dilemma*. New York: Hill and Wang Publishing, 1984.

Myrdal, Gunnar, *An American Dilemma* (Two Volumes). New York: McGraw-Hill Book Company, 1964. (Originally published in 1944)

Niebuhr, Reinhold, *Moral Man and Immoral Society*. New York: Charles Scribner's Sons, 1932.

Nolen, Claude H., *The Negro's Image in the South: The Anatomy of White Supremacy*. Lexington: University of Kentucky Press, 1968.

Perkinson, James W., *White Theology: Outing Supremacy in Modernity*. New York: Palgrave-Macmillan Publishing, 2004.

Raboteau, Albert J., *Slave Religion: The Invisible Institution in the Antebellum South*. New York: Oxford University Press, 1978.

Rahner, Karl, *Christian Faith: An Introduction to the Idea of Christianity*. New York: Crossroads Publishing, 1985.

Rauschenbusch, Walter, *A Theology for the Social Gospel*. Nashville: Abingdon Press, 1990. (Originally published by The Macmillan Company, 1917).

Salley, Columbus, and Ronald Behm, *What Color Is Your God? Black Consciousness and the Christian Faith*. New York: Citadel Press, 1988.

Scherer, Lester B., *Slavery and the Churches in Early America: 1619-1819*. Grand Rapids, Michigan: Eerdman's Publishing Company, 1975.

Smith, H. Shelton, *In His Image But...Racism In Southern Religion, 1780-1910*. Durham: Duke University Press, 1972.

Sullivan, Clayton, *Rescuing Jesus from the Christians*. Harrisburg, Pennsylvania: Trinity Press International, 2002.

Tawney, R. H., *Religion and the Rise of Capitalism*. New York: The New American Library, 1954.

Walker, David, *The Appeal to the Coloured Citizens of America*. Baltimore, Maryland: Black Classic Press, 1993. (Originally published in 1830).

Weber, Max, *The Protestant Ethic and the Spirit of Capitalism*. New York: Charles Scribner's Sons, 1958.

Williams, Delores S., *Sisters in the Wilderness: The Challenge of Womanist God-Talk*. New York: Orbis Books, 1993.

Williams, Eric, *Capitalism and Slavery*. Chapel Hill: University of North Carolina Press, 1994. (Originally published in 1944).

Wilmore, Gayraud S., *Black Religion and Black Radicalism: An Interpretation of the Religious History of African Americans*. 3/e. New York: Orbis Books, 1998. (Originally published in 1973).

Wilmore, Gayraud S., and James H. Cone, eds., *Black Theology: A Documentary History, Volume 1, 1966-1979*. New York: Orbis Books, 1979.

Wood, Forrest G., *The Arrogance of Faith: Christianity and Race in America from the Colonial Era to the Twentieth Century*. Boston: Northeastern University Press, 1990.

Zuckerman, Phil., ed., *DuBois on Religion*. Lanham, Maryland: Rowman & Littlefield Publishers, 2000.

Index

white male, 96; white person image
of, 103, 110
docile disposition, 29–31, 104–11
double consciousness, 133
Douglass, Frederick, 122, 169
Douglass, Kelly Brown, 68–69, 101, 107
DuBois, W. E. B., 1, 116, 146
Dussel, Enrique, 44

earthly toil, 156–57
egalitarian militancy, 181–82, 184–85
Emerson, Michael O., 184
England, 3–4
Ephesians, 120
Equality and inequality: Christian,
118–19; culturally different
meanings of, 88; God of,
85; God's stratified structure and,
86–87; racial, 174–75; relationships
of, 128–29
eschatology, doctrine of, 151; American
colonies emergence of, 154–55;
black dehumanization and, 160–66;
components of, 159–60; dimensions
of, 152; Greek culture origins of,
153–54; obedience rewarded in, 166;
otherworldly, 155–57, 162, 166;
questions raised by, 152; slaves and,
154–55
eternal bliss, 151–52
eternal damnation, 151–52
Europe: African's God and law
knowledge in, 37–38; African's value
to, 6;
Christian pedagogy in, 20–28;
productive living and Christianity in,
21; stations of life worldview of, 76
Eve, 67
evil female, 67

faith communities, 9–10
fatalism, 109
fear of God, 14–15
female evil, 67
floggings, 63
Fosdick, Harry Emerson, 180
Frazier, E. Franklin, 131
Fredrickson, George M., 6, 88

Free African Society, 138
freedom: black people's ungodly, 110;
Christian, 13–16; human, 158;
slave's, 14–15;
slaves denied physical, 119;
slavocracy construction of, 14; spirit
of, 137
free market commodities, 102
Freire, Paulo, 109, 184
Fuller, Richard, 134

Genovese, Eugene E., 142
Gibson, Edmund, 156
God: African people's knowledge of,
37–38; black community liberated
through, 179–85;
black community oppressed by,
171–72; black oppression sanctioned
by, 76–77, 79, 134; determinism of,
75–76; of egalitarian militancy, 181–
82, 184–85; equality and stratified
structure from, 86–87; fear of, 14–
15; laws of, 48; master-slave
relationship ordered by, 77; racial
stratification ordained by, 88–89,
143–44;
racist theocracy guided by, 181,
184–85; as Reformation tradition
charter member, 25; righteous
liberation from, 183; salvation
chosen by, 24–25, 172–73; salvation
through grace of, 107–8; servants
commissioned by, 141–42; slaves
destiny determined by, 157–58;
slave's eternal bondage from, 80;
slavocracy demand of obedience
from, 107; social stratification
favored by, 26–27; southern whites
resolve tested by, 91; as sovereign
Lord, 84–92; stations in life ordained
by, 89; ultimate equality from, 85;
white privilege condoned by, 89,
170–71; as white supremacist, 76–
84. *See also* Jesus; white Jesus
God-Jesus-Mary paradigm, 71
Godliness: black ungodliness and, 96;
of docility, 104–11; of white
supremacy, 96–104